About Island Press

Island Press is the only nonprofit organization in the United States whose principal purpose is the publication of books on environmental issues and natural resource management. We provide solutions-oriented information to professionals, public officials, business and community leaders, and concerned citizens who are shaping responses to environmental problems.

In 1994, Island Press celebrated its tenth anniversary as the leading provider of timely and practical books that take a multidisciplinary approach to critical environmental concerns. Our growing list of titles reflects our commitment to bringing the best of an expanding body of literature to the environmental community throughout North America and the world.

Support for Island Press is provided by Apple Computer, Inc., The Bullitt Foundation, The Geraldine R. Dodge Foundation, The Energy Foundation, The Ford Foundation, The W. Alton Jones Foundation, The Lyndhurst Foundation, The John D. and Catherine T. MacArthur Foundation, The Andrew W. Mellon Foundation, The Joyce Mertz-Gilmore Foundation, The National Fish and Wildlife Foundation, The Pew Charitable Trusts, The Pew Global Stewardship Initiative, The Rockefeller Philanthropic Collaborative, Inc., and individual donors.

Understanding
Environmental
Administration
and Law

To Albert K. Chase, Jr.

Understanding Environmental Administration and Law

Susan J. Buck

ISLAND PRESS

Washington, D.C. ● Covelo, California

Library of Congress Cataloging-in-Publication Data

Buck, Susan J.
    Understanding environmental administration and law/Susan J.
    Buck.—2nd ed.
        p.   cm.
    Includes bibliographical references and index.
    ISBN 1-55963-474-X (pbk.)
    1. Environmental law—United States. 2. Environmental policy—
United States.   I. Title
    KF3775.B83   1996
    344.73'046—dc20
    [344.30446]   96-826
                                                          CIP

Printed on recycled, acid-free paper ⊛

Manufactured in the United States of America

10 9 8 7 6 5 4 3 2 1

Contents

Afterword   185

Preface

This book springs from two basic premises. The first is that environmental managers need to understand the legal context of their work, and the second is that existing books are inadequate to the task.

Of course, most environmental managers understand the laws and regulations affecting their own jobs. However, they usually view these as constraints on their own autonomy. As the Boatman in *A Man for All Seasons* says, lamenting that the fee is the same for rowing upstream as down: "whoever makes the regulations doesn't row a boat." Most managers are taught their professional and scientific disciplines first, and their training for administration is on-the-job training. Thus they learn the "right" way to measure floodways or to harvest trees, and when state budgetary constraints preserve inaccurate maps or leave a prime stand of trees uncut, managers are outraged because they have not been taught that political factors are as valid as a basis for decision making as scientific measurements.

Setting aside the question of whether political issues *ought* to be considered, the fact remains that they *are* considered. Good managers need to understand how the legal and political process operates, in order to anticipate political changes and perhaps to channel their impacts in ways that are helpful to their own professional goals.

Environmental managers deal with the law every day. At the very highest level, statutes and executive orders define the boundaries of job responsibilities. At the lowest level, rules and regulations provide guidance and at times restrictions on bureaucratic activities. Somewhere in between is the middle manager, that fabled creature who must translate the larger commands into operations. At the middle manager's level, the law is both friend and master. The law is *flexible,* and a good manager learns how to use it to achieve the organization's policy goals.

Typically the middle manager has come up through the technical ranks and, as a reward for good technical skills, has become an administrator. At this point the infamous Peter Principle may come into play: employees rise to their level of incompetence. Administration is a skill, as much art as science, and it has its own special tools. One of the most important tools for an environmental manager is the law.

My second premise was that existing books do not provide an adequate explanation of the legal process for environmental managers. Of course, there are many excellent books on environmental law.* These are, however, casebooks suitable for law students; they do not provide insights into the practical application of law for managers. For example, in the case of *National Audubon Society* v. *Department of Water and Power of the City of Los Angeles* (1983), a California court held that a public trust protected the waters of Mono Lake. Los Angeles was required, under this decision, to reconsider its use of water from the lake. To a lawyer, this case is of great legal interest. To an employee of the Los Angeles water department, the case is a nightmare, providing no useful guidelines on whether, when, or how water may still be diverted from Mono Lake for the urgent water supply needs of the city.

The purpose of this book is to show how the policy process is infused with the legal process. I hope to demystify the law, to translate it from the law books, and to make it accessible to the nonlawyer. The law is like chess: a finite number of pieces, each with its own moves, resulting in infinite combinations and strategies. Here I hope the readers will find the pieces pictured and the moves defined. They must play their own game.

---

*Especially noteworthy are *Environmental Law,* Vols. 1 and 2 by Jackson Battle, and Vol. 3 by Mark Squillace (Cincinnati: Anderson Publishing Co., 1986 and 1988); *Environmental Law and Policy* by Zygmunt Plater, Robert Abrams, and William Goldfarb (St. Paul, MN: West Publishing Co., 1992); and *Cases and Materials on Environmental Law,* 4th ed. edited by Roger Findley and Daniel Farber (St. Paul: West Publishing Co., 1995).

Acknowledgments

I have been fortunate in having able and dedicated students to help with this writing project. John Ehmig verified the case and statutory citations; he also wrote the section on "Finding Case Law." Nancy Carlson prepared the case on Fisheating Creek. Christen Compton prepared the material on the environmental policy in the European Union.

I owe a special thanks to two federal employees. The section on the Pittman-Robertson and Dingell-Johnson Acts (which is drawn from another research project) could not have been written without the generous help of Claude Stephens of the Fish and Wildlife Service, who answered all my questions and then sent me an enormous—and enormously useful—package of material. The updated material on the wild horse and burro program was provided by Bob Bainbridge of the Bureau of Land Management; the material he sent to me arrived only two days after our telephone interview.

I am particularly grateful to Eric Goldstein of the Natural Resources Defense Council, who provided a detailed page-by-page commentary on the first edition; I profited a great deal from his suggestions. Several other reviewers also contributed useful suggestions for this edition: Mimi Becker (University of New Hampshire); John Freemuth (Boise State University); Jim Kimmel (Southwestern Texas State University); and Margaret Reams (Louisiana State University). Any error or flaw that remains uncorrected must be laid at my door.

Several students helped with the research for the first edition of this book. David Cushing's work was essential; without his efforts with interlibrary loan, the manuscript would have been years late. Dana Dooley prepared the bibliography and list of cases, saving me much time and trouble. Megan Schmid provided the full citations for the legislation. Three other students, Jeff Bimmer, Paul Bivens, and Joe Morgan, chose to write annotated bibliographies for this book in lieu of research papers; their excellent research eased my own task considerably.

I am especially grateful to two colleagues, Marlene Gaither and Harley Hiett, who wrote about actual cases to help present the practitioner's view of environmental law.

Chapter One

The American Legal System

While legal scholars over the centuries have offered many definitions of *law,* the definition that meets with the approval of most Americans is that of the nineteenth-century jurist John Austin: the law is the command of the sovereign backed by a sanction. In other words, the law is whatever the government says it is, and if we choose not to comply, the government will punish us. For citizens whose encounters with the law are largely limited to traffic police or the IRS, such a definition is adequate. But citizens whose daily work is bounded by a governmental structure of rules and regulations see more to the law than simply commands. Who gives the sovereign the right to issue commands? Are there areas of public or private endeavor in which the sovereign has no rights to issue commands? What is the range of penalties for noncompliance? Does it matter if the noncompliance is accidental or unavoidable? How does a citizen *discover* the latest governmental command?

All of these questions are pertinent to environmental managers. The scope of their administrative authority and the intent of the legislature in giving them that authority are important parameters. Managers in regulatory enforcement must know when they may or should compromise and when they must bring their full enforcement powers to bear on a violator. Resource managers must maintain the delicate balance between resource protection and resource use. Their arsenal is not restricted to the "sanctions" of the sovereign. They have persuasion, political pressure, and incentives on their side as well. To understand these managerial tools, managers must also understand the system in which they wield them.

This chapter explores the legal system in which American environmental managers must operate. The first section discusses the English roots of American common law and how this body of law became accepted in the new United States. It also discusses the other sources of law: statutes, rules and regulations, and the Constitution. How judges apply this law is discussed in the second section. The impact of our complex federal system on environmental administration and law is discussed in the third section.

Sources of Law

Western public law is based on one of two systems: English common law and the European civil law tradition, also called continental or codified law. The simplest way to distinguish between these two systems is to look at the judicial decision-making process. Common law is based on the idea of precedent: like cases are decided alike. The judge bases his decision not only on the applicable statute but also on how other courts have interpreted the statute. In some areas of the common law there are no controlling statutes, only rules set forth by appellate courts. By contrast, in the continental or civil system, the law is spelled out in detailed civil codes; the specific rules laid out in *Leviticus* are a familiar example of the civil code approach to the law. In the civil system, the judge locates the appropriate section of the code and then applies it to the situation at hand.

The Common Law

The common law system developed in the thirteenth century. When the English feudal system began to weaken and the cities to develop, the king sent royal judges to decide controversies in his name. This was done primarily to increase the king's power and authority as the power and authority of his feudal lords waned. Each feudal manor had its own customs, and the judges would weigh their own perceptions of fairness, the existing customs, and the political repercussions in reaching decisions. As we might expect, the decisions were often based on unclear reasoning, and cases that appeared similar might be decided in completely contradictory ways. The clerks accompanying the judges began to record decisions and reasoning; congregating back at the palace they compared notes, and gradually the judges started to refer to the decisions of their colleagues as another basis for decisions. Eventually the recording of decisions became regularized, and the judges were required to set out their reasoning for the formal record. Any deviation from precedent had to be justified. In this way the common law— the system of law common to the entire country—was established.

Today we take the English basis of our legal system for granted. In the early days of the republic, when the former colonies did not have their own cases to determine the precedents for judicial decision making, judges drew on the same English law that had governed their decisions prior to the Revolution.[1] At the time of the Revolution, there was debate about whether the new country would follow the English tradition: in some quarters the feelings were very strong that a complete break from England was the only correct approach. The legal system that was suggested to replace the common law tradition was the civil law approach that prevailed on the continent of Europe and was used by allies such as the French. The French colonies had retained the continental legal system, and even today Louisiana, a former French possession, is still governed by such a system.

Despite the radical proposals to change the law, the English system prevailed. Colonial lawyers and judges were trained in the common law, and contracts, property transfers, and all forms of legal transactions were already in the English style. Besides, despite the outpourings of anti-English sentiment immediately following the Revolution, most colonists still thought of themselves as English in spirit. Edmund Burke, the English statesman and philosopher, excused the American Revolution on the grounds that good Englishmen *should* rebel when treated unfairly. Common sense and common law prevailed, and the American legal system was based upon the English one.

One of the earliest environmental cases resting on common law traditions appeared before the United States Supreme Court in 1842. *Martin* v. *Waddell* originated with the contention by a New Jersey riparian landowner, Waddell, that he had exclusive rights to take oysters from the Raritan River. He based his assertion on a grant made by King Charles in 1664 to the Duke of York, which gave the duke "all the powers of government." Waddell claimed that his rights to the mudflats were directly descended from property rights transferred by the Duke of York and his managers. Waddell's opponent, Martin, argued that the king held certain resources (among them, mudflats) in trust for the people, and that the king's grant to the Duke of York required the duke to hold these resources in trust as well. Thus, despite language that might be interpreted otherwise, the duke did not have the power to transfer the mudflats to private ownership any more than the king did. The Supreme Court agreed with Martin that the original grant did not include the *exclusive* right to fish the adjacent waters. Of course, in the interim since the grant had been given to the Duke of York, the state of New Jersey had formed a new government, so the second question before the Court was whether New Jersey was similarly prohibited from granting private, exclusive rights to lands that under common law were public trust lands. Justice Taney (the same justice whose decision in *Dred Scott* helped precipitate the Civil War) found that the public trust doctrine had survived the Revolution:

[W]hen the people of New Jersey took possession of the reins of government, and took into their own hands the powers of sovereignty, the prerogatives and regalities which before belonged either to the crown or the Parliament, became immediately and rightfully vested in the State.[2]

Although *Martin* v. *Waddell* is not the only case where courts articulated the continuance of English traditions, it is one of the clearest. Of course, the changing social and economic situations in the United States led to many and frequent diversions from the English law, but the basis was firmly established.

In addition to the common law, which continues to develop, statutes, rules and regulations, and the Constitution are rich sources of American law.

Statutes and Ordinances

Statutes are the formal acts of legislation passed by Congress or the state legislatures. Similar enactments passed by county and city governments are often called ordinances or local laws. Sometimes statutes are very specific, setting, for example, the time limits on Superfund damage claims or the maximum permissible automobile emission levels. At other times, however, the legislatures establish broad guidelines and leave the details to the executive branch. This is done for several reasons. First, the legislators have neither the time nor the expertise to hammer out the details of implementation. Second, the legislative process is slow and cumbersome; it is designed that way so that the decisions are as free from circumstantial pressure as possible. Administrative actions are comparatively speedy, as will be seen in chapter 5. Finally, by passing the responsibility for detailed implementation to the executive branch, the legislature avoids much of the political repercussions of unpopular decisions. For example, when Bureau of Land Management (BLM) proposed raising the cost of federal land grazing permits to market levels, the resulting firestorm engulfed the BLM bureaucrats and not the Congress that had given them the authority to raise fees.

Rules and Regulations

Another source of American law is the rules and regulations promulgated by administrative agencies. Technically, under the Constitution only the legislature has the authority to make laws. However, in the American system the legislature has delegated some of their lawmaking authority to the executive agencies. From the late nineteenth century through the middle of the New Deal, the constitutionality of legislative delegation of authority was questioned, and even today some commentators argue that the Congress in particular cannot give rulemaking powers to the executive branch without very clear and restrictive guidelines. In practice, however, federal and many state agencies have the power to make rules and regulations that have the force of law. These rules must meet two constitutional standards: *procedural due process* (Did the agency follow the legal requirements of notice and hearing?) and *substantive due process* (Is the agency operating within its designated policy boundaries?). This will be discussed more fully in chapter 4. It is, however, important to note that any rule or regulation that is formulated with the proper procedures and is within the statutory authority of an agency has the same status as any piece of legislation passed by the legislature and signed by the executive.[3]

The Constitution

The Constitution plays a vital part in environmental regulation. For example, the common urban practice of zoning raises the constitutional question of whether zoning is a "taking" of an individual's property. We are accustomed to thinking of zoning as a way to regulate and to protect the welfare and orderly development of a community. However, the Constitution clearly states:

> No person shall . . . be deprived of life, liberty, or property without due process of law; nor shall private property be taken for public use, without just compensation (Amendment V).

Is zoning the equivalent of taking a person's property "for public use"? Suppose the zoning significantly reduces the value of the property or makes it unusable? Must the owner be compensated? Or is the act of zoning the use of "due process of law" and therefore exempt from paying just compensation? Until recent years, zoning has been consistently interpreted by the courts as a legitimate exercise of a state's police power: the obligation to protect public health, safety, and welfare. But court decisions in the 1980s and 1990s have found some forms of zoning to be a taking; this is partially a result of the increasing number of conservative justices now in the legal system following the Reagan and Bush years.

Another constitutional issue in environmental law is the legitimacy of agency rulemaking. Prior to the New Deal, agency rulemaking was viewed with deep suspicion by the legal profession. Some questioned the authority of Congress to delegate its legislative powers; others questioned the wisdom of allowing bureaucrats, who are not directly responsible to the people, to make binding rules and regulations. The issue seemed to be settled with the New Deal and the passage of the Administrative Procedure Act in 1946.

However, as the Supreme Court becomes more conservative, a majority of justices may choose to return to the position that Congress is neglecting its duties when delegating its legislative authority. Dissenting in *American Textile Manufacturers* v. *Donovan* in 1981, Justice Rehnquist wrote that in delegating rulemaking responsibility for cotton-dust standards to the Occupational Safety and Health Administration,

> Congress simply abdicated its responsibility for the making of a fundamental and most difficult policy choice. . . .That is a 'quintessential legislative' choice and must be made by the elected representative of the people, not by nonelected officials in the Executive Branch. . . . in so doing Congress unconstitutionally delegated its legislative responsibility to the Executive Branch.[4]

Justice Scalia is also inclined to encourage Congress to give clearer policy directions to the agencies.[5] The issue of delegation, far from having been settled in the middle of the twentieth century, seems likely to be a contentious issue well into the twenty-first century.

Other constitutional issues arise within agencies' procedures for appeals, investigations, and hearing procedures. These will be looked at again in the discussion of the Administrative Procedure Act in chapter 5.

Judicial Decision Making

In deciding the cases brought before them, judges are required to interpret the relevant statutes and regulations, to follow common law precedents, and to apply constitutional principles. One of the more difficult areas for judicial review is statutory interpretation.

Statutory Interpretation

Unlike the common law, which rests on facts and the idea of precedent, statutory law is the result of negotiations and debate. When, for example, a citizen challenges official behavior based on the accusation that the official has violated a statute, the first chore for the reviewing court is to determine just what the statute means. The court can do this by several techniques.

First, the court may examine the intent of the lawmakers in the language of the statute itself and as it is shown in the legislative history. The legislative history is the formal record of the evolution of the statute: testimony offered in support or opposition to the statute, or to parts of the statute; the debates on the legislation; and the amendment sequence. The best source of legislative history is the House, Senate, or Conference Report that accompanies the bill to the final floor vote.

Interpreting legislative history may sound simple, but it may be a judicial morass. First, the testimony is often conflicting. Second, the debates are *real* debates, during which legislators may become convinced that the position of the opposition has merit, so that on one day the legislator holds one opinion and on the next a different opinion. Because the legislative history is the chronological history of the act, it may record ideas or motivations that were ultimately utterly abandoned by the members. Third, the *Congressional Record,* which is the official organ of the Congress and records these testimonies and debates, is given to the members for correction prior to publication. Originally intended to allow members to correct grammatical slips of the tongue, the *Record* may now be substantially edited for the home constituents, and what is printed in the *Record* may bear only a superficial resemblance to what was said on the floor of the Congress.[6] In the 1990s, the conservative members of the Supreme Court are less anxious to delve into the legislative history and seek to decide the cases wherever possible based on the plain language of the act.

In interpreting statutes, the courts also look at contemporary administrative interpretations. The courts presume that if the agencies were very far off the mark in their application of the statute, the legislature would have corrected the mistake. In theory this is so, but in fact, only those aberrations that are brought to the attention of an elected representative with both the interest to do something and the position within the legislature to accomplish it are likely to be corrected. Nevertheless, the courts often continue to defer to agency interpretations of their own statutes, especially where the language is ambiguous and the agency interpretation has been consistent.

The courts will also consider nonlegislative changes that have taken place since the statute was enacted. For example, the Federal Communications Commission (FCC) was established long before cable television existed, but courts are required to determine the cable industry's compliance with the regulatory apparatus put in place by the FCC. The courts must look beyond the direct language of both the statute and the legislative history to find the *intent* of the legislature. This may be a very complex task. For example, when the Forest Reserve Act was enacted in 1891, the legal concept of "endangered species" had not been imagined. In 1989 and 1990, the spotted owl controversy forced legislators, judges, and Forest Service administrators to reconcile the 1891 Act with the Endangered Species Act (1973) requirements and with the demands of the troubled logging industry and environmentalists. How successfully this was accomplished may be indicated by the 1995 Supreme Court decision,[7] which allows federal regulation of private land to protect endangered species, and the high probability that the Endangered

Species Act will not be reauthorized by the 104th Congress without substantial amendment.

Finally, the courts examine past judicial opinions on the statute, partly to
search out the reasoning of other courts (in obedience to the dictates of the
common law) and partly again on the assumption that the legislature would
move to correct any misplaced judicial opinions.

Judicial Precedents

The theory underlying common law interpretation is deceptively simple:
judges determine the facts and then, finding previous cases with similar
facts, reason from analogy to reach their conclusions. In practice, of course,
this may be an amazingly complex process. Astute attorneys will find cases
that parallel their client's position, while the opposing attorneys, working
from the same set of facts, will offer as precedent an entirely different set of
cases that support an entirely opposite judicial conclusion. This is why common law decisions are often referred to as "judge-made" law, because the
judge uses his own discretion to choose between the competing precedents
offered to him. For example, in an Arizona case, *Spur Industries* v. *Del Webb
Development* (1972), Del Webb's company developed his Sun City community toward Spur's feedlot. Webb sued to close the feedlot on the grounds
that it was a public health hazard (i.e., a public nuisance). Spur relied on the
common law protection that Webb was "coming to the nuisance" (or in
kindergarten terms, Spur was there first!). There was no statute to help the
judge decide, and because this was a controversy between two private parties and hence no government involvement, there was no constitutional
question to be resolved. The court exercised the wisdom of Solomon and ordered Spur to move and Webb to pay for the move.

Applying Constitutional Principles

In cases that raise constitutional issues, the court must first consider the language of the Constitution itself. For example, the First Amendment states:

> Congress shall make *no law* respecting an establishment of religion, or pro-
> hibiting the free exercise thereof; or abridging the freedom of speech, or
> of the press; or the right of the people peaceably to assemble, and to peti-
> tion the Government for a redress of grievances [emphasis added].

Supreme Court justices Hugo Black and William O. Douglas were known as
"absolutists" because they refused to accept any restriction on First
Amendment freedoms: they insisted *"no law* means *no law."* Their col-

leagues on the bench did not accept this position, relying instead on another facet of constitutional interpretation: the intent of the Framers as reflected in documents from the Constitutional Convention and from the private and public papers of the men who wrote the Constitution. From these documents and papers it is clear that the Framers intended to protect political speech and broadsheet-pamphlet types of literature. Probably the Framers would be surprised to find their amendment protecting obscene photographs and the *National Enquirer.*

Most judges and legal scholars agree that the Constitution is a "living document" that must be allowed to change with changing conditions. For example, there is no right to privacy written into the Constitution, yet the Supreme Court has held that the Constitution confers such a right. This right to privacy was first announced by Justice Douglas in *Griswold* v. *Connecticut* (1965) when he concluded that the guarantees in the Bill of Rights implied a right to privacy because they could not be achieved without it.

Federalism

One of the most important characteristics of our political system often gets lost in our focus on national government activities. The United States is a federal system: it is an intergovernmental system of local governments, state governments, and the national or federal government.[8] Each level has some degree of autonomy, although the national level has been increasing in power for the last century and the states no longer have the same independence they once had. This can be attributed to several factors.[9] First, presidential candidates for the past century have believed in and campaigned for a strong national government; members of Congress achieved—often inadvertently—the same goals as they provide services to their constituents and thus earn reelection. Second, there has been a widespread disillusionment with the state governments. Many eastern states are dominated by rural interests, and the cities suffer in legislative allocations; as a result, the cities seek federal relief and further enlarge the national power. Third, the United States has had a series of national crises that were clearly beyond the abilities of the states as single government entities: World War I, the Great Depression, World War II, and the several "police actions" since. The expansion of federal social programs to cope with the Depression and the increase in defense spending from both active military engagements and the cold war have increased the power of the national government at the expense of the states. Since the mid-1980s, conservatives in the national government have advocated shifting responsibilities for some policy areas to the states; the states are concerned about bearing the costs of these programs, especially since the renewed emphasis on federalism is often linked to a national budget reduction.

Some environmental policies are set primarily at the state level; for example, certain aspects of wildlife management, such as setting hunting seasons, are state prerogatives although several federal laws restrict state autonomy in this area. (See chapter 6 for a full discussion of the relationship between the federal and state governments in this area.) Under the Tenth Amendment to the Constitution, "the powers not delegated to the United States by the Constitution nor prohibited by it to the States, are reserved to the States respectively, or to the people." However, the Constitution also provides that treaties "shall be the supreme law of the land. . . . any thing in the Constitution or laws of any state to the contrary notwithstanding" (Article VI). Federal exercise of the treaty power and the commerce clause have virtually eliminated absolute state control in any policy area.

Federalism is especially important in environmental law because typically the federal agencies rely upon the states to enforce environmental regulations. Even in nonregulatory areas, the federal presence of such agencies as the Bureau of Land Management, the Forest Service, and the National Park Service affects the states. These agencies manage most federally owned land, and in some states (especially in the West) large tracts of undeveloped land are owned by the national government. In Alaska, Colorado, Oregon, and Utah over half the land belongs to the federal government; in Nevada, 86 percent of the land is federally owned.[10] This has a substantial impact on economic development, tourism, recreation, and the tax base of the state and local governments.

Another reason that federalism is so important in environmental issues is that so many environmental problems cross political boundaries; for example, transboundary air pollution was addressed by the 1990 Clean Air Act Amendments, which created regional ozone transport commissions to deal with smog problems on a regional basis. Interstate compacts, described in the Constitution and subject to Senate ratification, provide another vehicle for state cooperation in many environmental areas. For example, the Potomac River Fisheries Commission is the regulatory body formed in 1963 from the Potomac River Compact (1958) between Maryland and Virginia. Under the compact, the river fisheries are managed in accordance with Maryland laws unless the commission decides otherwise. Although commission regulations may be challenged in court, the commission has never lost a court challenge. Regulations may be changed or revoked by a joint resolution of both the Maryland and Virginia legislatures, but this process has never been used. Although the commission must rely on the states for enforcement, the licensing power is so well established that effective regulation is easily achieved. Many other jurisdictions across the country, which must deal with transboundary issues of water quality, air quality, wildlife management, bridges, harbors, and conservation, choose to use such interstate compacts.[11]

Federalism has other, less obvious effects on environmental law. Lobby groups find their influence increased through federalism because multiple governments provide multiple points of access. State policymakers may be more vulnerable to lobbying because their state economies are more fragile. One western state, for example, has decided not to comply with the state natural resource trustee requirement of the Superfund Amendment and Reauthorization Act (SARA) for fear of alienating one of the major businesses in the state; that particular business would be a likely candidate for state resource damage suits were a trustee to be appointed.[12] During the 1970s, business lobbies often favored state control of pollution enforcement because they thought the states were more vulnerable to economic pressure. In the 1980s, as the Republican administrations of Reagan and Bush began to ease the federal burden on business, businesses found that many states were exceeding federal standards, creating an administrative nightmare for those companies with plants and offices in several states. By the early 1990s, they were back in Congress, advocating federal regulations that would set the ceiling (rather than the floor) for state actions.

Another factor that increases the access points for lobbyists is the staggered election campaigns in a federal system. With national elections held every two years for the House of Representatives, every four years for president, and every six years for the Senate, plus the various gubernatorial and state house elections, a busy lobbyist can be permanently involved with helping or hindering candidates' election prospects at all levels of government. The lobbyist can then pick and choose the races and the candidates that will be the most helpful to his organization's goals.

It is no accident that the national terms of office are so staggered. The Constitution is designed around a federal system. The House, allocated by population—the larger a state's population, the more representatives it has—is balanced by the Senate, which has two senators per state regardless of the state's land mass or population. Until 1913, senators were not even popularly elected but were instead chosen by their own state legislatures. This compromise, struck during the Constitutional Convention, was needed to accommodate the concerns of the states that each be fairly represented. One unanticipated result at times was to balance the states sufficiently to cancel each other, leaving a clear field for the president and his own policies.

Our national culture has changed from the predominately agrarian times of Jefferson. The increased urbanization and industrialization, the development of national transportation networks and international communications, and the increasing social problems, such as homelessness, drug use, and AIDS, are beyond the states' capacities to manage or even to coordinate. The civil rights movement, which could never have succeeded without federal, judicial, and legislative involvement, has also changed the relationship between the states and the national government. Finally, in the past century, state politicians have found it easier to get money from the federal government than to raise state and local taxes, thus endangering their own chances for reelection. And in intergovernmental relations (as well as practically everywhere else), he who pays the piper calls the tune.

Tangier Sound Watermen's Association v. *Douglas* (1982), discussed below, provides a good illustration of the complexities of intergovernmental involvement in resource management. This case also illustrates some of the points to be discussed in chapter 6: the state ownership of wildlife doctrine, conflicts with federal law, and limitations on state and federal authority to regulate.

Case Study: *Tangier Sound* (1982)

Tangier Sound is an area of the Chesapeake Bay that is especially rich in crab habitat. Unfortunately, the Virginia-Maryland state line runs through Tangier Sound; the crabs tend to live in Virginia while the local crabbers live in Maryland.

Prior to 1982, Virginia imposed a residency requirement on anyone seeking a license to fish in Virginia waters. This meant that the Maryland crabbers could not legally follow the crab supply out of their state jurisdiction. The Watermen's Association argued that the residency requirement created an improper barrier to interstate commerce ("Congress shall have Power. . .to regulate Commerce with foreign Nations, and among the several States. . . ." [Article I, Section 8]) and was therefore unconstitutional. They further argued that the only justification for such an interference with interstate commerce would be a legitimate and compelling state interest such as conservation, and Virginia clearly had no conservation interest since there was no limit on the number of Virginia residents allowed to have crabbing licenses. The watermen stated that the privileges and immunities clause of the Constitution ("The Citizens of each State shall be entitled to all Privileges and Immunities of Citizens on the several States," [Article IV, Section 2]) and the equal protection clause ("No state shall . . . deny to any person within its jurisdiction the equal protection of the laws," Fourteenth Amendment) protected their rights to work in Virginia water. Finally, the watermen noted that many of their fishing vessels were federally licensed and were therefore exempt from state restrictions.

Virginia argued that the state had a compelling state interest to allow the residency requirement to stand. First, effective enforcement of regulations required that only residents be allowed to crab. That enabled Virginia inspectors to check boats unloading in Virginia and to ensure court appearances of violators who otherwise must be either arrested or extradited. Second, the requirement was essential for conservation measures. By limiting crabbing to residents, each resident could use the most efficient possible gear, thus maximizing his catch. If nonresident crabbers were permitted, restrictions on gear would be required to protect the crab resource from stress. This in turn would reduce each crabber's catch, and a state may legitimately protect an internal industry. As an aside, Virginia offered the federalism defense: by restricting a state's control of its resources, the state is restrained from trying "novel social and economic experiments without risk to the rest of the country."[13]

Virginia dismissed the constitutional claims advanced by the watermen. The commerce clause was not violated because the residency requirement was not a barrier to *trade;* watermen were allowed to buy or sell crabs and to transport them in, out, or through the state. The only prohibition was against catching them in the state. The privileges and immunities clause was not violated; the watermen were not restricted from lawfully pursuing their trade because the trade itself was not lawful. In a desperate attempt to stave off the inevitable, Virginia advanced the trespass defense: since crabbing by necessity disturbs the bottom, any taking of crabs is also a trespass on state-owned land. (The states do own the submerged lands; it is navigation on the water above that is given into federal jurisdiction.)

Of course, what was truly at issue here is Virginia's desire to keep out-of-state crabbers (and in particular, Maryland crabbers, with whom a centuries-old feud existed) from profiting in Virginia wildlife. Virginia was really asserting state independence from federal interference in natural resource management. The federal presence in fisheries management in the Bay is felt in two areas: legal constraints such as were at issue in *Tangier Sound,* and in certain species-specific (for example, striped bass) management plans.

Neither state was particularly eager to enter into cooperative management plans (although in the late eighties those positions softened). Maryland was so reluctant that she entered the *Tangier Sound* case on the side of Virginia and against her own citizens. The arguments raised against cooperative management had four bases. First was the difference in political philosophy between the two states: Virginia was more reluctant to impose and to accept regulation than was Maryland, but once regulatory authority was delegated, the Virginia legislature was willing to rely upon administrative expertise. Second, Maryland's economic and political base was more dependent on fisheries than was Virginia's. This reduced Maryland's willingness to negotiate and to compromise. If Maryland and Virginia were to formalize a cooperative agreement through, for example, an interstate compact, some state control would be lost and a new center of power developed. The states were understandably reluctant to risk this. Third, the regulatory structures in place and the implementation strategies used varied greatly between the two states; they did not agree on season, catch limits, size limits, or even legal gear. Finally, the portion of the Bay under Maryland jurisdiction is biologically homogeneous to a great extent. In contrast, Virginia has separate ecosystems in each major river in addition to the great difference between the mouth of the Chesapeake Bay and the areas closer to the Virginia-Maryland state line. The Bay is a marine environment in its lower reaches that blends to a brackish one as it approaches the Susquehanna. Even if the Chesapeake were within only one political jurisdiction, its size and variability would make management difficult.

In 1982, the Federal District Court in Richmond decided in favor of the Watermen's Association, finding the residency requirement to be a violation of the commerce clause. Virginia did not appeal, and one more area of state autonomy was reduced in favor of broader resource management objectives.

Suggested Reading

Carter, Lief. *Reason in Law* (2nd. ed.). Boston: Little, Brown and Co., 1984. An elegant and pithy explanation of how judges think and how they *ought* to think.

Cox, Susan J. B. (Susan J. Buck). "Interjurisdictional Management in Chesapeake Bay Fisheries." *Coastal Management* 16 (1988): 151–166. This article elaborates on the issues raised in the *Tangier Sound* case.

Garraty, John (ed.). *Quarrels that Have Shaped the Constitution*. New York: Harper & Row (Torchbook), 1964. Sixteen landmark Supreme Court cases are presented in a "We were there" format. They are highly readable and give an indelible understanding of the cases. Especially relevant for environmental law are "The Dartmouth College Case," "The Steamboat Case," and "The Charles River Bridge Case."

Nice, David. *Federalism: The Politics of Intergovernmental Relations*. New York: St. Martin's Press, 1987. Academic but thorough.

Notes

1. The common law system is indeed *English* rather than *British*. Scotland, which joined England in 1707, has a form of law based on the continental system, a reflection of the long Scottish association with France.

2. *Martin* v. *Waddell*, 41 *U.S.* (16 Pet.) 367 (1842), at 416.

3. As a North Carolinian, I must add a caveat here, since the governor of North Carolina does not have veto power over legislation and his signature is not required for it to become law. However, for all other states and for the United States Congress, the signature of the executive is required.

4. *American Textile Manufacturers Institute, et al.* v. *Donovan, Secretary of Labor, et al.*, 452 *U.S.* 490 (1981), at 547–548.

5. See, for example, Scalia's dissent in *Mistretta* v. *United States*, 488 U.S. 373 (1989).

6. Changes to this editing process were proposed under the Republican House rules in the 104th Congress. Since each chamber sets its own procedures for the *Record*, Senate concurrence was not necessary. However, veteran *Record* watchers have not detected any significant change as of August 1995.

7. *Babbitt* v. *Sweet Home Chapter of Communities for a Greater Oregon*, 115 S. Ct. 714 (1995).

8. Examples of other federal systems are Canada, Australia, and Switzerland.

9. The following discussion is drawn from William Keefe, Henry Abraham, William Flanigan, Charles O. Jones, Morris Ogul, and John Spanier, *American Democracy: Institutions, Politics, and Policies* (Homewood, IL: Dorsey Press, 1983), Chapter 2.

10. Tom Arrandale, *The Battle for Natural Resources* (Washington, DC: Congressional Quarterly Press, 1983), p. 47.

11. V. Randall Tinsley and Larry Nielsen, "Interstate Fisheries Arrangements: Application of a Pragmatic Classification Scheme for Interstate Arrangements," *Virginia Journal of Natural Resources Law*, 6 (2), Spring 1987. 265–321.

12. Susan J. Buck and Edward Hathaway, "Designating State Natural Resource Trustees under SARA," in Michael Hamilton (ed.), *Regulatory Federalism, Natural Resources and Environmental Management* (Washington, DC: ASPA, 1990), pp. 83–94.

13. *New State Ice Co.* v. *Liebmann*, 285 U.S. 262 (1932), at 311, Justice Brandeis dissenting.

Chapter Two

Environmentalism in the United States

While American environmentalism is rooted in the works of philosophers such as Thoreau, preservationists like John Muir, and politically active conservationists like Theodore Roosevelt and Gifford Pinchot, the contemporary American emphasis on environmentalism as regulatory policy is of fairly recent origin. This chapter traces the environmental movement in the United States from the 1960s through the first two years of the Clinton administration. The keystone legislation of the thirty-year period from the sixties to the nineties is the 1969 National Environmental Policy Act (NEPA). The forces leading up to NEPA's passage and the intentions of Congress in passing it provide the second portion of the chapter. This section includes a discussion of the *Calvert Cliffs* case, which set the stage for the powerful impact of the Environmental Impact Statement (EIS) provision of NEPA. The third section takes a brief look at the Environmental Protection Agency, established in 1970. The last sections discuss the "environmental decade" of the seventies and the developments of subsequent years.

Beginnings of the Environmental Movement

In the fall of 1962, Rachel Carson's book *Silent Spring* was published with little fanfare. Formerly a biologist with the U.S. Fish and Wildlife Service, Carson had written wonderful, lyrical books about nature; this book took on the chemical industry in much the same way as Ralph Nader's *Unsafe at Any*

Speed took on the auto industry in 1965. The chemical industry predicted an early demise for the book: "It is fair to hope that by March or April *Silent Spring* no longer will be an interesting conversational topic."[1] The title was an act of genius, and the American imagination was caught by the vision of a spring devoid of birdsong or katydids or bullfrogs bellowing in the night. Carson's book is still an interesting conversational topic over a quarter of a century later. Its effects are larger than reducing the use of pesticides or saving the bald eagle. The book was a triggering event for the entire environmental movement because it mobilized the average American. Biocide *was* in everyone's backyard.

There were other forces at work as well in the sixties. The Vietnam War was provoking intense controversy and conflict in American society, and the related counterculture movement was prompting a romantic, back-to-nature perspective. The financial prosperity of the fifties, coupled with increasing mobility and leisure time, regenerated interest in outdoor activities. Causes were "in," and the environment, with its appeal to health and aesthetics and its underlying antibusiness philosophy, was a prime candidate to become a cause. This cause was embraced so thoroughly by the American people that it has now become one of our enduring American values, as Ronald Reagan discovered to his dismay when he misinterpreted his electoral mandate to include reduced environmental protection.

Looking back through the sixties, we can see the inexorable building of American consciousness toward Earth Day. In 1963, the Clean Air Act authorized federal hearings on *potential* air pollution problems; in 1964, the Wilderness Act set aside tracts of land and barred them permanently from development. A New York case, *Scenic Hudson,* for the first time admitted scenic and recreational criteria in legal actions. In 1966, the Endangered Species Preservation Act was passed, and in 1968, the spectacular American Apollo space flight that circled the globe produced moving photographs of a fragile planet.

Early in 1969, a major "trigger event" shocked the American public into demanding immediate action to protect the environment. On 28 January 1969, Union Oil Company's Platform A in the Pacific Ocean began to disgorge oil. Over eleven days, 235,000 gallons of crude oil spread out, ruining forty miles of Santa Barbara's beautiful Pacific beaches. Thousands of birds and mammals died; one dramatic photograph shows an oil-soaked bird surrounded by debris and gazing in a doomed stupor over the surf. The spill became a national event, searing the public conscience with images of ruined water and pathetic, dying animals. Five months later the Cuyahoga River in Ohio caught fire. One of President Nixon's aides wrote that the political mood in Washington engendered by the public outcry could only be captured by the word *hysteria*. On 1 January 1970, President Nixon signed the National Environmental Policy Act (NEPA), arguably the most important piece of environmental legislation in the century.

National Environmental Policy Act

Congress had five major objectives in passing NEPA. These objectives were spelled out in section 2 of the act:

> To declare a national policy which will encourage productive and enjoyable harmony between man and his environment; to promote efforts which will prevent or eliminate damage to the environment and biosphere and stimulate the health and welfare of man; to enrich the understanding of the ecological systems and natural resources important to the Nation; and to establish a Council on Environmental Quality.[2]

Mandating a National Policy

The first purpose of NEPA was to provide a clear mandate for all federal agencies, regardless of their mission or position within the government, "to create and maintain conditions under which man and nature can exist in productive harmony."[3] There were no exemptions for any federal agency; all were expected to comply and to cooperate with other agencies. NEPA provided a "welcome rationality mechanism" for an increasingly complex policy area, and the NEPA model has been adopted not only by numerous American states but also by other nations and some multilateral organizations.[4]

Establishing Action-Forcing Requirements

The second objective of the act was to establish action-forcing procedures for the federal agencies. It was not enough to contemplate environmental concerns; under § 102(2)(C), the agencies were required to write an Environmental Impact Statement (EIS) for all federal projects and to circulate the statements to local, state, and other federal agencies for their comments:

> Imagine the shock of Richard Nixon and many members of Congress when, early in 1970, they discovered that these apparently innocuous words of §102 could be the basis of very real lawsuits. §102, like a snake in the grass, contained the hidden but potent impact statement requirement.[5]

This provision exploded into a powerful weapon for the citizen lobbies to delay or to halt numerous projects; the *Calvert Cliffs* case presented at the end of this section was a major influence in shaping the power of the EIS requirement.

The act stipulated that the social sciences were to be integrated into the decision processes; no longer were the relatively simple physical data sufficient. This provision has not been fully utilized. For example, a model social impact assessment performed on the proposed Chief Joseph Dam considered the impact that an influx of several hundred unmarried construction workers would have on the recreation demands and social patterns in a rural town of less than two thousand. The Army Corps of Engineers analysts wrote that "patterns of adult entertainment of new citizens may be somewhat different" from those of the original residents.[6] This is certainly an understatement.

Other action-forcing requirements were that agencies must consider qualitative information, protect the global environment "where consistent with the foreign policy of the United States," and deliberately seek the least damaging alternatives. This last provision has conflicted with presidential efforts to impose cost-benefit analysis on environmental regulations. (The impact of these regulatory reforms is discussed later in this chapter.)

Council on Environmental Quality

Another objective of NEPA was the creation of the Council on Environmental Quality (CEQ). This council of three members appointed by the president is subject to Senate confirmation and has statutory obligations such as data collection and an annual report to the president which forms the basis of his annual Environmental Quality Report to Congress. In the 1990s, the Environmental Protection Agency (EPA) provides significant assistance to CEQ in preparing this report. Under NEPA, the federal government, and especially CEQ, is to foster the collection of data and indices of environmental quality. This is not as simple as it might sound. For example, the Chesapeake Bay is influenced by the District of Columbia and the states of Maryland, Virginia, and Pennsylvania. Only Maryland and Virginia have shorelines in the Bay itself. Several fisheries stocks migrate between the states and sometimes even into federal waters. Both states have sophisticated biological data collection systems but the two are not statistically compatible. The data collected in Virginia measure slightly different variables at different times in the life cycles or the calendar than do the data in Maryland. Statistical packages are being developed to integrate the data sets. This is a relatively simple problem dealing with one (admittedly large and varied) body of water and two state governments. Other problems are more complex. Some of the problems are simply not amenable to even the most cooperative of efforts. For example, the ecological systems associated with water supplies vary so extensively across several thousand miles of territory that no single data set can adequately describe them.

Reagan tried to abolish the CEQ early in his first administration but was thwarted by the statutory requirement for the council. He contented himself with cutting the Council's budget by 62 percent, thus reducing both its personnel and its reports. The election of a Democratic president did not presage a return to the glory days of the Carter administration. Indeed, early in his administration, Clinton proposed eliminating CEQ and replacing it with an environmental policy adviser. This was not done, and CEQ has regained some staff but "it has clearly ceased to be a major player in White House politics."[7] However, proposals to eliminate CEQ continue; for example, in July 1995, the House of Representative Appropriations Committee considered a bill that, in addition to imposing drastic budget cuts on EPA, eliminated CEQ.

The greatest impact from NEPA has come from the universal federal mandate to take environmental concerns into account and the action-forcing procedures exemplified by the EIS requirement. The first court decision to examine the underlying intent of NEPA was the *Calvert Cliffs* case.

The *Calvert Cliffs* Case (1971)

The case of *Calvert Cliffs Coordinating Committee, Inc.* v. *United States Atomic Energy Commission* (1971) arose when the United States Atomic Energy Commission (AEC) issued rules governing the granting of construction and licensing permits for nuclear power plants. AEC claimed that its rules complied with the procedural requirements of NEPA. However, the Calvert Cliffs Coordinating Committee, a Maryland public interest group trying to halt the licensing of a partially constructed nuclear plant on the Chesapeake Bay, sued on the basis that AEC did not adequately consider environmental issues when the rules were promulgated. The Calvert Cliffs group had four specific arguments. First, the hearing board within AEC that made the final determinations on permits and licenses was not required to consider environmental factors unless an outside party or the regulatory staff raised the issue during the review. Second, in an attempt to "grandfather" some facilities, nonradiological environmental issues were not allowed to be raised in cases where the hearing notice was published in the *Federal Register* prior to 4 March 1971. Third, if other federal agencies certified to AEC that their environmental standards were satisfied by the construction project, the hearing board was prohibited from considering the same environmental factors themselves. Finally, any facility with a construction permit issued before NEPA compliance was required could not be formally reevaluated until the contractors applied for an operating license.

One of the most important aspects of Judge Skelly Wright's decision was the distinction he drew between the substantive requirements of NEPA's Section 101 and the procedural requirements of Section 102, which contains the EIS provision. Section 101, he wrote, provided a broad, substantive mandate to all federal agencies to "use all practicable means and measures" to protect the environment. Environmental values were to become part of a pantheon of values that must be considered before any federal agency acted. Judge Wright found this mandate to be flexible, giving wide discretionary powers to the agencies. In contrast, he found the procedural requirements of Section 102 to be very strict. Unlike Section 101, with its "practicable means and measures" language, Section 102 compels the agencies to consider environmental factors "to the fullest extent possible":

> We must stress as forcefully as possible that this language does not provide an escape hatch for footdragging agencies; it does not make NEPA's procedural requirements somehow "discretionary." Congress did not intend the Act to be such a paper tiger. Indeed, the requirement of environmental consideration "to the fullest extent possible" sets a high standard for the agencies, a standard which must be rigorously enforced by the reviewing courts.[8]

The importance of this ruling can hardly be overestimated. By the time the EIS issue reached the Supreme Court, Judge Wright's opinion had been cited as precedent over two hundred times. The legal sophistication of the environmental lobbies is rooted in their response to the power of the EIS. NEPA changed from a bill viewed by most of its proponents as a "motherhood and apple pie" measure to an act that delayed the B-1 bomber and the Alaska oil pipeline. Major environmental groups and citizen plaintiffs have used NEPA and EIS to force federal agencies to consider all environmental factors when any federal action, however loosely defined, is contemplated.

Formation of the Environmental Protection Agency

The Environmental Protection Agency (EPA) was created by executive order in 1970. President Nixon's advisers saw EPA as a coordinating agency that would cut across existing agency lines to provide a coherent national policy for the environment. EPA has complete or partial jurisdiction over air pollution, water pollution, drinking water contamination, hazardous waste disposal, pesticides, radiation, and toxic substances.[9] It also participates in implementation of many laws administered by other agencies at both the national and state levels. EPA conducts its own research and, "by recruiting employees who value environmental protection, EPA has also developed a high level of cohesion."[10]

EPA is unique in its organization: all other regulatory agencies (as opposed to regulatory commissions that are not headed by a single political appointee) are housed administratively in some executive branch department, such as Department of Interior or Agriculture. The EPA administrator is appointed by the president and oversees the Washington staff and ten regional offices. EPA is relatively independent and has control over its own information sources, which usually enhances political power. This has not been the case for EPA.

Bureaucratic theory supports the prediction that such a mega-agency would fall victim in interagency battles for resources. EPA does not have an exclusive advocate in the Cabinet, it regulates powerful businesses, and its support constituencies must spread their resources across many other agencies. Despite a workforce committed to environmental protection, shortages of staff and other resources have led to selective enforcement and lowered morale. The unfortunate antics of senior political appointees, such as Anne Gorsuch Burford and James Watt, led to a crisis of confidence within the agency that was only partially dispelled with the return of William Ruckelshaus in 1983 as EPA administrator. Funding has been inadequate since the first Reagan administration. Even with increases made by President Bush in both staff and budget, staff levels in 1993 barely exceeded the levels in 1980, and the budget for FY 1993 was only 21 percent above the FY 1975 budget.[11] Threats of budget cuts continued under the Republican-controlled Congress of 1995: in July the House Appropriations Committee considered a bill that would cut EPA's budget by one-third.[12]

It is doubtful that EPA will ever return to the halcyon days when cabinet-level status seemed a possibility. Policy implementation at the agency is often driven by the need to comply with court orders,[13] and the agency is confronted with "a profound legislative distrust permeating almost all the Agency's congressional relationships."[14] To succeed in meeting its many congressional mandates, the EPA needs a massive infusion of resources, which, given its poor record in meeting statutory deadlines and its lack of success with such programs as Superfund, seems unlikely. The closing years of the century will prove a critical time for the agency.[15]

The Environmental Decade: The 1970s

The seventies have been called the environmental decade. Major pieces of legislation were put into place during the ten-year period between NEPA and the first Reagan administration. In 1970, the Resource Recovery Act

(Solid Waste Disposal Act) was passed, the Clean Air Act was amended, and EPA was established. The first Earth Day, 22 April 1970, was celebrated by millions of Americans who were also celebrating the apparent end to our involvement in Vietnam. In 1971, Barry Commoner published *The Closing Circle,* and the Alaska Native Claims Settlement Act authorized federal nomination of "national interest lands." In 1972, the Federal Water Pollution Control Act, the Federal Environmental Pesticide Control Act, the Ocean Dumping Act, and the Coastal Zone Management Act were all passed. After this, legislation was more often refined rather than initiated; the most impressive legislative achievement was the 1980 Comprehensive Environmental Response, Compensation, and Liability Act (CERCLA or Superfund).

Nonlegislative landmarks included the United Nations Conference on the Human Environment, which led to the United Nations Environmental Programme, and the publication of *Limits to Growth* by the Club of Rome and *Small is Beautiful* by English economist E. F. Schumacher. However, the environmental accomplishments of the seventies were overshadowed by the tragedies of Love Canal and Three Mile Island.

A third environmental crisis of the 1970s involved American dependence on foreign oil. In October 1973, the Organization of Petroleum Exporting Countries (OPEC) voted to cut its oil production by 5 percent, and the Saudis halted their oil exports to the United States, threatening to maintain their embargo until the Nixon administration changed its pro-Israeli stance. Fuel prices at the gas pump shot up, and Americans old enough to have been driving in 1973 remember long lines and quotas on gasoline. The "crisis" continued in one form or another through the Ford and Carter administrations; even when petroleum products were reasonably plentiful, the fear of a recurrence drove federal energy policy. Reagan was committed to deregulation even in energy policy, believing that a free market and regulatory relief would be most beneficial for the beleaguered energy industry. This brought his administration in direct conflict with environmentalists as federal lands and the Outer Continental Shelf were opened, or proposed for opening, for exploration.

Environmental Action in the Eighties

With many of Reagan's policies, what was perhaps bad for the environment was good for the environmental movement. During the seventies, environmental concerns became routinized and the dramatic events of the sixties faded from public memory. The scandals of the Reagan administration in the EPA, and the lightning rod activities of Reagan's Secretary of Interior James Watt, reignited general public concern.

Reagan's appointments of Anne Gorsuch (later Burford) to head EPA and of James Watt to be Secretary of Interior helped mobilize renewed support for environmental activists. Brilliant in their own ways, neither Gorsuch nor Watt was sympathetic to the conservation, preservation, and regulation ideologies of the environmental establishment. Warning bells were sounded when Reagan discovered "killer trees" robbing us of our oxygen. Watt explained during his Senate confirmation hearings that conservation was necessary only for one more generation, until the Second Coming, and changed the buffalo on the Interior stationery to face right instead of left. "Good science" was the excuse used to delay environmental decisions; even in the mid-eighties, the Reagan administration was refusing to acknowledge the damage done on this continent by acid rain, pending further scientific investigations. During Burford's administration, EPA became politicized, or at least it was perceived to be politicized, causing damage to its effectiveness with both the regulated industries and the Congress, neither of which now trusted its findings or accepted its decisions.

Despite these problems, several important pieces of legislation were passed or renewed during Reagan's tenure. In 1986, Superfund was reauthorized in the Superfund Amendment and Reauthorization Act (SARA). SARA did more than simply continue the 1980 Superfund legislation. It added, among other provisions, a community right-to-know provision that caught the attention—and conscience—not only of communities but also of the businesses within the communities. Now local communities must be informed of the location, nature, and volume of certain hazardous materials within their jurisdiction. Many corporations had simply never bothered to assemble this information, and at least one, DuPont, was so horrified at the aggregate data that they initiated a nationwide chemical reduction program. The focus of SARA expanded from simply cleanup to include the protection and management of natural resources. The new requirements for natural resource trustees for the first time included payment for habitat destruction and indirect damage to natural resources. This expanded focus required a degree of cooperation between the regulatory agencies and the resource management agencies at both the federal and state levels that was unprecedented.

Reagan's heir in the White House, George Bush, promised to be the environmental president. Bush needed to distance himself from Ronald Reagan, and in retrospect this promise was largely a campaign decision triggered by national events such as the fire in Yellowstone National Park.[16] Early signs were encouraging as he appointed William Reilly, president of the World Wildlife Fund and Conservation Foundation, as head of EPA. His choice of Michael Deland, former director of EPA's Region I office in Boston, as Chairman of CEQ was widely supported in the environmental communities. However, Bush's other nominations to environmental positions were not as well received. For example, James Cason, Bush's nominee to head the Forest Service, was not confirmed by the Senate because of charges he was biased toward mining and oil interests, and the appointment of Manuel Lujan from New Mexico as Secretary of Interior sent a strong signal that it would be business as usual in the West.

In his efforts to promote environmentalism, Bush was partly hampered by budget concerns; perhaps this is one reason he did little to prove that his proenvironment campaign position was more than just political rhetoric. With the federal deficit perceived by a majority of Americans as the most severe problem facing the country, and energy sources increasingly uncertain, generous environmental budgets were unlikely. As a good conservative, Bush favored market solutions to environmental problems and thus encountered opposition for new programs from a largely Democratic Congress. Although he seemed to prefer regulatory reform over deregulation (one might argue that not much remained to deregulate, leaving only reform as an alternative anyway), budgetary constraints inhibited the flexibility of either the President or the Congress to commit needed resources.

The optimism of environmentalists in 1990 soon faded. With the notable exception of William Reilly, most Bush appointees favored regulatory reform over strong environmental programs. Vice President Quayle soon chaired the White House Council on Competitiveness, a new organization used to weaken environmental regulations by imposing stringent cost-effectiveness criteria. Through no fault of his own, Reilly was unable to make the changes his supporters had anticipated:

> Reilly's efforts were often derailed by members of the White House staff, especially by former chief of staff John Sununu, who toned down EPA pronouncements on global warming and wetlands preservation, and by budget director Richard Darman, who once called Reilly 'a global rock star.'[17]

His spectacular and public disagreements with Bush over American participation in the 1992 United Nations Conference on the Environment and Development (UNCED) in Rio de Janeiro eroded relations between Bush and EPA even further:

> The chill blowing toward the EPA from the White House was unmistakable, a continuing effective obstacle to many environmental policy initiatives from Congress or the bureaucracy.[18]

Although serious environmental issues, such as wetlands protection and the *Exxon Valdez* spill in Alaska's Prince William Sound, arose during the Bush administration, perhaps the most serious problem came from the clash of environmental values and economic growth posed by the Endangered Species Act (ESA). The collision between the timber industry and the Northern Spotted Owl occurred on George Bush's watch. In 1989, the Secretary of Interior listed the spotted owl as an endangered species, raising the ire of loggers who saw old growth forests not as habitat but as economically unproductive timber ripe for harvest. As of 1995, when the Supreme Court declared in *Babbitt* v. *Sweet Home Chapter of Communities for a Greater Oregon* that Congress intended ESA to protect habitat on private as well as public lands, the battle over endangered species is still joined.

The environmental high point of Bush's presidency occurred with the passage in 1990 of the Clean Air Act Amendments; the amendments strengthened and extended the Clean Air Act, and Bush's leadership was essential for their passage. This was the only major environmental legislation passed during his term, and in the first two years of the 1990s, many environmental laws were weakened or themselves endangered. For example, despite Bush's campaign promise of "no net loss of wetlands," a new federal wetlands manual—written with the help of Quayle's Council on Competitiveness—redefined wetlands to permit some wetlands destruction.

By the end of the Bush-Quayle campaign against Bill Clinton and Al Gore, public opinion polls showed a high disapproval rating for Bush's record on the environment. During 1991 and 1992, Bush had opposed the reauthorization of most of the major environmental laws. This had the effect of delaying reauthorization of the Clean Water Act, the Resource Conservation and Recovery Act, and the Endangered Species Act, which pushed the reauthorization fights into the Clinton administration.[19]

The Final Decade of the Twentieth Century

The closing decade of the twentieth century began with environmental fanfare: the 1990 Clean Air Act Amendments on the national level and the 1992 UNCED in Rio at the international level. By 1995, there was less to celebrate. Russia had begun to reveal the horrifying extent of the environmental problems throughout the old Soviet bloc.[20] International action on biodiversity was proceeding without American participation. Meanwhile, President Clinton's administration struggled to protect landmark environmental legislation passed since 1970.

Clinton's administration got off to a strong environmental start. Although the environment was not a major issue in the 1992 campaign, those voters most concerned about the environment supported the Clinton-Gore ticket five to one.[21] Vice-presidential candidate Al Gore, the senator from Tennessee, gave an environmental luster to the ticket; his 1992 book, *Earth in the Balance,* was a best-seller.[22] Gore has not assumed the mantle of environmental leadership that many environmentalists thought he would. However, bureaucrats at CEQ and the Fish and Wildlife Service suggest that the appointment of key Gore supporters has quietly influenced environmental policy, for example, working to improve the government's biodiversity programs by encouraging multispecies and habitat conservation (dubbed the "ecosystem" approach[23]).

Just as Bush's appointment of William Reilly seemed auspicious, Clinton's appointment of Bruce Babbitt as Secretary of Interior was greeted with quiet jubilation by environmentalists. Babbitt, whose "family" dominate business and politics in northern Arizona, had a sterling environmental record as governor of Arizona. Then in April 1993, Clinton signed the Biodiversity Convention, which had opened for signature at the Rio Conference.

It is a bit early to evaluate the impact of the Clinton administration on environmental policy. Since the midyear elections, Clinton has been hampered by a recalcitrant Congress. The House, under the leadership of Speaker Newt Gingrich, was initially interested primarily in passing its "Contract with America." In the Senate, majority leader Bob Dole has one eye on his presidential campaign. It seems unlikely that Clinton will achieve any landmark environmental legislation to rank beside Bush's Clean Air Act Amendments. The Biodiversity Convention is stalled in the Senate Foreign Relations Committee, where chairman Jesse Helms of North Carolina has consistently opposed ratification. Probably the best that supporters of the Endangered Species Act can expect is for the act to be reauthorized without being eviscerated.[24]

Clinton inherited more than just the reauthorization fights from the Bush years. He was also left with the extremely volatile issue of environmental justice (also called environmental equity): the problem that locally undesirable land uses (LULUs) are sited disproportionately in low-income and minority communities.[25] For example, a predominately black community in Warren County, North Carolina, was chosen in 1982 as the site for a polychlorinated biphenyl (PCB) waste disposal facility; protests and demonstrations against the facility were unsuccessful in halting construction but did call attention to the problem. Subsequent research by the U.S. General Accounting Office (GAO) and the United Church of Christ Commission for Racial Justice found that race and economic status were significant variables in the location of commercial hazardous waste facilities.[26]

Some writers argue that minority groups are unable to stop damaging developments such as waste dumps in their neighborhoods because they lack political power, while others charge that this is evidence of deliberate racial discrimination. Some observers say that the conclusions of deliberate discrimination are not supported by the data. They note that the data do not indicate whether the poor or minority communities were in place at the time of the siting decision or if the poor community developed around the site because the facility's proximity lowered housing values. They also note that constraints such as zoning restrictions that are beyond the control of the siting decisionmakers may have affected the decision.[27] To respond to these and related issues, President Clinton issued Executive Order 12898 requiring each federal agency to

> make achieving environmental justice part of its mission by identifying and addressing, as appropriate, disproportionately high and adverse human health or environmental effects of its programs, policies, and activities on minority populations and low-income populations.

The order also directs the EPA administrator to form an interagency Federal Working Group on Environmental Justice to assist the other federal agencies to develop an environmental justice strategy.

A third inheritance from the 1980s was regulatory reform in the federal environmental bureaucracy.[28] Serious attention to the regulatory problems at EPA began with Lee Thomas, EPA administrator from 1985 to 1989; under his leadership, EPA published *Unfinished Business,* a comparison of the human risks associated with a number of environmental problems.[29] EPA's problems, discussed earlier in this chapter, are rooted in its organizational structure and the struggle for bureaucratic resources. Responding to these difficulties, in 1989, William Reilly ordered a second report, *Reducing Risk: Setting Priorities for Environmental Protection,* published in 1990.[30] This document set out Reilly's plans for changing the way EPA conducted its regulatory responsibilities. EPA's goals were to determine relative environmental risks through scientific analysis and then use the rankings to prioritize short-term and long-term programs; to rely less on "command and control" mechanisms and more on market strategies such as were established in the 1990 Clean Air Act Amendments; to increase EPA discretion in encouraging pollution prevention rather than relying on expensive cleanup projects (see chapter 3 for a discussion of administration discretion); and to emphasize source reduction as a waste management technique.[31] This continues to drive regulatory reform in EPA in the mid-1990s:

> Risk-based decisionmaking is now a centerpiece of EPA policy, but it has nevertheless undergone an important shift in meaning, reflecting changes both in the environmental policy agenda and in the use of risk assessment to address that agenda. These include changes in policy concerns . . . ; in the use of risk assessment itself, from quantitative analysis of particular substances to comparative analysis of risk priorities; and in policy re-

sponses to these new priorities, from pollution control to pollution prevention and from "command-and-control regulation" to a broader range
of "risk reduction tools."[32]

Economic rationality would suggest that a more flexible process, if prop-
erly designed, will ease the regulatory burden without losing environmental quality. Certainly this process has worked well in Great Britain, where
pollution control is both a political and a scientific question. Pollution control is conducted with "regard to local conditions, to the current state of scientific, technical and medical knowledge of the potential harm or nuisance
involved and to the financial implications."[33] In theory this allows sufficient
discretion on the part of the regulatory agencies to negotiate with offenders
in a reasonable manner rather than forcing compliance with rigid standards.

In absolute numbers, the improvement in Great Britain's environment in
the past has been impressive.[34] However, we must be careful when drawing
parallels between Great Britain and the United States. David Vogel attributes
the British success to three factors: "a highly respected civil service, a business community that was prepared to cooperate with government officials,
and a public that was not particularly mistrustful of large corporations,"[35]
all factors that are lacking in the United States. The relatively high social status of public officials allows them to deal with industrial managers on an
equal footing, and the presumptions of good intentions, on one hand, and
economic flexibility, on the other hand, enable the two groups to work cooperatively rather than as antagonists.

Still, as the federal government moves toward a new century, a cooperative attitude among business, government, and the environmental community may prove more successful than the previous one of distrust and an-
tagonism. It seemed that with the Bush administration, these three groups
were moving toward an accommodation. However, the sharp ideological
divisions between Congress and the White House, and within Congress,
have made environmental problems more visible and less amenable to compromise.

Suggested Reading

Anderson, Frederick. *NEPA in the Courts: A Legal Analysis of the National Environmental Policy Act.* Baltimore: Johns Hopkins University Press for Resources for
the Future, 1973. An excellent discussion of the purposes behind NEPA and of
its impact in the first three years after passage.

Clarke, Jeanne Nienaber and Daniel McCool. *Staking Out the Terrain: Power Differ-
entials among Natural Resource Management Agencies.* Albany: State University of

New York Press, 1985. An excellent study of bureaucratic behavior of five main federal resource agencies (Corps of Engineers, Forest Service, Bureau of Reclamation, Park Service, and the Fish and Wildlife Service). The authors develop a useful model of bureaucratic power that is based on the ability of agencies to expand resources and their jurisdictions.

Kaufman, Herbert. *The Forest Ranger: A Study in Administrative Behavior.* Baltimore: Johns Hopkins University Press, 1967. The classic study of socialization of Forest Service professionals into the bureaucratic norms of the Forest Service.

Lacey, Michael, ed. *Government and Environmental Politics: Essays on Historical Developments Since World War Two.* Washington, DC: Woodrow Wilson Center, 1991. Useful, topical essays on conservation, parks, land management, wildlife, nuclear power, and toxic substances. The list of authors is impressive and includes Samuel Hays, Joseph Sax, and Frank Gregg.

Lash, Jonathan, Katherine Gillman, and David Sheridan. *A Season of Spoils.* New York: Pantheon, 1984. Subtitled "The Reagan Administration's Attack on the Environment," this book exposes the excesses of the first Reagan administration. While it is certainly biased in its interpretations of the facts, the research is solid. The book is entertaining as well as informative.

Nash, Roderick. *American Environmentalism: Readings in Conservation History,* 3rd ed. New York: McGraw-Hill, 1990. Superb collection of original documents in American conservation history with clear introductory comments. Be sure to get the third edition, as the first two are not edited as crisply.

Sale, Kirkpatrick. *The Green Revolution: The American Environmental Movement 1962–1992.* New York: Hill and Wang, 1993. Concise, solid and well-written summary of three decades of environmental struggle with an analysis of what it means for the future.

Shabecoff, Philip. *A Fierce Green Fire: The American Environmental Movement.* New York: Hill and Wang, 1993. Best of the 1990s crop of one-volume surveys of the nation's environmental movement from pre-Revolutionary times to the present, written by the former national environmental reporter for the *New York Times.*

Vogel, David. "The Politics of the Environment, 1970–1987: A Big Agenda." *Wilson Quarterly* 11(4) (Autumn 1987): 51–68. A graceful summary of the political influences on major environmental actions during the seventies and eighties.

Notes

1. Ted Williams, "'Silent Spring' Revisited," *Modern Maturity* (October-November 1987), p. 48.

2. 42 U.S.C. § 4321.

3. 42 U.S.C. § 4331.

4. Zygmunt Plater, Robert Abrams, and William Goldfarb, *Environmental Law and Policy: Nature, Law, and Society* (St. Paul, MN: West, 1992), p. 600.

5. Plater, Abrams, and Goldfarb, p. 601.

6. A. A. Harnisch, et al. *Chief Joseph Dam Columbia River, Washington Community Impact Reports*. IWR Reports 78-3 and 78-R2. (Fort Belvoir, VA: U.S. Army Engineer Institute for Water Resources, 1978), p. 413.

7. Walter A. Rosenbaum, *Environmental Politics and Policy* 3rd ed. (Washington, DC: Congressional Quarterly Press, 1995), p. 119.

8. *Calvert Cliffs Coordinating Committee, Inc.* v. *United States Atomic Energy Commission* (1971), 449 F.2d 1109 (D.C. Cir.) at 1114.

9. Kenneth J. Meier, *Regulation: Politics, Bureaucracy, and Economics* (New York: St. Martin's Press, 1985), p. 140.

10. Meier, p. 140.

11. Michael Kraft and Norman Vig, "Environmental Policy from the 1970s to the 1990s: Continuity and Change," in *Environmental Policy in the 1990s* 2nd ed. Edited by Norman Vig and Michael Kraft (Washington, DC: Congressional Quarterly Press, 1994), pp. 18–19.

12. This cut of $2.4 billion would leave EPA with an annual budget of $4.87 billion. Ecological Society of America, "Environmental Policy Update, July 17, 1995," esanews@umdd.umd.edu.

13. Rosemary O'Leary, *Environmental Change: Federal Courts and the EPA* (Philadelphia: Temple University Press, 1993).

14. Rosenbaum, p. 115.

15. For a complete discussion of the problems faced by EPA, see Walter A. Rosenbaum, "The Clenched Fist and the Open Hand: Into the 1990s at EPA," in *Environmental Policy in the 1990s* 2nd. ed. Edited by Norman Vig and Michael Kraft (Washington, DC: Congressional Quarterly Press, 1994), pp. 121–143.

16. Norman Vig, "Presidential Leadership and the Environment: From Reagan and Bush to Clinton," in *Environmental Policy in the 1990s* 2nd ed. Edited by Norman Vig and Michael Kraft (Washington, DC: Congressional Quarterly Press, 1994), p. 80.

17. Jacqueline Vaughn Switzer, *Environmental Politics: Domestic and Global Dimensions* (New York: St. Martin's Press, 1994), p. 62. The "global rock star" quote is from "William Reilly's Green Precision Weapons," *The Economist* 30 March 1991, p. 28.

18. Rosenbaum, p. 96.

19. Vig, p. 86.

20. D. J. Peterson, *Troubled Lands: The Legacy of Soviet Environmental Destruction* (Boulder, CO: Westview, 1993).

21. Vig, p. 87.

22. Albert Gore, *Earth in the Balance: Ecology and the Human Spirit* (Boston: Houghton Mifflin, 1992).

23. Some federal officials and wildlife professionals are quietly amused at this "new" designation since they have been managing under an ecosystem approach for decades.

24. Reluctance to ratify the Biodiversity Convention is connected to ESA reauthorization. The convention is modeled in part on the ESA, and ratification would provide a federal treaty obligation to protect endangered species and habitats in ways which closely parallel the ESA. Should the convention be ratified, a watered-down ESA might provide relief only as long as it took the environmental lobby to run several convention cases through the federal courts.

25. The Bush administration had, to its credit, tackled this thorny issue as early as 1990, when William Reilly appointed an EPA task force to investigate charges of inequity. It issued a report in 1992 that confirmed the possibility of discriminatory decisionmaking (see USEPA, Office of Policy, Planning and Evaluation, *Environmental Equity: Reducing Risk for All Communities, Vol. 1: Workgroup Report to the Administrator* (Washington, DC: EPA, June 1992), cited in Rosenbaum, p. 182, n. 58.

26. U.S. General Accounting Office, *Siting of Hazardous Waste Landfills and Their Correlation with Racial and Economic Status of Surrounding Communities,* GAO/RCED-83-168 (June 1, 1983); United Church of Christ Commission for Racial Justice, *Toxic Wastes and Race in the United States: A National Report on the Racial and Socio-Economic Characteristics of Communities with Hazardous Waste Sites* (New York: Commission for Racial Justice United Church of Christ, 1987). Both cited in Roger Findley and Daniel Farber, *Cases and Materials on Environmental Law,* 4th ed. (St. Paul, MN: West, 1995), pp. 51–52.

27. Vikki Been, "Locally Undesirable Land Uses in Minority Neighborhoods: Disproportionate Siting or Market Dynamics?," *Yale Law Journal* 103 (1994): 1383–1422. Quoted and summarized in Roger Findley and Daniel Farber, *Cases and Materials on Environmental Law,* 4th ed. (St. Paul, MN: West, 1995), pp. 54–55.

28. The best discussion of the role of science and risk assessment in environmental policy is found in Rosenbaum, Chapter 5.

29. USEPA, *Unfinished Business: A Comparative Assessment of Environmental Problems* (Washington, DC: EPA, 1987), cited by Richard Andrews, "Risk-Based Decisionmaking," in *Environmental Policy in the 1990s* 2nd ed. Edited by Norman Vig and Michael Kraft (Washington, DC: Congressional Quarterly Press, 1994), p. 222, n. 28.

30. USEPA, Science Advisory Board, *Reducing Risk: Setting Priorities for Environmental Protection* (Washington, DC: USEPA, September 1990), cited by Walter A. Rosenbaum, "The Clenched Fist and the Open Hand: Into the 1990s at EPA," in *Environmental Policy in the 1990s* 2nd. ed. Edited by Norman Vig and Michael Kraft (Washington, DC: Congressional Quarterly Press, 1994), pp. 121–143.

31. Rosenbaum, pp. 135–140.

32. Richard N. L. Andrews, "Risk-Based Decisionmaking" in *Environmental Policy in the 1990s* 2nd ed. Edited by Norman Vig and Michael Kraft (Washington, DC: Congressional Quarterly Press, 1994), pp. 220–221.

33. Central Directorate of Environmental Protection, *Pollution Control in England* (London: Department of the Environment, August 1984), p. 1.

34. Between 1958 and 1978, urban ground concentrations of sulfur dioxide fell by 50 percent. From 1958 to 1981, industrial smoke decreased by 94 percent while in the same period domestic coal smoke was reduced by 80 percent. Water quality has improved; in 1958, 86.1 percent of Great Britain's rivers had both fish and water that was potable after treatment. In 1975, 91.4 percent of the rivers met those standards. Between 1958 and 1980, the kilometers of "grossly polluted" and "poor quality" nontidal waterways decreased by 39 percent, and the length of polluted tidal waterways was reduced by 42 percent. David Vogel, *National Styles of Regulation: Environmental Policy in Great Britain and the United States* (Ithaca, NY: Cornell University Press, 1986), pp. 22, 153, 157.

35. Vogel, p. 242.

Chapter Three

The Public Policy Process

Beloved by social scientists, models of how the world works are at their best only approximations. Public policy process models are no better—and no worse. The process described in this chapter appears to be an elegant and linear process, but be forewarned that public policy is in reality a complex, confused, and confusing Rube Goldberg device into which an infinite variety of ingredients are poured, and out of which comes . . . a surprise.

Still, as a heuristic device, a linear description of public policy can be helpful. The four basic types of public policy—distributive, competitive regulatory, protective regulatory, and redistributive—have their own set of policy actors and characteristics. These four types and their relationship to environmental policy are discussed in the first section of this chapter. The remaining sections discuss the mechanics of the public policy process. First, government reactions to the 1969 Santa Barbara oil spill mentioned in chapter 1 provide an overview of the policy process. The second section describes the three stages of the policy process: agenda-setting, policy formulation and legitimation, and policy implementation and evaluation.

Types of Public Policy

Domestic public policy can be divided into four major categories: distributive, competitive regulatory, protective regulatory, and redistributive.[1] Many policies have some characteristics of more than one of these policy types; nevertheless, the categorization is useful because it highlights the different policy actors and policy processes associated with each type.

Distributive Policy

Distributive policy supports private activities that are beneficial to society but that would not usually be undertaken by the private sector. For example, certain kinds of medical research are expensive and have little, if any, financial reward for the companies involved; the government may subsidize such research. Farmers need support through the bad times if they are to be able to produce agricultural products on a regular basis; the federal government instituted price supports. In the nineteenth century, settlement of the American West was physically dangerous and economically risky; the government, eager to encourage western expansion, gave away land and leased federally owned lands at below-market prices. This subsidy of western cattle ranchers continues today.

Distributive policies usually have low visibility. The people involved (e.g., the ranchers and Bureau of Land Management [BLM] officials) maintain cordial relations, and unless some unexpected event triggers media interest, the decisions governing this sort of policy are made by *subgovernments,* also known as *iron triangles.* A subgovernment is a coalition of three groups of actors: the affected interest group, the relevant agency in the executive branch, and the appropriate congressional committees or subcommittees. They are quiet and stable networks of policy actors with similar interests and goals.

Distributive policy is not often the focus of public controversy, and the subgovernments are king. When controversy does arise, the subgovernments disintegrate, only to re-form when the dust settles. During the first Reagan administration, some western states attempted to obtain control of the federal lands within their state boundaries. This "Sagebrush Rebellion" pitted BLM against their normal allies, the cattlemen. In previous times, the environmentalists and BLM had been bitter enemies, the environmentalists claiming that poor management and overgrazing were ruining the public lands of the West. One BLM official told me that he would never have believed a year before the Sagebrush Rebellion started that he would be leaking advance information to the environmental lobby. However, the environmentalists were, for once, on the same side as BLM as they both fought to keep the federal lands out of the control of what they perceived as rapacious state developers. Once the controversy subsided, the environmentalists and BLM found themselves again on opposite sides of the fence, figuratively if not literally.[2]

Competitive Regulatory Policy

The control of radio broadcasting by the Federal Communications Commission (FCC) is an example of competitive regulatory policy. Several parties *compete* for the right to broadcast on a certain frequency; the successful applicant is then *regulated* by the agency. Thus, competitive regulatory policy limits the provision of specific goods and services to a few who are chosen from a group of competitors, and the selected companies are then regulated. Other examples are television station licensing and, in the pre-Reagan days of intense industry regulation, airlines and trucking company route assignments. The regulation of trucking companies was so extensive at one time that trucking lines were told specifically which goods could be carried between two points and in what direction. Airlines had to agree to service feeder lines in order to be awarded major, profitable runs.

Since deregulation, the importance of competitive regulatory policy has diminished considerably. These are usually low visibility policies, and decisions are made at the bureau level, or by independent regulatory commissions such as the FCC or the Securities and Exchange Commission, or by the courts. Often the regulated industries have a great deal of input into the regulatory decisions. This leads to the problem of the *captured agency,* an agency that identifies so closely with the interests of the regulated industry that it forgets its responsibilities to society. For several years after the commercial development of cable television, the FCC was accused of being a captured agency in thrall to the Big Three of broadcasting: ABC, CBS, and NBC. Critics of the agency attribute the slow acceptance of cable television to the networks' ability to influence FCC decisions.

Protective Regulatory Policy

This form of policy protects the public by regulating private activities. Unlike the other forms of policy, this may be an active policy, not only prohibiting certain actions (such as emitting sulfur dioxide into the atmosphere) but also requiring some activities (building tall smokestacks or inspecting automobiles or recycling waste). When a banker tells his loan customers the total price of a car (including interest), he does so because of protective regulatory policy, not because he has a big heart.

The main actors in the protective regulatory policy are the committees and subcommittees of the Congress, the full House and Senate, executive agencies, and business interest groups. Many of these policies cannot be relegated to a subgovernment level; for example, an announcement by the surgeon general of the United States about the medical dangers of secondhand smoke is front-page news. Usually, however, these policies have only moderate visibility, and the parties involved work out their decisions through bargaining and compromise.

Most environmental policy falls into the protective regulatory category. Some observers of the environmental scene blame the slow improvement of the nation's environment on the federal choice of protective regulatory policy as a vehicle for compliance, rather than distributive policies. By defining pollution control as punitive, allowing certain amounts of pollutants to be released or generated and stored and then punishing any excess, the federal government provides corporate America with little incentive to develop waste reduction policies or to look for alternate production methods. Critics suggest that more progress would be made by rewarding recycling, material conservation, and waste reduction than by continuing an adversarial, litigious approach.

Redistributive Policy

The most controversial type of public policy is redistributive, which seeks to change the allocation of valued goods or services—money, property, rights—between social classes or racial groups or genders. It is the most controversial because in this policy, unlike the others, there are usually clearly defined winners and losers. Most often the winners are from disadvantaged groups in society; for example, affirmative action is a redistributive policy. Because of the high visibility of this type of policy, the political actors also have high visibility: the president, the congressional leaders, and large interest groups.

Environmental Policy

Most environmental policy fits either the protective regulatory policy category (for example, air and water pollution policies) or distributive policy (for example, national parks). Sometimes a policy may overlap categories. For example, the burros at Grand Canyon National Park were a nuisance and also destroyed habitat needed for native species. Unfortunately for the Park Service, burros are cute; one in particular, Brighty, had been the subject of a very popular children's book and had a statue erected to him on the South Rim.[3] In order to preserve the canyon ecosystem, the Park Service decided to shoot the wild burros, prompting an avalanche of protest. The Park Service ultimately compromised, allowing animal protection groups to rescue many of the burros before shooting the rest. Clearly the Park Service, usually categorized as a distributive policy agency, was not engaged in distributive policy when it decided to destroy wild burros to protect native species. Another example of crossover is in the federal food stamp program. Federal food stamps are used as a common example of redistributive programs, but they actually originated as a distributive program to buy surplus food during the New Deal.

Sometimes astute politicians can sell a program as one politically acceptable form of policy, knowing all the while that the real impact will be otherwise. Urban renewal is such a program. Advertised as a redistributive program to help the poor of the inner cities, in fact the poor were pushed out and high-rise offices and expensive condominiums replaced the slums. The poor simply shifted to more crowded and less convenient tenements. Instead of being redistributive, the program was distributive, subsidizing urban real estate speculators.

As might be expected, agencies that cope with overlapping policy types face especially difficult administrative problems. Since each policy type involves different sets of actors, the complexities of political bargaining, budget protection, and client services are multiplied. The troubles of the Environmental Protection Agency are partly caused by such dual responsibilities, since the EPA administers grants and contracts as well as enforces regulatory statutes.

The Mechanics of Public Policy

One of the unfortunate truths about the depth of our political concerns is that we care most about those incidents that are closest to us. When an airplane crashes on an international flight, the media reports the number of *American* dead or injured, and if the plane is filled entirely by foreign nationals, the crash has only the briefest mention on the national media and is then forgotten. Just so do environmental issues come into the national consciousness. For most Americans, the first really big oil spill was the January 1969 Santa Barbara spill. However, on 18 March 1967, the *Torrey Canyon*, a 970-foot tanker with 117,000 tons of crude oil in its storage tanks, ran aground fifteen miles west of Land's End in Cornwall, northeast of the Isles of Scilly. Initially, about 40,000 tons of oil were released by the ruptured tanks, but salvage efforts were futile, and all 117,000 tons of oil spilled into the western end of the English Channel. Eventually the oil washed up on the holiday coasts of England and France.

American environmentalists were a small but hardy band in the late sixties, and they watched the *Torrey Canyon* incident with horror. Oil experts, however, noted the narrowness of the Channel, and the peculiarity of the prevailing winds and currents and assured the American public that such an accident would not happen in American waters. Environmentalists received similar assurances about oil wells off the Pacific coast. The general public was not very worried, but the environmental activists were, and when the Santa Barbara well blew, they were quick to take advantage.

Rapidly an interest group called GOO (Get Oil Out) was formed. The American media were much more concerned with the destruction of forty miles of Southern California beaches than with the holiday sites of France and England. Within three days, GOO had collected more than fifty thousand signatures on petitions asking the president to stop deep-sea coastal oil drilling. Attention focused on the federal Outer Continental Shelf (OCS) oil leasing program administered by the Bureau of Land Management (BLM), although two other federal agencies—the U.S. Geological Survey and the Federal Water Pollution Control Administration—were also involved. The leasing program was temporarily halted by Interior Secretary Walter Hickel.

The incident also drew attention to the growing problem of other forms of marine oil pollution. Twenty percent of oil in the world's water comes from shipping, including accidents, bilge water dumping, and emptying ballast tanks. Natural oil seepage from the ocean floor contributes 15 percent, while offshore production is responsible for only 5 percent.[4] In the North Sea and North Atlantic alone, scientists estimate that as many as 450,000 marine birds die each year from chronic oil pollution.[5] The public uproar over the Santa Barbara spill led to the passage of the National Environmental Policy Act in December of the same year; it was signed into law on 1 January 1970. It also had long term repercussions for the federal oil leasing programs. Despite the oil crisis in the early seventies, OCS leasing goals were never met. The coastal states and communities were reluctant to have oil rigs drilling off their coastlines, and the political pressures caused by a constant stream of small spills and a few major disasters like the *Exxon Valdez* (which poured 11 million gallons of oil into Prince William Sound in Alaska) kept the public interested in the impact of oil development in the marine environment. In 1978 the Outer Continental Shelf Lands Act Amendments incorporated the coastal states into the planning process for OCS development. Since then, although OCS oil production exceeds that of the dry lands, the political influences have prevented massive exploitation of OCS.

Here we have a microcosm of the policy process. A trigger event (the Santa Barbara spill) is used by policy initiators or policy entrepreneurs (environmental lobbyists) to induce policy formation and legitimation (passage of NEPA) to achieve policy goals (de-emphasis on OCS wells and re-emphasis on environmental protection) that are implemented throughout the country (EPA regulations and state involvement in OCS planning).

The environmental policy process is exceedingly complex. What appears as a relatively straightforward process is actually an iterative process. Evaluation, or predicting impacts and outcomes, begins with the agenda-setting process, and interest groups dissatisfied with the predicted outcomes begin immediately to reforge the agendas. Formulation and legitimation are shaped in a fluid system that reflects the constant activities of interest groups and the bureaucracies, which all the while are conscious of the possibility of judicial intervention. Evaluation strategies are chosen and rejected on the basis of their projected political outcomes.

What is necessary to negotiate the political process successfully? Political experience, flexibility, an acceptance of the validity of political decision making, and, above all, the realization that nothing is ever final. The next three sections discuss in more detail the various stages in this process, beginning with the setting of the public policy agenda.

Agenda Setting

Why do citizens strive to get their issues on the public agenda? Why not be satisfied with convincing their own circle of friends and colleagues of the correctness of their position? They strive to have their preferences turned into public policy for three reasons. First, public policy is legitimate. Government policies are usually regarded as legal obligations that citizens have a duty to uphold. The big exceptions—speed limits, Prohibition—are notable because they are exceptions. Nongovernmental groups and institutions may generate important policies (for example, corporate investment decisions or church rules on female clergy) that may be regarded as binding on the members of the organizations, but these policies have no authority for people who are not members. Only government policies are *legally* binding, and only government policies are legitimate almost automatically.

A second characteristic of public policy that encourages citizens to work for their own preferences is the universality of government policies. Membership in other policy-generating groups is voluntary, and these groups make policy only for their own members. But government policy applies—or may apply—to everyone.

Finally, only the government has the power to force compliance with its policy decisions. Government has a monopoly on coercion in society; other organizations can legally exercise only limited sanctions. Only government can imprison (or even execute) individuals for refusing to obey its directives, although we have laws that protect us from the government using coercion arbitrarily; for example, the Fifth Amendment states that no person (not *citizen* but *person*) "shall be . . . deprived of life, liberty, or property, without due process of law."

So, because government actions are legitimate, enact societywide policies, and enforce these policies, people work to have their policy preferences become public policies.

Systemic and Institutional Agendas

In public policy there are two basic forms of agendas: systemic agendas and institutional or decision agendas.[6] The systemic agenda consists of all the issues that a political community agree need to be resolved and that they also agree are within governmental authority. These are the issues that wax and wane in the public attention until finally the issue recurs often enough or becomes sufficiently problematic that it can no longer be ignored. When this occurs, policymakers place the issue on their institutional agenda: the list of issues they plan to consider actively and seriously.

Systemic agendas are fairly abstract and fluid. Issues may appear on the systemic agenda for years before actually reaching the institutional agenda; some issues never do make it. Systemic agendas identify problem areas but rarely propose concrete alternatives and solutions. As a general rule, the more people are interested in and concerned about an issue, the more likely that issue is to reach the systemic agenda and perhaps the decision agenda as well. Rarely, however, does an issue suddenly become a topic of general conversation; dramatic trigger events (see below) such as the Chernobyl reactor disaster are the exception. Usually concern for an issue moves through predictable stages of public concern before reaching the systemic agenda.

The narrowest kind of public is the *identification group,* people with a detailed awareness of specific issues. Local groups concerned to stop a nuclear reactor in their neighborhood form identification groups. *Attention groups* focus on the broader implications of the issues concerning identification groups: antinuclear power groups are attention groups. Unlike the identification group, which is interested only in the reactor threatening their community, the attention group opposes nuclear reactors everywhere. The *attentive public* is the generally informed and educated layer of society. These are the people who, once they are convinced that an issue is important, inform the wider public. They may not have a passionate opposition to nuclear power, but Three Mile Island and Chernobyl have convinced them that nuclear power is a danger. They will write articles, make speeches, join protests, lobby their elected representatives, and discuss the issue at church suppers. The combined effect will be to bring the issue to the attention of the general public. The general or *mass public* is the last segment of the public to become involved in pacing an issue on the systemic agenda. These people are less active, interested, and informed than any of the other kinds of public. Getting their attention requires highly generalized and symbolic issues, and keeping their attention for any length of time is difficult. However, without their concurrence, reaching the institutional agenda is virtually impossible.

Institutional agendas are specific, concrete, and limited. They identify the problem and its alternative solutions; often institutional agendas work within strict time constraints. Usually an issue must first be placed on the systemic agenda, although sometimes an issue is so critical that it moves immediately to the institutional agenda. It is, however, important to note that some issues are on the institutional agenda without passing through this process each time. The Congress (and indeed, most legislatures) deals with four kinds of problems: chronic problems, such as the federal budget that recurs annually; sporadic problems such as reauthorizing environmental legislation; crisis problems, such as the savings and loan bailout that plagued the Congress in the early 1990s; and finally discretionary problems.[7] This discretionary agenda is chosen by legislators for many reasons: perhaps they have an ideological commitment to the issue, like Paul Rogers of Florida, who struggled for strong emission standards during the fight over the 1977 Clean Air Act amendments, or there are rewards to be gained in the political fray (paying old debts or creating new ones) or in subsequent elections (Rogers, for example, represented a south Florida constituency desperately concerned with respiratory problems of the elderly).

Reaching the Decision Agenda

Issues reach the decision agenda in a variety of ways. One way is through individuals or coherent groups working deliberately to have their concerns addressed by government;[8] another is less deliberate, seeing policy proposals as ingredients in a "policy primeval soup" where ideas and solutions blend, sink to the bottom, or rise to the top before being skimmed off by government and served up on the decision agenda.[9] Often the agenda is reached by a combination of the two. To extend the metaphor, the individuals may stir the soup, vary the ingredients, or add a few spices to tempt the appetites of the decision makers.

According to the instrumental view, there are four ways to create issues and four corresponding categories of initiators or policy entrepreneurs (people who use situations to place issues on the agenda); these categories may overlap. "Readjustors" may perceive an inequality that affects them; they then strive to have the inequality reduced. For example, rural residents, who do not themselves generate low-level nuclear waste, fight to stop waste disposal sites from being sited in their communities. "Exploiters" manufacture issues for their own gain. For example, when George Bush made an issue of the pollution in Boston Harbor during the 1988 presidential campaign, he was probably acting as an exploiter. "Circumstantial reactors" take advantage of unanticipated events or "trigger events" to create or to magnify issues. For example, the Santa Barbara oil spill was used to halt OCS development; the crash of a fixed-wing aircraft filled with tourists led to regulations prohibiting below-rim sightseeing flights in the Grand Canyon; the terrible forest fires that ravaged Yellowstone National Park in 1988 led to a reevaluation of the controlled burn policies of the federal resource management agencies. Finally, "do-gooders" use events to publicize issues but gain no personal benefit from the issue. They may use inequalities or unanticipated events, but their motivation differs from the readjusters or circumstantial reactors. For example, the Greenpeace activists arrested in 1995 for protesting French nuclear testing in the Pacific are not motivated by private gain or perceived inequalities.

Some issues never reach the mass public and yet manage to be placed on the institutional or decision agenda. This often requires desperate measures by the identification and attention groups. Issues that are confined to an identification group gain the institutional agenda when the group members threaten to disrupt the system; an example of such disruption is monkey-wrenching carried out by radical environmental groups that despair of the traditional political process. Issues that are confined to attention groups are brought to the decision agenda by threatening legislators with legitimate sanctions, such as recalls, and withholding contributions or votes. When an issue can only reach the attentive public, access is easier because the attentive public tends to have political power by virtue of their social and economic status. Here political brokerage techniques or controlling the media will bring an issue to the institutional agenda. The media is, of course, available to and used by the identification and attention groups, but the attentive public often has formal control of the media.

Timing is critical in gaining the attention of the policy decisionmakers. Policy problems may exist for quite a long time before a politically acceptable solution is found, and even then, if the decisionmakers have other priorities, the issue may not make it to the decision agenda. All three of these "process streams" of problems, policies, and politics must meet for an issue to reach the agenda of government.[10] When they do often because an initiator has taken some critical action—a window of opportunity is opened, and the issue is under active and serious consideration by government officials. The passage of the Endangered Species Act in 1973 is an example of the three streams coming together to open a window of opportunity:

> Its passage resulted from a fortunate combination of circumstance: a powerful environmental lobby backed by an aroused public, a legislative urge for association with environmentalism, enormous ignorance about the political consequences of its implementation, growing scientific advocacy of species protection, and (no trivial matter) the threatened extinction of the American bald eagle, the national symbol.[11]

Small wonder that the Endangered Species Act passed almost unanimously.

Policy Formulation and Legitimation

While the entire policy process is political, the formulation and legitimation phases are the most intensely political. Many actors are involved in the formulation stage. The bureaucracy, although most involved in the implementation phase of public policy, has a role in formulation by suggesting policies to the legislature and providing information on the strengths and weaknesses of proposed solutions. The bureaus are given this role because they have, or are perceived to have, technical expertise that the elected officials and their staff lack, although the bureaus often have their own organizational needs to be satisfied by the policy process (budgetary constraints, personnel demands, program protection and expansion). The bureaucracy most often reflects the president's policy position, but the president and the bureaucracy may have separate goals in the policy process. Many times during the first Reagan administration, for example, the staff at EPA were at odds with the goals and initiatives of the political appointees and of the president. In fact, the accusation that the bureaucracy could not be trusted with the conservative agenda was a constant complaint of the administration. It took powerful and clear messages from the mass public to convince the president that the commitment to a protected and healthy environment was now a fixture in American values.

The media are also involved in formulation and legitimation as well. While they may create issues, as they did in the Watergate scandal and often do on television programs such as *60 Minutes,* the media are most often used by other actors to influence public or political opinion. Special interest groups watch the process carefully and intervene in those issues that affect their own concerns.

Problem Definition

One of the first difficulties in policy formulation is problem definition: legislators must first agree on the parameters of the problem before they can begin to formulate solutions. An example of the difficulties in problem definition may be found in the issue of tropical rain forest destruction. This destruction occurs in four main stages: road building and lumbering; colonization (made easier by the development of roads and the clearing of timber tracts) and crop planting (since the new settlers cannot live off the forested areas); soil exhaustion (because there is no dormant season); and grass planting and cattle grazing (inefficient, marginally profitable, and a contributing factor for soil erosion). Assuming that the governments having jurisdiction over the rain forests want to halt the destruction, or that the developed countries are convinced that this issue is important enough to justify interference in the activities of a sovereign nation, how might this problem be defined? The problem definition will guide the solutions to be attempted.

As a start, this might be defined as a timber problem. Obviously, one incentive to reduce rain forest destruction would be to reduce the world market for rain forest lumber. In a world where even expensive eyeglass frames are made from mahogany, reducing the demand for fine furniture seems unlikely. A second definition might be as a problem of population pressures. If the developing countries with rain forests could house, feed, and employ their own populations within the urban or already existing rural environments, these people would not need to move into the rain forest areas denuded by the lumber companies. Unfortunately, there seems to be little political will to reduce populations; the developing countries sometimes perceive attempts to require reductions in the birth rate as hidden genocide.

Perhaps the rain forest destruction is a problem of agricultural techniques. The indigenous people of the forest survive very nicely without destroying the trees: the new settlers might be taught the indigenous farming practices. However, unlike the new settlers, the native peoples are unaccustomed to the luxuries of urban life: soft drinks, blue jeans, boom boxes. Their farming methods are labor intensive and generate little cash crop. The food they do produce is neither familiar nor appealing to the settlers' palates. What about replenishing the soil so it does not become exhausted? Fertilizers are expensive and bring their own potentially harmful environmental effects.

Finally, the problem might be defined again as a market problem. By reducing world beef consumption (although hogs or sheep would do equally well—or poorly—on deforested land) or banning beef produced on deforested land (much as the European Economic Community [EEC] banned American beef fed growth hormones), the final stages of deforestation might be avoided.

None of these problem definitions or problem solutions alone seems useful. As the issue of the rain forest becomes expanded to wider publics, policymakers are going to be forced to find some way to address and to define the issue. "Stop the destruction of the rain forest" is an agenda-setting strategy with emotional appeal; *how* to stop the destruction becomes the formulation problem.

Formulation

Once a problem has been defined, the solution that emerges is the result of bargaining and compromise by various factions within government, each of which believes it has the answer to the problem. One strategy that often emerges from the political negotiation process is the "good science" strategy employed so effectively by the Reagan administration. When a problem appears intractable, the appointment of a study commission is a sure way to delay, and perhaps ultimately to avoid, a decision. Another strategy is to pass resolutions condemning the undesirable activity, while actually doing nothing. Negotiations may hinge on issues not directly related to the policy problem; Congressional logrolling—trading political favors—frequently governs policy formulations. The process of negotiation and bargaining does not stop with passage of initial legislation; it continues in the formulation of subsequent amendments and reauthorizations of the original legislation. The 1977 amendments to the Clean Air Act are a good example of this continual renegotiation process.

In 1977, Congress considered amendments to the 1970 Clean Air Act.[12] At issue was the auto industry's attempts to delay by five years their compliance with the auto emission standards imposed by the original act. They had already had three one-year extensions. Democrats led both sides of the battle in the House. Paul Rogers of Florida, chairman of the House Subcommittee on Health and the Environment, pushed for compliance within the extended time limits already agreed upon. John Dingell, representing Detroit with its blue-collar autoworkers and their threatened jobs, was joined by a majority of the Republicans in asking for the extension. Dingell usually was on the side of environmental legislation, but in this case his constituents' needs were paramount.

Rogers defined the issue in terms of health: respiratory problems in the elderly, developing respiratory problems of children. Dingell defined it as jobs and the protection of an essential American industry. By the time the issue emerged from the subcommittee, the issue had been defined as: "How can we clean up the air at the lowest possible cost?" This was a substantial victory for the auto industry: Rogers really did not care how much it cost, but in order to get the opposing forces to compromise, he accepted their definition of the problem. By the time the final vote came on the floor of the House, Rogers had been forced to give even more ground. President Carter's energy policy had fueled Dingell's allies, and the automakers and sellers had exerted great lobbying pressure on all members of the House. Dingell's forces carried the day, although their victory was somewhat diminished by the subsequent changes made in the conference with the Senate.

By defining the problem and then using negotiation and compromise, the policy was formulated. It was also legitimated by the same process. Although no one member of either the House or the Senate was truly satisfied with the outcome, all accepted it as legitimate because in the American political system, the public generally accepts as legitimate the decisions made by the government.

Legitimation

Legitimate policies have the authority of the state (in the American system, the authority of the people) attached.[13] Legitimacy is "a belief on the part of citizens that the current government represents a proper form of government and a willingness on the part of those citizens to accept the decrees of that government as legal and authoritative."[14]

Legitimacy is largely psychological. There is nothing that the government can do to force citizens to accept its policies as legitimate. Legitimacy is substantive as well as procedural; there are certain areas in which the citizens feel the government should not meddle, although examples of these areas are increasingly difficult to find.[15] For example, a legislative decision to ban red meat would not be perceived as legitimate, regardless of any predicted positive impact on world food supplies and American coronary disease rates. Finally, legitimacy is variable. Governments that are either consistently outside the areas of public acceptance or that violate the public trust may become illegitimate; this loss of legitimacy was a major factor in the resignation of President Nixon. In the American system, legitimacy is achieved through the legislative process, the administrative process, the courts, and—rarely direct democracy. The legislature is the source of primary legislation. Elected by the people, the legislators are expected to represent their constituencies.[16] As long as they collectively do not violate the wishes and expectations of the electorate, and they follow the procedural guidelines for their own legislative body, the laws they pass are legitimate to the voters.

The administrative process, being of fairly recent origin and handicapped by not being in the Constitution, has been subject to criticisms of its legitimacy from the earliest days of the administrative state. However, the rulemaking process or "secondary legislation" is generally accepted as legitimate. If the agencies follow the correct procedures, usually as laid down in the Administrative Procedure Act, their rules have the force and effect of legislative law. There is frequent opportunity for public input and influence in the administrative decision process, and while citizens may complain about a "fourth branch of government," administrative decisions are usually accorded legitimacy.

Court decisions, while subject to appeals or changes due to changing circumstances, are also legitimate. Court decisions are especially powerful because they have a direct Constitutional connection and judges are, at most levels, less vulnerable to political pressures. Judges rarely need to compromise. The decisions of the United States Supreme Court are particularly influential in legitimating government decisions because they are *not* subject to further appeal and the justices may rule on the constitutionality of the actions of another branch of government. Only Congress can nullify a Supreme Court decision, either through legislation or by removing a disputed issue from the Court's jurisdiction.[17]

The final source of legitimacy is direct democracy, most often expressed in referenda or initiatives. In recent years, stringent demands have been placed on many state budgets by taxpayer initiatives, and these have had an inevitable effect on state environmental programs. Nuclear power issues have occasionally been taken directly to the people, but the use of direct democracy to make a policy decision or to legitimate policy is unusual.

Implementation

Implementation occurs when the policy goals are translated into governmental actions that affect other branches of government or the citizens. Although implementation may be hampered by poor policy design or a lack of commitment by policymakers, once responsibility for the policy passes to the hands of the administrators, other factors come into play. Bureaucratic resources and administrative discretion are two of the most important factors.

Bureaucratic Resources

It is in implementation that bureaucracy shows its greatest influence.[18] The resources available to bureaucracies are considerable. The initial source of their power comes from their legal authority to implement legislation. Congress delegates its legislative authority to agencies, thus providing the legal justification for administrative rules and regulations. Bureaucratic power is also enhanced by the indispensable nature of the bureaucratic activity: modern government would be impossible without the agencies. The agencies are also empowered by their technical expertise and support of their constituencies.

The technical expertise of senior or mid-level agency administrators is especially important in the environmental agencies; usually these administrators are first trained in their substantive fields and then promoted to increasingly important administrative posts. In the Park Service, for example, the interpretation and historic preservation employees are trained in history, journalism, and related fields while the management employees have degrees in forestry, marine biology, environmental science, and similar technical areas. Superfund site administrators must be knowledgeable about chemical, physical, and biological processes. Many of the environmental agency staff have graduate degrees in their professional areas. Although rarely trained in administrative skills, the technical expertise of the bureaucrats and the intimate knowledge of their own policy areas far outreach the knowledge base of even the most well-informed congressional staff. Despite the information available from the Congressional Research Service and the Office of Technology Assessment, the Congress is almost forced to rely upon information and analyses provided to them by the bureaucracy.

There is a negative side to the issue of technical expertise. Because agency personnel rarely have professional administrative experience, they often view the interjection of political ideas or values as a corruption of the decision-making process. This rejection of political influence is not limited to the agencies. Environmentalists deplore the position of lumber companies in the Pacific Northwest that bring political pressure to bear on the Congress and the Forest Service to allow them to clear-cut. Timber companies ridicule the claims of the Native Americans and the environmentalists to protect rare animals with no apparent commercial value. And government specialists, trained in the sciences, are outraged that Superfund sites take years to clean because the state and local governments insist on approving all EPA and responsible party agreements. This is one area in which professional socialization is needed for the administrators. Political factors are a reality, and in a representative democracy, political factors are a legitimate balance to the technical side of the decision process.

The constituencies that each agency develops are a second resource. This is the obverse side of the "captured agency" coin. Any regulatory or management agency works closely with interest groups. These groups become accustomed to the working habits of the agency and learn effective patterns of negotiation and compromise. "Better the devil you know than the devil you don't" is their operating theory. They are reluctant to upset the stable relationships they have developed, and so a threatened agency may rely on its interest groups for protection in times of budgetary crisis or changing political leadership. These client groups often have prestige and political influence, and they are a powerful factor in consolidating the position of the agencies. While they are not often called upon to defend the agency or to exercise influence on the agency's behalf, their very existence increases the authority of the agencies.

Administrative Discretion

A third factor that cannot be underestimated is the discretionary power of the agencies. While some commentators would like to limit discretion as much as possible, or even to eliminate it entirely, discretion is essential for an effective administration. Legislatures cannot possibly draft legislation in the detail that is necessary for implementation. They lack the technical expertise that is such a powerful resource for the bureaucracy. And even if they had the necessary staff and expertise, the cumbersome legislative process of negotiation and compromise would bog down the governing process.

Discretion also gives administrators leeway to fit policy decisions to individual cases, to "humanize" the governmental process. It enhances their flexibility, allowing administrative law to evolve incrementally and to be checked or changed without the fanfare that accompanies legislative activity. Finally—and this is especially true in environmental administration—discretion compensates for changing technology. As scientific data accumulate, or drought endangers national forests, or new species are discovered, the discretionary powers of administrators can accommodate the changes.

This is not to say that governing necessarily continues to improve as discretionary powers increase. Too much discretion, which can lead to corruption, favoritism, or simple confusion, can be as harmful as too little discretion. The advantages of bureaucratic government rest in part on the regularity and predictability of government activity. A good administrator is able to strike a balance.

Administrators make three kinds of discretionary decisions: substantive, procedural, and complex. *Substantive* discretionary decisions are those in which an administrator makes a decision or promulgates a rule on a policy issue. These substantive decisions are one method for agencies to distribute benefits to their client groups. Agencies exercise this discretion in several ways. They decide, for example, where to locate research stations or unit headquarters that are frequently major sources of employment in small communities. In the late eighties, the Forest Service proposed consolidating the administrative offices of the Prescott and Coconino National Forests in northern Arizona. The impact on the town of Williams, a very small community already endangered by an interstate bypass, was enormous, and the political fallout was great enough that the Forest Service shelved its plans, at least temporarily. A more subtle use of substantive discretionary power is in wording rules and regulations either to create client groups or to shape the benefits for which they are eligible. Sometimes discretion is at the "street level." In granting wetland permits, for example, state investigators have a wide latitude in interpreting potential soil erosion or habitat destruction.

Procedural discretionary decisions relate to the selection of the processes used to gather information or to make decisions. A procedural discretionary decision might be whether to hire consultants or to use in-house personnel to develop a forest plan. Finally, *complex* discretionary decisions, like the hybrid rulemaking process discussed in the material on the Administrative Procedure Act in chapter 5, combine the features of both substantive and procedural decisions, for example, will the forest plan be based on timber industry data or agency data or a combination of both? Administrative officials are given a wide latitude in their decisionmaking and actions; this increases their flexibility and improves the efficacy of the administrative state. However, administrative officials can exceed their authority or misuse it. When this occurs, they may be individually liable for tort actions brought against them by citizens. The liability of individual employees to lawsuits is one of the more complex issues in environmental law.

Under the ancient common law doctrine of sovereign immunity, the government and its employees were absolutely immune from prosecution for actions related to their governmental functions. The doctrine has its origins in the ancient divine right of kings: God ordains the king, God can do no wrong, the king can do no wrong. However, even divine kings recognized that their subordinates could make mistakes (or that, for political reasons, the king might want to dissociate himself from some subordinate's action), and so the custom evolved that the king could give permission for the government to be sued. However, in the twentieth century the immunity of government officials from liability suits has changed. Immunity ranges from absolute immunity (for such activities as legislating) to none (no more immunity than is borne by a private citizen). In the middle range is qualified immunity: an employee is acting in "good faith" who is immune from individual tort actions.

State employees may be held personally liable under state laws and regulations. For example, the liability of state water quality managers discussed next is a complex mix of professional standards, citizen public relations, and state regulations.

Case Study: Water Quality Systems in Arizona

In addition to other environmental rules, the Arizona Department of Environmental Quality (DEQ) was empowered by the legislature through Arizona Revised Statutes 49-253 to develop and to enforce rules governing water systems. The rules provide that plans must be submitted and the construction of water systems must be inspected by a Professional Engineer.

The owner of a water system must protect the water system and keep it in proper operating condition. The owner must also sample for various pollutants. Operation not in accordance with departmental rules may subject the water system owner to an administrative order, an injunction, and, if these fail, to fines for contempt of court.

However, responsibility for the water system rests partially with the engineer as well. If the engineer who designs and inspects the construction of a water system is negligent, the State Board of Technical Registration, which licenses professional engineers, may take disciplinary action, such as the suspension or revocation of the engineer's license, and may assess administrative penalties not to exceed $2,000.

In addition, if someone were injured because of the improper design, construction, or operation of the water system, the engineer or system owner could become liable in a private action for the tort of negligence. Sometimes, it may be shown by an injured party's attorney that the engineer or system owner violated a rule of the department. In that case, the law of torts holds that such violation of a governmental rule is evidence of negligence that can be presented to a jury.

The expansion of a water system in Navajo County, Arizona, was designed by a consulting engineer whose professional license was granted not by examination but through action of a grandfather clause. The plans were found to be unworkable by the contractor and DEQ field engineer. It was necessary for the system owner to threaten the consulting engineer with a complaint to the Board of Technical Registration before plans were redesigned. Following the consulting engineer's death, his estate filed a lawsuit for payment in excess of what the system owner anticipated. The owner then alleged that the consulting engineer's original design was improper and the design contract's scope was exceeded. It was important that DEQ's field engineer could demonstrate that the original plans would not work and the rules of the department were violated. The owner's attorney could then use this information in an attempt to show the consulting engineer was negligent in designing the system expansion. The suit was settled out of court.

Variables Affecting Implementation

Successful implementation is very difficult, partly because it involves a number of interdependent actions that must be accomplished almost simultaneously.[19] Implementation actions include acquiring resources (such as money, land, personnel, or equipment); interpreting directives, rules, and regulations; planning programs; organizing activities; and extending benefits and applying restrictions.

The implementation process is characterized by many complicating factors. First is the multiplicity of actors. At a minimum, bureaucrats are responsible to two masters: the president or his political appointee, and the Congress, which has authorized the agency's existence and which continues to hold the purse strings. Bureaucrats must also satisfy their client groups or, failing that, be able to defend their actions to the elected officials who receive the client groups' complaints. Some agencies have advisory groups with varying degrees of impact on the agency activities. There is always the possibility of judicial review, which even for the victorious agency is a process that consumes time and resources and perhaps even political goodwill.

Another complicating factor is the federal context of environmental administration mentioned in chapter 1. Each of the fifty states has its own bureaucratic organization to cope with environmental policy. In some states, there are as many as eight state agencies with some environmental responsibilities; no state has less than three.[20] This obviously complicates efforts by the states or the federal government to encourage interstate coordination in environmental administration. In addition, the state bureaucracies, although often given implementation responsibilities for federal programs, must also respond to the political pressures of their own state legislatures.

Because of the numerous agencies and policymaking bodies involved, the goals of any one policy may be diffuse, multiple, and competing. For example, the Forest Service is often frustrated by its multiple-use mandate. Trained as silvaculturists, foresters view trees as a crop, to be nurtured and then harvested when mature. The Forest Service was established partially to ensure a steady, affordable, flexibly priced source of timber for the American construction industry. Being forced to allow old stands of timber to decay for habitat protection, when by forestry standards they should have been cut years ago, goes against the grain of responsible foresters. Equally dismayed is the entrepreneur who invests in patents for a new biological form of pest control only to find that, while one federal agency grants him a patent, another refuses to let him sell his product. Or take the case of power plant operators forced to change reactor design long after approved construction has taken place. This "ratcheting" afflicts many industries subjected to EPA regulations.

Finally, there are unforeseen circumstances—hurricanes and floods, broken dams, decreasing ozone layers, economic recessions, the fall of the Berlin Wall—which can skew the best designed and best intentioned implementation strategies. Flexibility is key to effective implementation, but too much flexibility allows unacceptable waivers and weak enforcement.

Implementing Environmental Policy

The two most common types of environmental policies are distributive policy and protective regulatory policy. Each policy type generates its own set of issues during implementation.

Although generally stable and dominated by subgovernments, *distributive policy* may erupt into conflict and difficulties for the implementing agencies. One problem arises when new responsibilities are added to existing, well-established policies. From the agenda setters' perspective, new issues may often be resolved by tacking them onto existing remedies. From the implementors' perspective, this shakes the comfortable coalitions, bringing in new client groups and usually necessitating a redistribution of resources. Another problem may occur when the elected officials change priorities. In theory, bureaucrats should be responsive to the political will of the electorate, which is expressed to them by the political appointees. However, responsive changes are difficult to accomplish after years of sunk costs and interest group expectations.[21] This becomes especially complicated when the will of the executive differs from the will of the legislature. Finally, changes in society, either through technological advances or resulting from socioeconomic differences, may force bureaus to rethink their allocation of distributive benefits.

Protective Regulatory Policy

Protective regulatory policy is inherently controversial and highly visible, a real tinderbox for the bureaucrat implementing the policy. As technology and economic conditions change, routines for enforcement must also compensate. Congress remains closely involved in implementing protective regulatory policy because its members hear so frequently from their regulated constituents. The president is also likely to become involved, as President Carter did during the passage of the 1977 Clean Air Act amendments that extended the automakers' deadline to comply with emission standards. Bureaucrats find themselves under pressure from industry and businesses to cut back on enforcement while the environmentalists push for enforcement that often seems punitive.

Case Study: Coconino County License Revocation

An example of implementation of a protective regulatory policy is a county government's revocation of a restaurant license. The following discussion shows how the administrative process may be used by environmental managers to achieve policy goals—in this case, continued public health. It also demonstrates the importance of record keeping in effective administration and affirms the necessity of creating a good record during administrative enforcement proceedings.

In October 1987, the Coconino County (Arizona) Health Department held its first administrative hearing; the purpose of the hearing was to revoke the Mandarin Restaurant's health permit. During the first part of October, the restaurant was inspected by two Health Department agents. The facility received a low score (45 out of a possible 100) with numerous critically weighted violations, including improper food and facility temperatures, tainted ground beef, and damaged canned goods. They were also found to be reserving leftovers such as tea, rice, and fried wontons to re-serve to customers.

The two health inspectors closed the restaurant immediately because of the many serious violations and its overall poor condition, which posed an imminent health hazard to the public. The officers discussed the inspection report with the owners, reviewing all marked violations. During the inspection, food found at improper temperatures was discarded and damaged canned goods were embargoed as evidence. The operator signed the inspection reports, and the restaurant was closed until further notice.

After review and evaluation of the file, the Health Department decided to suspend the Mandarin Restaurant permit, and revocation proceedings were begun. The decision to move for revocation came about in part because the file showed that the restaurant had been closed twice before for imminent health hazards and repeated violations.

To revoke the operator's permit, the department had a choice between a judicial proceeding or an administrative hearing. An administrative hearing was chosen, partly to save money but primarily because it was the fastest and most effective way to protect public health.

Organizing an administrative hearing was a real challenge for the staff since this was the first time that the department had taken steps to revoke a food operator's permit. Everything had to be researched, from the sending of a revocation notice to the hiring of an administrative hearing officer. Each detail had to be carefully considered in order to prevent the case from being thrown out on a technicality.

In preparation for the hearing, department staff painstakingly reviewed the regulations for compliance procedures from the County Food Code and the chapter on administrative procedure from the Arizona Revised Statutes. The County Food Code provided for an administrative hearing, outlining violations and the length of time an operator was given to correct them. The state statutes outlined the parameters for notice and hearing, including the admissibility of evidence, due process, fairness of the hearing, hearing officer, counsel, and witnesses.

The revocation notice was sent, and the hearing date was set for the end of October. The department then had the task of selecting a hearing officer. A judge from the city of Flagstaff was chosen because of his experience with city court cases and because he was not employed by the county nor was he personally or financially involved with the restaurant.

Another important element in the preparation for the hearing was the meetings held with the County Attorney's office. These were crucial in the department's interpretation of the law governing the procedures for holding an administrative hearing. It was equally important to familiarize the attorney's office with the Food Code so the department could be effectively represented at the hearing.

One of the most important aspects of the department's preparation for the hearing was establishing the findings of fact and organizing the evidence to be presented, since the outcome of the hearing would rest on these facts

alone. The department's successful prosecution of this case may in large part
be due to their extensive efforts to make the written evidence as clear and
concise as possible. This was especially challenging, since eight handwritten
inspection reports had to be reviewed for each repeated violation. This experience emphasized the importance of the clear and accurate documentation of violations recorded by the health inspectors.

The representative from the county attorney's office came well prepared
for the hearing. He was knowledgeable about the Food Code and had reviewed the findings of fact thoroughly. The department also provided the
hearing officer with a copy of the Food Code well in advance of the hearing.

The food operators' testimony was weak and ill prepared; they came to
the hearing with an incomplete record of the inspection reports on their
restaurant. They had been told they could be represented by an attorney
but elected not to have one, and their problems with the English language
interfered with their understanding of the proceedings.

The hearing officer ruled in favor of the Health Department.

If the department is ever faced again with a license revocation hearing, it
will probably place more emphasis on the collection of evidence, such as
photographs of the facility. Additional preparation is likely to include the
acquisition of more food samples, damaged food equipment, and even in-
sects or rodents (if present). While all this evidence was not necessary in this
revocation hearing, had the operators been represented by an attorney, the
evidence might have been needed.

Despite the difficulties the department encountered in this case, the experience was of enormous value to the department because it revealed the
basic steps required to organize and to hold an administrative hearing.
These procedures were documented for future reference. While it is recognized that each situation with a food operation will differ in particulars, the
essential steps of collecting evidence, documenting the findings of fact, and
presenting the case within the parameters of a hearing remain the same.

Evaluation

Evaluation is not simply the end stage of the policy process during which
analysts measure actual outcomes against desired one; it occurs throughout
the policy process.[22] Evaluation is of two types: formative and summative.
Formative evaluation takes place while the policy is being formulated and
implemented. It allows mid-course corrections if the policy goals are being
bypassed or if new and unintended consequences seem imminent. It is flexible and encourages policy outcomes that fit policy intentions. *Summative
evaluation* is used when a policy or program is completed. Analysts isolate

the goals of the program and then observe how closely the program achieved the goals.

As complicated as implementation may be, evaluation is even more problematic. It is difficult to isolate the precise, actual goals of many policies. Perhaps the legislation was vague, or the goals were impossible to attain, given existing technology. The action-forcing provisions of NEPA discussed in chapter 2 raise just such problems: how should progress toward goals be evaluated? Policy goals may change between the time the policy reaches the systemic or institutional agendas and the time it is evaluated. Even if achieved, goals may have unintended consequences; did Congress really intend the Endangered Species Act to be used to halt a federal project such as the Tellico Dam? Finally, stated goals may not be the true goals of a policy. For example, in 1984, the state of Maryland declared a moratorium on taking striped bass. One possible explanation for the controversial moratorium was a new state initiative, which had recently been implemented by the governor, to reduce pollution in the Chesapeake Bay. The moratorium would increase striped bass populations, which is an indicator in the public mind of water quality, regardless of the effectiveness of the cleanup program. Thus the state program (and the governor) would appear effective even if the cleanup effort were unsuccessful.[23]

A second set of problems involves measurement of outcomes. Some environmental activities have no direct market value and various techniques of shadow pricing must be used to derive their monetary value. How, for example, does an evaluator put a price on a day at Yellowstone National Park? Most people would agree that there are some values that cannot be measured, such as the utility of a life or the last dusky seaside sparrow, but the demands of regulatory analysis may require that some market value be assigned. Other management programs and directives may have competitive or synergistic effects.

Bureaucrats must also deal with a third set of problems: the dynamic between efficiency and effectiveness. It is often easier to measure efficiency in delivery than effectiveness in achieving goals. A park may increase its visitor-days and claim legislative applause for serving more citizens per dollar spent. However, if the purpose of the park—or even its partial purpose—was to provide a satisfying experience of the natural environment, information simply on the number of citizens served is not adequate.

Coping with the values of individuals and organizations involved in the policy process is the last problem in evaluation and is perhaps the least amenable to solution. Organizations have values (for example, the Park Service traditionally supports preservation values while the Forest Service advocates conservation and use); professions within organizations have values (such as the silvaculturists' desire to cut old timber); and clients and the general public have values (such as the preservation of wilderness and simultaneous access to the wilderness). Even the evaluator has his own values and expectations.

Suggested Reading

General public policy

Kingdon, John W. *Agendas, Alternatives, and Public Policies*. New York: Harper Collins, 1984.

Mazmanian, Daniel, and Paul Sabatier. *Implementation and Public Policy*. Glenview, IL: Scott, Foresman and Company, 1983.

Ripley, Randall, and Grace Franklin. *Congress, the Bureaucracy, and Pubic Policy* (4th ed.). Homewood, IL: Dorsey, 1991.

————. *Policy Implementation and Bureaucracy* (2nd ed.). Chicago, IL: Dorsey, 1986.

Environmental policy

Harris, Richard, and Sidney Milkis. *The Politics of Regulatory Change: A Tale of Two Agencies*. New York: Oxford University Press, 1989. A wonderful discussion of the impact of deregulation on the FTC and EPA.

Rosenbaum, Walter A. *Environmental Politics and Policy* (3rd ed.) Washington, DC: Congressional Quarterly Press, 1995. Primarily an undergraduate text, this furnishes as excellent overview of several areas of environmental policy: air pollution, water supply and pollution, toxic and hazardous wastes, energy, and public lands. The discussions on the relationships between science and politics alone make the book worthwhile.

Vig, Norman, and Michael Kraft. *Environmental Policy in the 1990s: Toward a New Agenda*. Washington, DC: Congressional Quarterly Press, 1990. This book provides recent analyses of environmental activity in Washington. Most of the articles are specialized but rewarding if one perseveres.

Notes

1. The material that follows is drawn primarily from Randall Ripley and Grace Franklin, *Congress, the Bureaucracy, and Public Policy* (Homewood, IL: Dorsey Press, 1984), esp. Chapter 1.

2. Another perspective on the temporary coalition of BLM and environmentalists is found in Susan J. Buck, "Cultural Theory and Management of Common Property Resources," *Human Ecology* 17 (1989): 101–116.

3. Marguerite Henry, *Brighty of the Grand Canyon* (New York: Rand McNally, 1953).

4. Penelope ReVelle and Charles ReVelle, *The Environment: Issues and Choices for Society* (Boston: Jones and Bartlett Publishers, 1988), p. 429.

5. G. Tyler Miller, Jr., *Living in the Environment* 5th ed. (Belmont, CA: Wadsworth, 1988), p. 473.

6. The material on agenda setting is from Roger Cobb and Charles Elder, *Participation in American Politics* (Boston: Allyn and Bacon, 1972), esp. Chapters 5–9, and from John Kingdon, *Agendas, Alternatives, and Public Policies* (New York: HarperCollins, 1984).

7. Jack Walker, "Setting the Agenda in the U.S. Senate," *British Journal of Political Science* 7 (October 1977), pp. 423–445.

8. Roger Cobb and Charles Elder, *Participation in American Politics* (Boston: Allyn and Bacon, 1972), esp. Chapters 5–9.

9. This charming analogy is from John Kingdon, *Agendas, Alternatives, and Public Policies* (New York: HarperCollins, 1984), Chapter 6.

10. Kingdon, Chapter 4.

11. Walter A. Rosenbaum, *Environmental Politics and Policy* 3rd. ed. (Washington, DC: Congressional Quarterly Press, 1995), p. 333.

12. This material comes from an excellent documentary, *An Act of Congress* (Learning Corporation of America, 1979).

13. The discussion of legitimation that follows is drawn from Guy Peters, *American Public Policy: Promise and Performance* 2nd ed. (Chatham, NJ: Chatham House Publishers, 1986), Chapter 4.

14. Peters, p. 63, notes omitted.

15. One of the side effects of consumer rights and the incredible expansion of personal injury litigation has been involvement of government agencies into personal lives in ways even our grandparents would find incredible. To force an unwilling store owner to prohibit smoking on his premises, to assign financial penalties for illegitimate children, to pass a leash law for *cats*—all of these are responses to demands that government do something about everything. This is not what the Framers had in mind for limited government. As a result, there are fewer areas in which American citizens will not accept government activity.

16. This is known as the "delegate" theory of representation: that the elected representatives vote their constituents' wishes. An opposing view is the "trustee" theory of delegation, which assumes that legislators, having access to better information, should vote their own consciences, regardless of the wishes of the folks back home.

17. Congress is, of course, subject to constitutional checks in this process.

18. The discussion which follows on bureaucratic resources and implementation, unless otherwise noted, is drawn from Randall Ripley and Grace Franklin, *Policy Implementation and Bureaucracy* 2nd ed. (Chicago: Dorsey, 1986), especially Chapters 1 and 2.

19. A very clear explanation of the implementation process is found in Daniel Mazmanian and Paul Sabatier, *Implementation and Public Policy* (Glenview, IL: Scott, Foresman, 1983), esp. p. 22.

20. National Standards Association, *National Directory of State Agencies* (Bethesda, MD: National Standards Association, 1987), tabulating under natural resources, water resources, health, environmental affairs, water pollution, air pollution, and solid waste.

21. One excellent definition of *sunk costs* is found in NEPA, § 102(C)(v), which refers to "irreversible and irretrievable commitment of resources."

22. This discussion of evaluation is from Peters, Chapter 7.

23. This speculation on the motives underlying the moratorium is based on numerous conversations between 1985 and 1988 with resource managers in the Chesapeake Bay and with political analysts interested in Maryland-Virginia conflicts.

Chapter Four

Legal Concepts in Environmental Law

Every discipline has basic techniques and skills. A miter joint is the same for a picture frame as for a house. Basic stitches must be mastered before sewing a hand towel or a suit. So it is with the law. This chapter explains the basic stitches of the law.

The first part demonstrates how to distinguish between the facts of a case and the point of law it establishes. Briefing or summarizing a case is the best way to distinguish between facts and law. A brief for *Tennessee Valley Authority* v. *Hill* is used to illustrate how to write a law school brief.[*]

The second section discusses due process, a concept that is important in the implementation and enforcement of regulatory policy. Other sections deal with concepts especially applicable to environmental law: standing, nuisance, property, and the public trust doctrine.

Understanding Case Law

One of the most difficult ideas to grasp in following legal cases is that often the facts of the case are less important than the point of law decided by the court. Facts provide the context for the decision, such as the policy area, the

---

[*]Readers who need to locate particular cases should consult "Finding Case Law" by John Ehmig at the end of this book.

precedents that might be followed, or mitigating circumstances. They frequently tell a tantalizing story, and it is frustrating to ask for "the rest of the story" and to be unable to discover what happened to the parties in the case.[1] However, readers of court opinions are often looking for legal "holdings" or the legal precedents that are set. The holdings are the core of the case; the most critical technique in using the law is knowing how to find the point of law for each case. Perhaps the easiest way to remember how cases should be used is to place ourselves in the role of a prosecuting or defending attorney. How would this case support our argument?

To illustrate the importance of the point of law and the lesser importance of the facts of the case, consider two cases, *Boyce Motor Lines* v. *United States* (1952) and *Dalehite* v. *United States* (1953). Boyce Motor Lines was a trucking firm that transported, among other things, explosives. The regulations of the Interstate Commerce Commission (ICC) prohibit carrying explosives through tunnels, for the obvious reason that a tunnel explosion not only endangers more lives than an explosion on an open highway, but in an underground or—even worse—an underwater tunnel, the damage would be extensive. Unfortunately for Boyce, the ICC also has a rule that requires trucks carrying explosives to move between the pick-up and delivery points as quickly as possible, which usually means traveling by the shortest route. Boyce, a New York City firm, chose to take carbon bisulfide, an explosive, through the Holland Tunnel in Brooklyn, reasoning that avoiding the tunnel would keep the truck on the road for many more miles and minutes than was safe. The third time Boyce used the tunnel, the load exploded and about sixty people were injured. Boyce was indicted for violating the tunnel regulations; the district court dismissed the indictment but the appeals court reinstated. Boyce appealed to the Supreme Court, arguing that the two rules were conflicting, that the ICC had not given clear guidance, and that it was impossible to transport explosives into Brooklyn without traveling on some dangerous, congested thoroughfare. The basis of Boyce's argument was that the regulations were impermissibly vague; the Court disagreed. Although three members of the Court dissented, the majority upheld the ICC and thus Boyce's indictment.

A second case dealing with explosives is *Dalehite* v. *United States* (1953). Both explosives and fertilizer contain ammonium nitrate, and after the Second World War, the Army converted fifteen of its ordinance plants to fertilizer production as part of the American effort to rebuild the agriculture of Europe and Japan. In 1947, the harbor of Texas City, Texas, exploded: two ships loaded with the Army's fertilizer caught fire and blew up. Five hundred and sixty people were killed and over three thousand more injured; Texas City practically disappeared. In a class action suit, Dalehite and others sought damages from the government, claiming the government had acted negligently in its handling of the potentially explosive materials. In 1953, when the case finally reached the Supreme Court, existing law exempted the government from liability when the government was performing discretionary actions; to do otherwise would be to discourage government officials from making decisions with any element of risk in them at all. The Army argued successfully that the procedures it had followed in labeling and shipping the materials were discretionary, and Dalehite lost the case. Congress later redressed the damages by passing a relief bill.

At a superficial level, these two cases seem similar. They both deal with explosions and with the safe transportation of explosives. Yet they cannot be categorized as "explosives" cases. The legal issue in *Boyce* is the alleged vagueness of two ICC regulations, while the legal issue in *Dalehite* is government liability for accidents that result from the exercise of legitimate discretion. The harm in *Boyce* is caused by a private carrier; the harm in *Dalehite* is caused by the government. Although a superficial reading of these two cases would find them to be similar, their legal impact is quite different. A careful reading, which tried to distinguish the precedent established by each case, would distinguish between regulatory vagueness and administrative discretion.

One way to ensure that cases are understood is to make a *case brief*. There are two kinds of briefs: lengthy legal memoranda written by lawyers and filed with the courts to support motions, and the standard law school brief which is a written summary, in a standard format, of the important facts and decisions of each case. The law school brief is a useful practice for managers to summarize key facts and the legal holding of each case. Briefing a case helps the reader grasp the essentials of the law determined in the case. While managers do not need all the information in a case brief, the habit of briefing is useful in a profession that rests so much on administrative law. Learning to brief a case may seem to be only an academic exercise, but the habit of figuring out the reasoning behind an opinion and the point of law is of incalculable value. Without a sense of the progression of legal thought, the legal concepts that our regulatory and management processes rely upon will be difficult to grasp. Legal concepts are fluid, varying with time, justices, and substantive areas.

Managers preparing new rules or planning to implement a program need to be able to predict, or at least to explain, judicial reactions to their behavior. By following judicial guidelines, managers may avoid problems. After the *Calvert Cliffs* decision (discussed in chapter 2), federal agency managers had no doubts about the requirements of the EIS provisions of NEPA. Understanding case law also helps managers interact with the attorneys in their agencies and in the private sector institutions with which they must deal. While the entire scope of environmental law is impossible for one person to master, the specific case law applying to any given agency's activities is accessible. Being able to distill the importance and impact of judicial decisions for themselves, and then to integrate their knowledge of recent cases with existing laws and agency regulations, puts managers in control of the law rather than at the mercy of others.

Briefing a Case

The first thing to understand about law school briefs is that they are short, hence the word *brief*. A formal brief starts out with the full name and legal citation of a case, including the year. (See the sample brief of *Tennessee Valley Authority* v. *Hill* [1978].) For administrators, the year a case is decided is very important, because the technology, social conditions, and political temper of the time the case is decided are critical to understanding how the case may be applied in current situations. The citation, or source, provides the volume number, the name of the series that reports the cases of the deciding court, and the page on which the court opinion begins. For example, in the *TVA* case, the opinion begins on page 153 of volume 437 of the United States Reports (the official government publication for Supreme Court decisions). You will find a list of the more common reporters and their abbreviations following the list of acronyms.

Second is the summary of the essential facts of the case. These are the behaviors and decisions that led to this particular case or controversy coming before the court. Was a species declared an "endangered species"? Was a cement plant constructed using the best available technology? Will individual members of the Sierra Club be affected when a recreational facility is built in Mineral King Valley? Only those facts necessary to understand the judicial reasoning in the opinion, concurrences, or dissents are included. This section also catalogs how the case comes before the court that wrote the opinion. Have administrative appeals been exhausted? Which court heard the case originally and how did those judges rule? What has been the history of the appeals process for this case?

Next the issues of the case are stated in the form of a question or questions that can be answered "yes" or "no." For example, in the *Boyce* case, the question is: are the ICC regulations governing transportation of hazardous material impermissibly vague? The judicial response to this particular question, which is the next piece of information in a brief, is "No." The court's response to each issue is followed by the action it ordered, if any.

A summary of the legal reasoning used by the judge writing the opinion follows. In a law school brief, only the reasoning that directly supports the opinion is included. Judicial excursions into interesting tangents are not put into a brief. The name of the judge writing the opinion is important because judges often develop a chain of reasoning over a series of cases or form tem-

---

Example of Law School Brief

Tennessee Valley Authority v. *Hill*
437 U.S. 153, 15 June 1978

Facts

Construction began on Tellico Dam in 1967. August 1973: a new perch species (snail darter) was discovered in the river behind the dam site. December 1973: the Endangered Species Act was passed. November 1975: the snail darter was listed as endangered. April 1976: seventeen miles of the Little Tennessee River behind the dam was declared critical habitat for the snail darter. February 1976: trying to save the snail darter, Hill brought suit in federal district court for an injunction to halt construction and was denied the injunction. On appeal, the Court of Appeals reversed the district court and ordered the injunction. TVA appealed to the United States Supreme Court.

Issues

1. Would TVA be in violation of the Endangered Species Act if it completed and operated the Tellico Dam as planned? Yes.
2. If "yes," is an injunction the appropriate remedy? Yes. The decision of the Court of Appeals is affirmed.

Reasoning

Justice Burger for the Court: The language of the act and the legislative history are clear. Congress intended to "halt and reverse the trend toward species extinction, whatever the cost," and the act "reveals a conscious decision by Congress to give endangered species priority over the 'primary missions' of federal agencies" (184).

Concur

None

Dissent

Justice Powell joined by Justice Blackmun: Congress has funded the Tellico Dam project for twelve years and continued this funding even after the Endangered Species Act passed. There is no indication that the Endangered Species Act was intended to be retroactive. While Congress will probably exempt the dam from the act, the Court should not force the congressional hand.
Justice Rehnquist also dissented.

Summary

Barring explicit congressional exemptions, the Endangered Species Act is a bar to any federal project that threatens the survival or habitat of a listed species.

---

porary alliances with other judges. How the individual judge views an issue may be a key factor in anticipating later judicial reactions. Also, the opinions of some judges are more respected than others, so that the prestige of the judge writing the opinion may give more weight to the decision.

Next are noted concurring and dissenting opinions, if any, and their reasoning. On courts in which more than one judge gives an opinion (usually appeals courts), a judge may agree with the outcome of the case but not agree with the reasoning by which it was reached; he may write a *concurring opinion* in which he explains his own reasoning or changes the emphasis of the court's reasoning. A judge may disagree with the outcome and write an opinion in dissent. It is in concurring opinions and dissents that we sometimes find the clearest expressions of judicial opinions because judges are under no obligation to write either concurrences or dissents. In a court opinion, the author is often fusing the decisions and rationales of more than one judge, but in a concurrence or dissent, the author is unfettered by such considerations. Since the manager needs to understand the *reasoning* as a guide to his own behavior, it is important to understand all the legal motivations of the judges who are sufficiently concerned about an issue to write a concurrence or a dissent.

Finally, the author of the brief should summarize the related principles and distinguish them, if necessary, from related cases.

It is critical that environmental managers do not carelessly assume that legal decisions and concepts from other policy areas also hold true for environmental policy. A good example of this is the concept of standing. The criteria used to establish standing in environmental matters are not the same as the criteria in, for example, product liability cases.

Standing

Traditionally, standing is the right to have one's case heard before a tribunal, that is, the right to "stand" before the judge. To have this right at common law, one must have suffered an actual injury in fact to a legally protected right. In federal cases, the requirement that a party bringing an action must have standing, or a sufficient stake or connection to the litigation, arises from the United States Constitution's "case or controversy" requirement (Article III, Section 2).[2] The *Fontainebleau* case illustrates some of the common law considerations for standing.

The Fontainebleau Hotel, built in 1954, was one of the grand hotels of Miami Beach. Its rival, the Eden Roc, was built next door in 1955. The owners of the Fontainebleau planned to add a fourteen-story addition that would shade the Eden Roc's beach, cabana, and pool after 2:00 P.M. The Eden Roc's owners obtained an injunction to stop the construction, and the Fontainebleau appealed. The appeals court supported the Fontainebleau because under Florida law, the Eden Roc's owners had neither a statutory right nor a state or federal constitutions right to the sunshine.[3] They could not bring a suit because they had no standing: no legally protected right of the hotel owners had been infringed.

This venerable common law view of standing changed as the administrative state evolved. In 1946, the Administrative Procedure Act (APA), which is discussed in chapter 5, broadened access to judicial review of agency actions:

> A person suffering a legal wrong because of agency action, or adversely affected or aggrieved by agency action within the meaning of a relevant statute, is entitled to judicial review thereof. 5 U.S.C.§ 702

This section of the APA liberalized access to judicial review of agency actions. Standing is a very complex issue, and judicial interpretations of standing vary with the policy area being reviewed. Several United States Supreme Court decisions since 1970 illustrate the evolving standing doctrine in environmental law. The first of these is *Association of Data Processing Service Organizations* v. *Camp* (1970), in which the association attempted to reverse an administrative decision allowing banks to provide data processing services to their clients. The question of the association's standing to bring the suit was raised. In this case, the Supreme Court significantly altered the criteria for standing to two questions: (1) is the person bringing the suit "aggrieved in fact" and (2) is the interest to be protected "arguably within the zone of interests to be protected or regulated by the statute or constitutional guarantee in question?"[4] *Data Processing* thus effectively eliminated the test of "legally protected right" in cases of judicial review of administrative action.[5]

A second case is the famous *Mineral King* case, *Sierra Club* v. *Morton* (1972). The Sierra Club tried to halt development of a $35-million recreation facility by Walt Disney Enterprises on national forest land in Mineral King Valley. The Sierra Club did not allege any actual injury to its members; it instead asserted a right to be heard because of its organizational interests in protecting the environment. The Supreme Court relied on *Data Processing* and refused to grant the Sierra Club standing, but the Court clearly spelled out how standing might be achieved: all Sierra Club had to do was to assert that some of its members would be unable to enjoy their usual outdoor recreational pursuits if the Disney resort were built. It is in this case that Justice Douglas wrote his famous dissent suggesting that even trees should have standing. He noted that American law already gave legal standing to some inanimate objects, such as ships, and even to some organizations, such as corporations, and he asserted that environmental objectives would be enhanced if litigators could sue on behalf of the trees or valleys or rivers.[6]

In 1973, the Court took its expanded notion of standing to new heights in *United States* v. *Students Challenging Regulatory Agency Procedures* (SCRAP).

Five Washington State students had formed an organization to challenge an ICC decision to allow across-the-board rate increases for the railroads.[7] The ICC already had in place a higher rate for recycled materials. The students argued that by increasing the rates, recycled materials would be even less profitable to ship, thus discouraging recycling and increasing the litter in the parks they enjoyed near their home city of Seattle. They also claimed that the lowered demand for recycled materials would cause an increase in logging and mining (to provide raw material for new products), thereby reducing their pleasure in the surrounding countryside. Improbably, the Supreme Court granted standing, although the challenge to the regulation was unsuccessful.

This decision to grant standing rested on reasoning that must have been a shock to the ICC. The Court said that SCRAP's argument was strengthened by the notion that many people would be affected and that the rather minimal nature of each person's harm was not a relevant factor. This is the opposite of the argument that was accepted by the Court for years as an absolute bar to taxpayer's suits: there are so many taxpayers, and the individual harm done by one new tax to the economic status of any one taxpayer is so small that taxpayer suits against the government are unacceptable.[8]

After *SCRAP,* the Court seemed to pull back from its liberal interpretation of standing in nonenvironmental cases. However, in environmental issues it continued to accept rather tenuous arguments for standing. *Duke Power Co. v. Carolina Environmental Study Group* (1978) challenged the Price-Anderson Act, which limited the liability for damages caused by nuclear power companies to $560 million for any one accident. The Carolina Environmental Study Group claimed that their damages from an accident would probably exceed the Price-Anderson limit, which meant that the statute was depriving them of property (their projected damages) without compensation. The nuclear power plants, they also contended, would never be built without the Price-Anderson protections, and the reactors were harming the environment. The Court granted standing, finding that the Price-Anderson Act was an acceptable substitute for common law remedies for damages.

There are several reasons why the courts were initially more liberal in granting standing in environmental cases than in nonenvironmental ones. First, in the early seventies and following on the heels of NEPA and Earth Day, the courts were eager to give environmentalists a chance to be heard, although being allowed to bring the suit did not guarantee victory for environmentalists. The Sierra Club in *Mineral King* was denied standing at first, although the Court carefully pointed out what they needed to do to establish standing, and they immediately and successfully refiled. The students in *SCRAP* lost their challenge to the ICC regulations. And Duke Power continued to build its reactor. The courts are as sensitive as any other branch of government to public opinion (although they are less vulnerable to expressions of public ill-will), and in these cases they were willing to open the judicial doors for discussion of issues.

Second, during the early 1970s, the Supreme Court had a number of liberal, activist justices; Justice Douglas was an ardent environmentalist and often brought his fellow justices along with him. Finally, in most cases the decisions required involved statutory interpretation (and justification for standing established in the Administrative Procedure Act), and the judges were not asked to interpret (and perhaps to amend informally) the Constitution in their decisions. Thus one of their traditional barriers to review—a reluctance to reach constitutional issues—was almost certain to be avoided.

In recent years, as the Court has become more conservative, it has indicated that it might want to tighten the liberal standing requirements a bit, holding in *Lujan v. National Wildlife Federation* (1990) that vague allegations of a connection between the environmental group members and federal lands with which they were concerned were not sufficient to convey standing. However, at present, to be granted standing a person must satisfy four general requirements.[9] First, they must be within the "zone of interest" covered by the statute. Second, they must establish that they have suffered an "injury in fact."[10] Third, they must show that the agency action is the cause of the harm. Finally, they must demonstrate a substantial likelihood that a judicial relief will reduce the injury.[11]

Allegations of environmental harm have always had remedies available at common law, and courts are inclined to follow this tradition. Although the circumstances of the environmental harm have changed, judges still have the common law and its precedents upon which to draw for remedies. One of the common law concepts that applies to environmental cases is that of nuisance.

Nuisance

The concept of nuisance also has a distinguished pedigree in common law. In general, nuisance involves a suit by one neighbor against another or by the public prosecutor suing on behalf of the public. The general rule at common law for nuisance is that no one may act so as to unreasonably interfere with the property rights of another person. There are two kinds of nuisance: private nuisance and public nuisance. A private nuisance is the unreasonable interference with the use or enjoyment of one's land, but it does not include physical invasion or trespass, for example, throwing trash over the fence. Playing drums at dawn or polluting a neighbor's well would be private nuisances.[12]

A public nuisance is an activity that adversely affects the health, morals, safety, welfare, comfort, or convenience of the public in general. Large-scale air and water pollution may be considered public nuisances. It is sometimes difficult to distinguish trespass from nuisance; for example, air pollution technically involves particulate matter falling in inappropriate places and is therefore really trespass, but the law tends to treat it as a nuisance. This allows a governmental remedy rather than requiring individuals to sue for damages from trespass.

Whether or not an activity is a nuisance may depend on its location. Rural areas are typically more lenient in the kinds of undertakings they will permit. A hog farm in rural Vermont does not impair the neighbors' use of their property, but transported to Boston, the same hog farm would be cast out. Residential areas tend to be the most restrictive, and even when the "nuisance" was in place first, often the residential use may have priority, as illustrated in the following case of *Spur Industries* v. *Del Webb Development* (1972).

In 1954 a suburban Phoenix development catering to retirees was established west of Phoenix, Arizona. Two years later, in 1956, a feedlot, later sold to Spur Industries, was started about two miles south of the development. In May of 1959, Del Webb began to develop Sun City, building south from the first retirement community. As Sun City grew, so did the feedlot, and by December 1976, the two were only five hundred feet apart. Although Webb had chosen to develop south and at least in the early years did not consider Spur to be a problem, by 1967 he was having trouble selling residential lots near Spur. Not even Sun City could tolerate thirty thousand head of cattle and a million tons of wet manure per day baking in the Arizona heat. Webb sued to close Spur, alleging that Spur was both a private and a public nuisance.

Spur contested the action with the defense of "coming to the nuisance": Spur Industries had preceded Del Webb into western Phoenix, and Webb had known all along that the feedlot was there.

The court was sympathetic to the interests of the people living in Sun City and found that Spur constituted a nuisance. The court ordered Spur to move but also ordered Webb to pay for the costs of the move. The court reasoned that in the interests of public health and enjoyment of property, Spur must move, but since Webb had put himself and his home buyers in the predicament, he must pay to extricate them.

Not all such cases do end so satisfactorily. Usually when an activity is economically beneficial and yet still a nuisance, the courts find themselves using the "balancing of hardships" or "balancing of the equities" doctrine. In *Boomer et al.* v. *Atlantic Cement Co.* (1970), a large cement plant was spewing dirt and smoke into the surrounding neighborhood and vibrating the ground. The neighbors claimed this was a nuisance and asked for an injunction to have the nuisance halted. The court agreed that the plant was a nuisance, but unfortunately, since the plant was already using the best available technology, the only way to stop the nuisance was to shut the plant. This plant had cost $45 million to build and employed over three hundred local residents. The court weighed the hardship to the community if the plant closed against the hardship to the home owners if the nuisance continued. The court allowed the plant to continue to operate but required the plant to pay damages to Boomer and his neighbors. One judge dissented, writing that to allow the nuisance to continue was the equivalent of giving the power of eminent domain to any private company that chose to pollute.

As is often the case with common law remedies, the exigencies of the situation may confound our ideas of equitable settlement. The benefits of allowing a nuisance to continue must be balanced with the costs of the nuisance. Who is to blame for the problem? What are the relative hardships for each of the parties? Are there third parties or the public involved?

The next section deals with a concept dear to the heart of Americans; we place it in the pantheon of national values, side by side with life and liberty.

Property: Issues of Land Use Law

The concept of property is rooted in English common law.[13] Although the notion of property has expanded since the 1960s to include entitlements such as welfare, this section focuses on real property—land and the economic issues related to land.

The first section, Origins of Land Use Control, looks at the changes in land tenure systems from feudal days to the Industrial Revolution in the United States. Next is the discussion of eminent domain, the ancient right of the sovereign to take private property for public use. In American law, this right is constrained by our notions of due process, both procedural and substantive. Due process is discussed in the third section of the chapter. Zoning, the regulation of private property uses, is the topic of the fourth section; some argue that this is really a taking or exercise of eminent domain. A discussion of regulation versus taking, which requires compensation, concludes the section on property.

Origins of Land Use Control

The concept of land use controls or regulations is not a phenomenon of the twentieth century, despite the resistance to zoning and other forms of regulation in rural areas. The regulation of land extends through Anglo-Saxon common law to ancient times; the earliest code of Roman law, dating to 451–450 B.C., provided for setbacks in housing construction.

Land use law is not constant; as social and economic conditions change, the law must adapt to protect new arrangements of land use and ownership and to encourage the policies preferred by the authorities. In the eleventh and twelfth centuries, English villages were largely feudal and had "common" land for the villages to use for grazing their livestock. Our modern-day notions of *common* as a public right does not accurately describe the medieval commons.[14] In the commons system, either by common law right as a freehold tenant or through usage and grants, a villager was entitled to pasture limited numbers of specific animals on the land not otherwise used by the feudal lord. The villager also had rights to cut wood, to fish, and to cut peat or turf for fuel. Even from the beginning, the use of the common was restricted: "Common pasture of stubble and fallow was a feature of open-field husbandry from the start . . . and with it went communal control."[15] The villages determined what kinds of animals and how many might be put on the common, the time of year they could be set loose, how long they might graze, and when they must be removed.

Although the commons system lasted for centuries, abuses of the system by the wealthier landholders were frequent. In the sixteenth, seventeenth, and eighteenth centuries,

> the poor owning rights may largely be kept out of their rights by the action of large farmers who exceed their rights and thus surcharge the common to the detriment of all, or by the lack of winter feed in the absence of which summer grazing could be of little worth. Again, jobbers would hire cottages in order to obtain, as it were, a right of entry to the common and then proceed to eat up the common; or new cottages would spring up near the common, and though legally without rights, would encroach in practice on those to whom the common really belonged.[16]

The unfortunate poor tenant was denied his remedy at law for the illegal abuses of the more powerful landowners. The ultimate conclusion was the enclosure of the common land, mostly between 1720 and 1880. Political demands for land reform were frequently no more than a sophisticated landgrab, justified in part by the admittedly striking increase in productivity of enclosed common land.

The increased productivity was often touted by land reformers—wealthy or otherwise—as proof of the evils of the commons system. However, the change was the result of many factors and not just of enclosure. Some of the increase would probably have occurred without enclosure, but enclosure hastened the process. The common land was not the best land. The lord's waste was often reclaimed land, cultivated from forest and marsh. Enclosure took the better land and subjected it to the new and improved methods of agriculture that had been all but impossible under the common system, for the management of the common could not be changed unless all commoners agreed and, just as important, remained agreed. Improved roads and transportation facilities made marketing easier, and, of course, the land had fewer people to support.

Economies of scale made it profitable to use improved stock. In 1760, Robert Bakewell, the founder of modern methods of livestock improvement, began selective breeding of farm animals. Previously forbidden by ecclesiastical authorities as incest, inbreeding of animals with desirable qualities soon led to dramatic improvements in stock. Planting the enclosure with nitrogen-fixing crops, such as clover, improved the soil; drainage improved livestock health. Animals were disturbed less by driving to and from pasture land. All of these factors combined to improve the productivity of the formerly common land. Economic pressures from abroad encouraged enclosure, and by the end of the eighteenth century, the commons system was effectively gone.[17]

While the system of communal land control was changing in rural areas, the urban landscape was also under examination. Urban crowding reached unthinkable heights, and in London, the Great Fire recorded by Samuel Pepys in the seventeenth century produced building codes and land use restrictions.

The American colonists brought with them an acceptance of land use controls, but they found such regulations were not necessary in the New World. Land was plentiful, and only when the Census of 1890 declared the American frontier officially closed did Americans really begin to come to grips with the need for land reform and regulation.

Conflicts over land use were at first easy to settle. Usually the common law remedy of nuisance was sufficient to settle private disputes. Initially, the strength of the concept of property rights, and the Lockean notion that if a person had worked for something, and paid for it, it was his to do with as he wished, overrode any suspicion that the public might be better served if certain activities were prohibited or restricted. However, as the American cities grew, public controls became necessary. Cities began to pass ordinances restricting certain kinds of activities (such as tanneries, or candle makers, or slaughterhouses with their attendant odors and refuse) to particular parts of town. The source of the power to regulate such activities is the *police power*. Although the term "police power" is not specifically mentioned in the federal Constitution, it refers to the inherent power of a state, subject to constitutional limitations and due process to promote order, public health, safety, morals, and general welfare. Early objections to the exercise of the police power generally rested on the notion of "taking" (the government was taking an individual's property for public use), but in the nineteenth century, charges of taking only meant the actual physical seizure of property. This notion of "taking" is discussed more thoroughly later in this chapter.

Most controls on land use come from government regulation, but some arise at common law. One is the concept of nuisance, discussed in the preceding section. Another is the notion of *waste,* which can arise when people share interests and rights in a resource. Waste is committing acts upon the land that are harmful to the rights of the party not in possession. A tenant who cut down all the trees in his landlord's yard would be guilty of waste. Waste can be affirmative (cutting down the trees) or permissive (allowing a roof to deteriorate so that rain damages the interior of the house). The remedy for waste can be money damages, an injunction to stop the conduct that is causing the harm, or some combination of the two.

There are also some private law or contractual devices to control property, such as easements and covenants. An easement is the legal right to use or traverse someone else's land and must be transferred when the property is transferred. Often utility companies have easements across private property for power lines or telephone wires or water pipes. Covenants are restrictions that "run with the land." Unlike easements, which in effect allow a physical trespass on the owner's property, covenants restrict the uses to which the land may be put. These covenants are voluntary, in the sense that buyers do not have to buy if they do not like them, but they are usually binding and also transfer with the property. Examples of covenants include prohibitions on children in retirement communities, restrictions on the types and heights of fences that may be erected around property, and minimum house sizes. Covenants that are discriminatory, such as banning racial or religious groups from owning property in a neighborhood, are not legal.

Eminent Domain

The right of the state to take private property is ancient. All property at one time belonged to the Crown, and in England today this is still technically true. When the sovereign took a subject's property, he was simply reclaiming property that already belonged to him. The sovereign was not required to use due process nor was he required to pay compensation. In the United States, the Fifth Amendment to the Constitution imposes an obligation on the national government to exercise due process of law in taking private property, as well as an obligation to pay for it:

> No person shall . . . be deprived of life, liberty, or property, without due process of law; nor shall private property be taken for public use, without just compensation.

From an analytic perspective, there are several critical factors in interpreting the Fifth Amendment. First, the amendment protects *persons* and not just *citizens;* some sections of the Constitution (for example, the Eleventh Amendment) apply only to citizens. Second, the amendment does permit persons to be deprived of life, liberty, or property; the restriction is that such persons must have "due process of law." What is "due process"? As described later, due process embodies society's fundamental concepts of legal fairness. At a minimum, due process includes the right to a hearing; just what kind of hearing is required is discussed later in this section. The government does in fact deprive persons of life (capital punishment), liberty (imprisonment), and property (taxes). There is, however, a restriction on taking real property; the last part of the amendment states that private property may not be taken for public use without just compensation; in other words, if the federal government wants a person's farm for a military base, it may take the farm but must pay a reasonable price for it. The power to do this is known as the power of eminent domain. It is not, however, essential for the exercise of eminent domain that the government be taking property for actual use by the government; "public use" can mean either actual use by the public (beaches, new military bases) or use for public advantage (for example, easements for electric power lines). In the nineteenth century, the federal government even gave the power of eminent domain to the railroads as an incentive for them to build a transcontinental line.

The Fifth Amendment is found in the federal Constitution and until the end of the nineteenth century was held to apply only to the actions of the federal government. Although many states had similar clauses in their state constitutions, in 1868 when the Fourteenth Amendment passed, five states still lacked the requirement for just compensation when the state seized private property. The Fourteenth Amendment reads in part:

> All persons born or naturalized in the United States and subject to the jurisdiction thereof, are citizens of the United States and of the State wherein they reside. No State shall make or enforce any law which shall abridge the privileges or immunities of citizens of the United States; nor shall any State deprive any person of life, liberty, or property, without due process of law; nor deny to any person within its jurisdiction the equal protection of the laws.

Through a long series of Supreme Court cases that do not concern us here, the Court has held that the Fourteenth Amendment incorporates virtually all of the Bill of Rights, that the protections the citizens have from the federal government apply as well to state government actions. While this has been of interest primarily in criminal cases, in environmental law the application of due process rights can be critical. Through the nationalization of the Bill of Rights, the national constitutional protections for property also apply to the states. This has important ramifications for issues of zoning and other forms of land-use regulation; states must use due process when taking property, and owners whose property is taken by eminent domain must receive just compensation.

Just compensation is usually determined by fair market value: what a willing buyer would pay a willing seller to put the land to its highest and best use. If only part of the property is taken, and the value of the remainder is changed, compensation is adjusted to include the loss or increase of value. A simpler calculus that is sometimes employed is to pay the difference between the value before the taking and the value after. There are other kinds of property rights that must be compensated; people other than the owner may have vested rights in the property. For example, some states still have dower rights, which give the wife a certain percentage of the value of all of her husband's real property, regardless of when or how he acquired it. When this property is taken, the dower rights must also be compensated. A lessee may need compensation, as may a person holding an easement across the property or someone with other rights such as mineral rights. Who is entitled to compensation and how that entitlement is calculated is a complex issue that varies widely between political jurisdictions.

Due Process

There are two forms of due process: procedural and substantive. Procedural due process is concerned with the forms and procedures followed by government when exercising its legitimate functions, while substantive due process is concerned with the legitimacy of government action in a particular sphere. Usually a reference to "due process" refers to *procedural* due process. Substantive due process is rarely invoked, although it is of more importance in environmental policy than in many other policy areas.

Procedural Due Process

Any government action that will affect a person's property requires some form of hearing before the action is taken. Environmental management usually involves administrative hearings before government agencies rather than court proceedings; there are important differences between the two. In an administrative hearing there is no right to a trial by jury. Evidence is presented in a less formal manner than in court. The decisionmaker is not totally independent of the agency holding the hearing; unlike Article III judges (judges who derive their powers from Article III of the Constitution, the article establishing the federal judiciary), administrative law judges are civil servants and vulnerable to transfers, salary changes, and some political pressures. Usually the individual affected in an administrative hearing has the option to appeal the decision but in most cases he must first exhaust nonjudicial remedies before being allowed to take his case to the courts. Some statutes even forbid judicial review of agency decisions.

The Coconino County restaurant license revocation described in chapter 3 is an example of an administrative hearing.

The case that lays the constitutional foundation for hearings in the administrative decision process is *Londoner* v. *Denver* (1908). The Colorado legislature had authorized the city of Denver to order street paving and to apportion costs to the adjoining property owners. The city did not allow a hearing for the property owners. The Supreme Court decided that when a tax is determined by a *subordinate body* (that is, an administrative agency acting under delegated legislative authority), constitutional due process provisions give the taxpayer the right to a hearing. Later cases restricted the taxpayers' right to a hearing,[18] but the important point here is that when an administrative agency is acting under delegated legislative authority, its actions may constitutionally require a hearing.

The precise nature of the required hearing differs dramatically, depending upon the nature of the issue and the parties involved. A school child may be entitled to due process before being suspended from school, but his hearing can be a simple conference in the hall with his school principal. A chemical company challenging new EPA regulations will probably receive a full-scale trial-like administrative hearing.

Although an agency may be required to provide a hearing, the adversely affected person is not required to take advantage of the offer. In fact, the right to a hearing may be waived and usually is. Although the percentages vary among federal agencies, fewer than 5 percent of the parties eligible for a full-scale hearing actually have one.[19]

Substantive Due Process

Substantive due process is of particular interest in environmental administration because so much of the environmental law deals with regulation. At least in the early years of the republic, the courts were willing to argue that the legislative power did not include economic regulation.

For the judges who endorsed natural law as generating fundamental rights entitled to judicial protection from legislative interference, property was one of the three basic rights of individuals (along with life and liberty). In *Lochner* v. *New York* (1905), the Supreme Court invalidated a New York law regulating the hours of bakery workers on the grounds that it interfered with the right of contract between employers and employees. From 1905 to the mid-1930s, substantive due process provided justification for the courts to invalidate many state laws involving economic regulation, especially labor legislation, price regulation, and limitations on entry into business. In 1934, because of such actions, the court was on a collision path with President Franklin Roosevelt and the New Deal programs. Roosevelt prevailed; the first change occurred in 1934 when in *Nebbia* v. *New York,* the Court refused to invalidate a New York law that fixed the selling price of milk. By 1941, the about-face was complete:

> [T]he Supreme Court has consistently maintained that, so far as the due process and equal protection clauses are concerned, legislative policy in economic matters is solely for the legislature. It has repeatedly taken the position that it will not review the legislative judgment in such matters and has denounced as overruled, or no longer in good standing, the leading due process decisions of the earlier 1905–1934 era in which the Court struck down significant economic legislation by substituting its judgment for that of the legislative bodies.[20]

This posture has given both the federal and the state legislatures a freer hand in regulating businesses for environmental reasons. Business and industrial interests have tried unsuccessfully to claim that the legislatures lack the authority to regulate their enterprises, but proponents of environmental regulation have usually prevailed.

The "Due Process Explosion"

One of the greatest expansions in legal rights in the administrative state has come from the "due process explosion": the transformation of entitlements to property rights. The key case is *Goldberg* v. *Kelly* (1970), which established that welfare was a property right that may not be taken away without due process. Just when a government benefit becomes a right was spelled out in *Board of Regents* v. *Roth* (1972). In that case, the Court held that in order for a due process hearing to be required the interested person first must have more than a unilateral expectation of the benefit; he must have a legitimate claim of entitlement. Moreover, this entitlement must originate in some independent source, such as a law or already existing rules and regulations.

The expansion of entitlements to property rights is rarely at issue in environmental law. However, it is possible to argue that in some states, citizens have a property right, protected by due process, in a healthy environment. Some states have established statutory rights to clean, safe environments; others have written such rights into their state constitutions. If these changes create entitlements for citizens, then administrative agencies may be required to exercise due process safeguards when managing or regulating the environment. Usually constitutional safeguards are designed to protect citizens against government actions, but interpretations of the due process clause may create positive obligations to act:

> The courts have struggled with the issue of imposing liability for state inaction because they have failed to identify any workable Constitutional standard. But in fact the Supreme Court developed such a standard when it set forth the due process requirements for the withdrawal of statutory entitlements. Even assuming that a state has no obligation to provide protection in the first place, it may violate the due process clause when it assumes such an obligation and then fails to fulfill it.[21]

A special problem arises because of the general nature of environmental protection. Some government benefits, such as police protection, do not create property interests because there is no special class of citizen entitled to the benefits. However, one might argue that environmental protection is not analogous to police protection, which states must provide, but rather that the provision of environmental protection is voluntary and therefore creates rights. A supporting argument is found in a 1971 California case, *Marks* v. *Whitney,* in which one party sought to build a marina that would have limited the access of his neighbor to the ocean. The neighbor's standing—the right to bring suit (discussed later)—was challenged when he objected. The California Supreme Court held on appeal that the neighbor had standing because if the plaintiff were allowed to build his marina, he would be "taking away from [his neighbor] rights to which he is entitled as a member of the general public."[22]

Zoning

The first comprehensive zoning plan in the United States was passed by New York City in 1916.[23] Since then the validity of zoning has repeatedly been upheld by the courts as a legitimate use of the police power. Zoning is invalid only if it is unreasonable, or arbitrary or capricious—the usual standards against which administrative action is judged—or if it deprives the owner of all or practically all of the use of his property. The general rule is that to be valid, zoning must be authorized by enabling statutes; comprehensive zoning is usually governed by statute and therefore is better able to withstand judicial challenge than incremental or piecemeal zoning.

The landmark case for comprehensive zoning is *Euclid* v. *Ambler Realty Company* (1926). This was the first case in which the Supreme Court directly addressed the constitutionality of zoning. Ambler Realty owned property abutting an industrial area. When the property was zoned residential, its value was cut by two-thirds. Ambler sued the city on the grounds that the zoning restriction was an unconstitutional taking without either due process or compensation. The Supreme Court upheld the use of the state's governmental police power.

Why would this case rest on an exercise of *state* power when it was the village of Euclid that had enacted the zoning ordinance? The reason rests on a peculiarity of American land use law. Counties and cities have no sovereign status.[24] The powers that they have are given to them by the states, and so the exercise of land regulation is indirectly an exercise of a state power.

The basis for many zoning challenges is that the localities exceeded the authority given to them by their state governments. However, because the zoning process is based on state legislative authority, a local zoning ordinance will usually not be overturned unless it is found to be arbitrary or capricious.

Regulation versus Taking

A big quandary in land use law is distinguishing between (1) a permissible use of the police power to regulate land use for the general welfare and (2) government action that takes a person's property and requires compensation. One way to distinguish between regulation and taking is to examine the purposes of government actions. The government action may be regulatory if it interferes with the property to prevent *harm* to the public, but if the interference were for the public's benefit, then the action may be a taking and require compensation. Thus a zoning decision that inhibited housing development to protect a watershed would be regulatory, but a similar decision to provide parking for a football stadium would be a taking.[25]

The line between regulation and taking is not fixed. In 1978, the Supreme Court decided in *Pennsylvania Central Transportation Co.* v. *New York* that "taking" must meet a three-part test. First, a taking probably exists if there has been a physical invasion of the property, for example, running a power line. Second, a taking may exist if the restriction on the property does not produce widespread public benefit or it is not applied to all property in similar situations. Finally, the third test examines the extent to which the property owner is restricted from earning a reasonable rate of return on his investment in the property.

Cases in the late eighties brought into sharper focus the concerns of municipal and state planning authorities over the exercise of their land use powers. In *First English Evangelical Lutheran Church of Glendale* v. *City of Los Angeles* (1987), the Supreme Court gave damages to the landowner for income lost as the result of land use regulations. Also in 1987, the Court ruled in *Nollan* v. *California Coastal Commission* that the Coastal Commission requirement for public access to the beach over Nollan's property was a taking.

In the early 1990s, the federal courts have continued to restrict the power of government to regulate private property in such as way as to reduce its economic value. In *Lucas* v. *South Carolina Coastal Council* (1992), the Court held that the state's Beachfront Management Act (enacted after the devastation of Hurricane Hugo to increase the protection of coastal areas) rendered Lucas's housing lots valueless and therefore constituted a taking. In effect, a regulation that eliminates all economic value of a property now entitles the owner to compensation. More recently, in *Dolan* v. *City of Tigard* (1994), the Court held that requiring a public easement as a condition for a building permit was a taking, and unlike the *Nollan* case, the Court placed the burden of justifying the regulation on the government rather than the landowner.

The law on takings versus legitimate regulation remains unclear. A conservative "property rights" movement began in the 1980s; it was "mostly a rural phenomenon with a limited following, a disorganized crusade carried on in farmhouse kitchens and small-town diners where disgruntled landowners swapped horror stories."[26] Led by Speaker Newt Gingrich, in 1995 the House of Representatives passed a bill to require compensation when wetlands or Endangered Species Act regulations reduced the value of property by more than 20 percent. Twenty states passed property rights bills between 1992 and 1995; four of these states (Florida, Louisiana, Mississippi, and Washington) have laws that entitle property owners to compensation when state and local restrictions on the use of land reduce the value of the property.[27]

As the conservative members of the federal bench become more plentiful and more powerful, "property" is beginning to reassert its position in the hierarchy of protected rights. Justice Rehnquist wrote for the majority in *Dolan*:

> We see no reason why the Takings Clause of the Fifth Amendment, as much a part of the Bill of Rights as the First Amendment or Fourth Amendment, should be relegated to the status of a poor relation.[28]

Public Trust Doctrine

The notion of the public trust, which dates in American law to *Martin* v. *Waddell* (1842) discussed in chapter 1, is based on the common law doctrine that the navigable rivers and waterfronts are held by the sovereign for the use of all the people.[29] Traditionally restricted to embrace only these water-related resources, the public trust doctrine in the United States has come to include other natural resources. Much of the debate on public trust resources is concerned with alienation, that is, relinquishing publicly owned resources into private hands.

The landmark case in public trust is *Illinois Central Railroad Company* v. *Illinois* (1892). In 1869, the state of Illinois had granted some submerged Chicago shorefront lands in Lake Michigan to the Illinois Central Railroad. Four years later, repenting of its gift, the state repealed the grant. The state then filed suit to "quiet the title" so the chain of ownership would be clearly recorded. Understandably, the railroad objected: the state retaking title to land that was privately owned seemed to raise the constitutional question of a violation of due process. However, the Supreme Court cleverly avoided the constitutional question by finding the original grant of land to be invalid because it violated the public trust obligations of Illinois. This case established the central tenet in public trust litigation:

> When a state holds a resource which is available for the free use of the general public, a court will look with considerable skepticism upon *any* governmental conduct which is calculated *either* to reallocate that resource to more restricted uses *or* to subject public uses to the self interest of private parties [emphasis added].[30]

Traditionally the public trust has applied only to tidelands and waters used in navigation, water-related commerce, and fisheries; under the original English common law, inland resources were the property of the Crown and were not within the public trust.[31] The public trust doctrine has, however, been expanded to include national parks, inland lakes, and wildlife. As with many of the common law doctrines accepted from England but modified to fit New World needs, the public trust doctrine is unclear and its application varied:

> Public trust law is not a sophisticated or well-coordinated branch of the substantive law. The use of wetlands for navigation, fishery, or commerce may conflict with one of the other public trust uses. . . . The confusion in public trust law derives partly from state legislatures' leaving to the courts the role of defining public trust use and of establishing a hierarchy of preferred uses. The courts, left to fashion the law from a hodgepodge of fact situations, have understandably been unable to formulate a comprehensive body of law.[32]

Traditionally the public trust doctrine has been put to a variety of uses. It may be used to challenge a government action (such as alienation) or as a defense by a citizen against government action (for example, to resist a condemnation or to assert a public use). Citizens may use the doctrine against other citizens. Government may exercise the trust either to recover damages from private parties or from other units of government or to protect its legislative prerogatives to define and to exercise the trust.[33]

Under current law, the public trust doctrine is invoked only when a violation of the public trust is alleged. There is no traditional use of the action to compel agency activity without some triggering event. For example, in *National Audubon Society* v. *Department of Water and Power of the City of Los Angeles (Mono Lake)* (1983), the trust doctrine was invoked to halt the city of Los Angeles from drawing municipal water from Mono Lake, and in the *Redwood National Park* litigation, *Sierra Club* v. *Department of the Interior* (1974, 1975, and 1976), logging on private lands adjacent to a national park triggered the lawsuit.

The public trust includes "an affirmative protective duty of government—a fiduciary obligation—in dealing with certain properties held publicly."[34] Some authorities go even further: one said that resource managers "have to view the [public trust] as the Bank of America trust officer would for a trust you set up for your children—strict adherence to trust principles."[35] Public trust resources

> are protected by the trust against unfair dealing and dissipation, which is classical trust language suggesting the necessity for procedural correctness and substantive care. . . . The public trust doctrine demands fair procedures, decisions that are justified, and results that are consistent with protection and perpetuation of the resources.[36]

At least one state court has found that the public trust in natural resources is an active trust. In 1927, the Wisconsin state Supreme Court ruled that:

> The trust reposed in the state is not a passive trust; it is governmental, active, and administrative. . . .[T]he trust, being both active and administrative, requires the lawmaking body to act in all cases where action is necessary, not only to preserve the trust, but to promote it. . . . A failure so to act, in our opinion, would have amounted to gross negligence and a misconception of its proper duties and obligations in the premises.[37]

Suggested Reading

Bean, Michael J. *The Evolution of National Wildlife Law.* New York: Praeger, 1983. This is the only comprehensive book that I know of on this topic; fortunately for us all, it is a clear, complete, and well-written treatise.

Cooper, Phillip. *Public Law and Public Administration* (2nd. ed.). Englewood Cliffs,

NJ: Prentice-Hall, 1988. This is *not* a casebook, which makes it a rarity among books on administrative law. I think it is the best administrative-law book available; a third edition is rumored to be forthcoming.

Friedman, Lawrence M. *A History of American Law* (2nd. ed.). New York: Simon & Schuster, 1985. The widely praised, definitive introduction to the topic.

Hoban, Thomas More, and Richard Oliver Brooks. *Green Justice: The Environment and the Courts.* Boulder, CO: Westview Press, 1987. This book is a mixture of casebook and explanatory text. The authors have a scarcely concealed antiregulatory bias, but the general discussions are excellent.

Kerwin, Cornelius. *Rulemaking: How Government Agencies Write Law and Make Policy.* Washington, DC: Congressional Quarterly Press, 1994. An extremely thorough, well-documented study of rulemaking in the federal government. Hardly light reading but well worth the trouble.

Schuck, Peter. *Foundations of Administrative Law.* Oxford: Oxford University Press, 1994. An invaluable collection of classic articles in the field of administrative law.

Notes

1. A case I find particularly frustrating is *Shaughnessy* v. *United States* ex rel. *Mezei,* 345 U.S. 246 (1953). Mezei was an alien resident who remained abroad for nineteen months and upon attempting to return to the United States was excluded for overstaying. He had gone to Europe to visit his sick mother and been caught by World War II. No other country would receive him, on the logical grounds that if the United States would not let him in, there must be a good reason, and he was confined to Ellis Island for twenty-one months. I have been unable to find out what happened to poor Mezei. Was he ever allowed to return to his home of twenty-five years? Did he return to Europe?

2. Some environmental statutes grant citizens the right to bring suit without needing to demonstrate an actual physical or substantial economic injury. Among the acts providing for citizen suits are Toxic Substances Control Act; Endangered Species Act; Marine Protection, Research, and Sanctuaries Act of 1972; Federal Water Pollution Control Act Amendments of 1972; Deepwater Port Act of 1974; Safe Drinking Water Act; Clean Air Amendments of 1970; Noise Control Act of 1972; Energy Policy and Conservation Act; and Resource Conservation and Recovery Act of 1976. Most of these acts permit citizen suits only when the agency actions are not discretionary, but there are some exceptions. For example, the Endangered Species Act of 1973 allows a citizen to sue the Secretary of the Interior "to compel application of prohibitions against the taking of resident endangered species or threatened species." 16 USCA 1540(g)(1)(B).

3. The Eden Roc tried to establish a right, arguing that one existed at common law, and invoking the doctrine of "ancient lights." The court rejected both arguments. There was, they said, no common law easement given to the Eden Roc, and the hotel

had not been built long enough to claim an automatic easement from length of usage. The ancient lights doctrine, which states that after twenty years, the windows of a building may not be shadowed, has never been an accepted doctrine in American law. Thus, while common sense would argue that no beachfront hotel should be allowed to build a shadow over its competitor's pool, the common law did not agree.

4. *Data Processing,* 397 U.S. 150 at 153.

5. It is important to emphasize that this holding would not have affected *Fontainebleau* because in that case there was no question of an improper administrative action. The old standard was still good because it was a civil action between two private parties, not between an aggrieved party and the government.

6. Responding to Douglas's dissent was John Naff:

> *If Justice Douglas has his way—*
> *O Come not that dreadful day—*
> *We'll be sued by lakes and hills*
> *Seeking a redress of ills.*
> *Great mountain peaks of name prestigious*
> *Will suddenly become litigious.*
> *Our brooks will babble in the courts,*
> *Seeking damages for torts.*
> *How can I rest beneath a tree*
> *If it may soon be suing me?*
> *Or enjoy the playful porpoise*
> *While it's seeking habeas corpus?*
> *Every beast within his paws*
> *Will clutch an order to show cause.*
> *The courts, besieged on every hand,*
> *Will crowd with suits by chunks of land.*
> *Ah! But vengeance will be sweet*
> *Since this must be a two-way street.*
> *I'll promptly sue my neighbor's tree*
> *for shedding all its leaves on me.*

John Naff, *Journal of the American Bar Association* 58 (1972): 820, in Christopher Stone, *Earth and Other Ethics* (New York: Harper & Row, 1987), p. 5.

7. I can't locate a source for the story that this case began as a law school class assignment, but true or not, it's a lovely story.

8. The Court had liberalized the absolute bar against taxpayer suits in *Flast* v. *Cohen,* 392 U.S. 83 (1968), but replaced the bar with a stringent test of a constitutional link between the taxpayer's harm and the government action. *Flast* challenged the 1965 Elementary and Secondary Education Act providing public funds to religious schools, alleging that the act violated the constitutionally mandated separation of church and state.

9. Jeffrey M. Gaba, *Environmental Law* (Black Letter Series) (St. Paul, MN: West, 1994), pp. 38–39.

10. *Mineral King* established that environmental groups whose individual members have suffered an injury may bring suit, although in *Lujan* v. *Defenders of Wildlife* (1992), the environmental group was not granted standing to challenge changes to FWS and National Marine Fisheries Service regulations applying the Endangered Species Act to the actions of federal agencies taken overseas. Defenders of Wildlife argued that two of its members with established records of overseas travel justified the suit, but the Court disagreed, noting that if one of the members had been a scientist working on a foreign endangered species, or if they had even had tickets to travel, the outcome would have been different. An interesting sidebar to this case was the "ecosystem nexus" approach, which maintains that the use of any part of a contiguous ecosystem justifies a defendable right in the entire ecosystem. Justices Black and O'Connor were the only justices to accept this argument.

11. Although it is not an environmental law case, the best example I know of these last two requirements is found in *Simon* v. *Eastern Kentucky Welfare Rights Organization* (1976). The Internal Revenue Service had changed its regulations, reducing the amount of free care a hospital had to provide in order to have a tax-exempt status. The welfare rights organization and several individuals sought judicial review on the grounds that their members and the individuals were denied free medical care. The Court denied standing because it was not clear that they would have received free care even if the rule were still in place (lack of causality), and even if the IRS were forced to reinstate the rule, there was no guarantee that the hospitals would continue to seek a tax-exempt status (no clear judicial relief).

12. In England, where the rights to fish a particular stream are property rights that may be bought and sold, the doctrine of nuisance has been used to force upstream industrial polluters to stop their activities. Since the anglers' associations have a property right in the fishing, the pollution that impairs the fishing is actionable for monetary damages, and the prospect of reimbursing a group of trout fishermen often leads to prompt remedial action by the polluters.

13. Unless otherwise noted, the discussion on property is from Robert R. Wright and Susan Webber Wright, *Land Use in a Nutshell* (St. Paul, MN: West, 1985).

14. See Susan Jane Buck Cox, "No Tragedy on the Commons," *Environmental Ethics* 7 (Spring 1985): 49–61, for a more detailed discussion of the medieval commons and the causes of the success of enclosure.

15. W. O. Ault, *Open-Field Farming in Medieval England* (London: Allen and Unwin, 1972), p. 17.

16. E. C. K. Gonner, *Common Land and Inclosure* 2nd ed. (London: Cass, 1966), p. 306.

17. Elimination of the feudal commons system is often cited as an example of the inevitable failure of community control of resources. The famous article by Garrett Hardin, "The Tragedy of the Commons," (*Science* 162: 1243–1248) is based on just such erroneous analysis. In the past twenty years, a large, empirically based literature on common property management has demonstrated the utility of community management of common pool resources (see, for example, Elinor Ostrom, *Governing the Commons* [Cambridge: Cambridge University Press, 1990]). This is not to say that

Hardin's "tragedy" never occurred, but it is not the dominant model and in fact did not occur on medieval English commons.

18. Notably *Bi-Metallic Investment Co.* v. *State Board of Equalization,* 239 U.S. 441 (1915), in which the city had increased the valuation of all taxable property without affording individual property owners the right to a hearing. The Court ruled that when a taxing action applied to all taxpayers (rather than a definite subset as in *Londoner*), no hearing was required. This is not a surprising decision in light of the absolute bar to taxpayer suits that was the rule until *Flast* (see Note 12, *supra*).

19. Florence Heffron and Neil McFeeley, *The Administrative Regulatory Process* (New York: Longman, 1983), p. 268.

20. William B. Lockhart, Yale Kamisar, and Jesse Choper, *The American Constitution: Cases-Comments-Questions* (St. Paul, MN: West, 1970), p. 332.

21. Lisa Heinzerling, "Action Inaction: Section 1983 Liability for Failure to Act," *University of Chicago Law Review* 53 (Summer 1986): 1063.

22. *Marks* v. *Whitney,* 6 Cal.3d 251, 491 P.2d 374, 98 Cal. Rptr. 790 at 797 (1971), quoted in David B. Hunter, "An Ecological Perspective on Property: A Call for Judicial Protection of the Public's Interest in Environmentally Critical Resources," *Harvard Environmental Law Review* 12 (1988), p. 372, Note 288.

23. Unless otherwise noted, the discussion of zoning is drawn from Robert Wright and Susan Webber Wright, *Land Use in a Nutshell* (St. Paul, MN: West, 1985), especially Chapter 6.

24. Although in many states the cities are subordinate to counties, in some, such as Virginia, the cities are governments independent of the counties in which they are found.

25. Readers who wish to read the early developments in the judicial attempt to strike a balance between regulation and taking should look at the following cases: *Pennsylvania Coal Co.* v. *Mahon,* 1928 (Pennsylvania law forbidding mining that causes subsidence of residential property is a taking of the coal company's subservice mining rights), the original landmark case for this policy area; *Miller* v. *Schoene,* 1928 (requirement that grove of ornamental trees be removed to protect apple trees from disease is legitimate regulation to protect the public from economic harm), this case vindicated Justice Brandeis's dissent in *Pennsylvania Coal; Morris County Land Improvement Company* v. *Township of Parsippany-Troy Hills,* 1963 (regulations restricting the use of filled land constitute a taking); *Just* v. *Marinette County,* 1972 (ordinance requiring permit to fill wetlands is valid exercise of public trust and police power); *Pennsylvania Central Transportation Company* v. *New York,* 1978 (restrictions on designated historic landmarks do not constitute a taking, sets three-part test for takings).

26. David Foster, "Property Rights Gains Ground," *Greensboro News & Record,* 30 July 1995, A11.

27. Foster, A11.

28. *Dolan* v. *City of Tigard,* 129 L. Ed. 2nd 304, 321.

29. Unless otherwise noted, this discussion is drawn from William H. Rodgers, *Handbook on Environmental Law* (St. Paul, MN: West, 1977), pp. 170–186.

30. Joseph Sax, "Public Trust Doctrine in Natural Resource Law: Effective Judicial Intervention," *Michigan Law Review* 68(3), January 1970, p. 490.

31. Charles Wilkinson, "Public Trust Doctrine in Public Land Law," in *The Public Trust Doctrine in Natural Resources Law and Management*. Edited by Harrison Dunning, (Davis: University of California, 1981), p. 169 (notes omitted).

32. Marianne K. Smythe, "Environmental Law: Expanding the Definition of Public Trust Uses," *North Carolina Law Review* 51 (1972): 322.

33. William H. Rodgers, Jr. *Handbook on Environmental Law* (St. Paul, MN: West, 1977), pp. 175–176.

34. Joseph Sax, "Introductory Perspectives," in Dunning (ed.), p. 6.

35. James Trout, "A Land Manager's Commentary on the Public Trust Doctrine," in Dunning (ed.), p. 57. At the time of this statement, Mr. Trout was the Assistant Executive Officer for the California State Lands Commission.

36. Rodgers, p. 172.

37. *City of Milwaukee* v. *State,* 193 Wis. 423, 214 N.W. 820 (1927) at 830, quoted in Helen Althaus, *Public Trust Rights* (Washington, DC: GPO, November 1978), p. 157.

Chapter Five

Pollution Control and Hazardous and Toxic Substances

Regulating the production, use, and disposal of harmful substances is a responsibility shared by the national government and the states. This chapter presents the administrative framework within which such regulation occurs. The chapter begins with a discussion of the Administrative Procedure Act (APA). Although APA does not deal directly with environmental matters, it is the basic legislation that governs all federal agencies. Most states have similar legislation, so to understand the framework that informs environmental legislation, it is necessary first to grasp the basic points of APA.

The second section discusses the legal liability of administrative officials. The next section presents the basic legislation aimed at controlling air and water pollution. The fourth section focuses on hazardous and toxic wastes and outlines the regulation of pesticides, the provisions of the Clean Air Act and Clean Water Act that deal with hazardous and toxic substances, the Toxic Substances Control Act, and Superfund and SARA.

The Administrative Procedure Act

The Administrative Procedure Act, passed in 1946, was the culmination of years of anxious debate among government officials, legal scholars, and the business community. Although the administrative state had been growing since the late nineteenth century, the New Deal led to a proliferation of both independent agencies and the overall bureaucracy. Some lawyers were especially concerned as power shifted from the courts to the executive agencies. They were being closed out of the decision process by Roosevelt's bright young men in the agencies.

In 1934, the second year of the New Deal, the American Bar Association (ABA) formed an administrative law committee that issued annual reports stressing the reduced power of the judicial branch. Joining these critical voices were the conservatives who used complaints about fairness, due process, and conformity to the common law to cloak their opposition to Roosevelt's economic and social policies. Some of the critics, however, were genuinely concerned about what they perceived as threats from the administrative process to traditionally protected rights. Their basic question was how the political system could maintain justice and the constitutionally mandated separation of powers if one person or agency acted as legislature (making rules), prosecutor (investigating infractions), judge (conducting hearings), and enforcing agent. As it became increasingly clear that the agencies were involved in *making* policy as well as interpreting legislative policy, concerns about the substantive law increased as well.

The Special Committee on Administrative Law of the ABA had managed in 1935 to engineer the passage of the Federal Register Act. The *Federal Register* for the first time provided a daily record of the administrative activities of the executive branch; for example, it contained the texts of executive orders and proposed and final rules. Encouraged by this success, the committee lobbied successfully for the Walter-Logan Bill, which was passed by Congress in December 1940. Proponents of the bill defended it as providing safeguards for individual liberties, unsullied by technical expertise: "Judicial review deals not so much with technical facts as with fairness of hearing—a matter not for technical experts but for impartial courts."[1] It was felt that a rigid procedural code would remove political pressures from the agencies by providing standards upon which to base decisions and by promoting rulemaking rather than case-by-case adjudication.

However, although the bill passed Congress, President Roosevelt vetoed the bill. Opponents of the bill charged that the act was nothing more than a blatant attempt to wrest control of the administration from the president. In his veto message, Roosevelt singled out for opprobrium two particular groups: lawyers and large business interests: "The bill that is now before me is one of the repeated efforts by a combination of lawyers who desire to have all processes of government conducted through lawsuits and of interests which desire to escape regulation."[2]

Roosevelt had another, more mundane reason for his veto. The Final Report of the Attorney General's Committee on Administrative Procedure was almost complete. The work of this committee was unique; instead of merely taking testimony and generating a report, it conducted primary investigations and produced legislation. For the first time, the administrative process was studied on the

> basis of knowledge rather than of hypothesis or preconceived ideas. . . . [The Committee] studied the administrative establishment from the inside, thoroughly and dispassionately. Its acute discussion of the characteristics of the administrative process, its conclusions as to defects existing in the process, and its proposals to remedy them all sprang from and were buttressed by facts laboriously ascertained and carefully weighed.[3]

The Attorney General's Report affirmed the necessity for and value of the administrative process. It found that agencies were an inevitable development that were essential for the effective management of a modern, industrial government. This was at least the view of the majority report; the minority extended the recommendations of the majority report in an attempt to impose a uniform code of administrative behavior on the agencies. The majority felt that the substantive issues dealt with by the various agencies were so complex and idiosyncratic that no uniform code could govern them all; the minority disagreed, and it is their bill that actually provided the basis for the APA.

Although extensive hearings were held in the summer of 1941 on the proposed administrative legislation, America's entry into World War II delayed further consideration of any administrative procedure legislation. Close to the end of the war, the ABA began again to agitate for legislation, and in 1946, the Administrative Procedure Act was passed.

The major impact of the act was that it codified existing practice and law; in other words, it found a common ground among the agencies. The APA has six major portions, all of which have relevance to environmental administration and law: definitions of terms used in the act; the rules for fair information practices; guidelines for rulemaking; cost-benefit analysis; procedures for adjudication; and provisions for judicial review of agency actions.

Definitions of Terms

The first section of the APA defines the terms used in the legislation. While this definition of terms is important in any legislation, it is especially important in the APA because it provides a point of reference for the agencies. Any agency that used different phrases to describe agency activities could turn to this section and discover the common terminology.

Fair Information Practices

One sign of the amazing success of the APA is how little it has been amended since 1946. The second section contains virtually all of the amendments, and they are primarily in the form of additions made in the sixties and seventies as a response to criticisms of governmental abuses of power. Section 552 is the Freedom of Information Act; Section 552(a) is the Privacy Act of 1974; and Section 552(b) is the Government in the Sunshine Act.

Rulemaking

The third section is perhaps the most important. It provides the guidelines for the federal rulemaking procedures.[4]

> "[R]ule" means the whole or a part of an agency statement of general or particular applicability and future effect designed to implement, interpret, or prescribe law or policy or describing the organization, procedure, or practice requirements of an agency and includes the approval or prescription for the future of rates, wages, corporate or financial structures or reorganization thereof, prices, facilities, appliances, services or allowances therefor or of valuations, costs, or accounting, or practices bearing on any of the foregoing. 5 U.S.C. §551(4)

It is important to distinguish between rulemaking and adjudication. Rulemaking is the administrative equivalent of legislation: it is sometimes called "secondary legislation." Rulemaking establishes *future* standards of *general* applicability; rules cover a class of people or actions and are not particularized like adjudication. Adjudication is the administrative parallel to the judicial process. It takes place after some activity had occurred; rulemaking prescribes the activity before it happens. Agencies can make policy either through rulemaking or adjudication; the courts prefer rulemaking. Agencies can also make policy by informal actions, such as the summary action taken by EPA in 1979 when it banned 2,4,5-T (dioxin) without a hearing and on an emergency basis just before the spring crop spraying season.[5]

The courts are more likely to review rules on procedural due process grounds than substantive due process. Regulations and rules must stay within the statutory authority given to the agency by the legislature. This authority is often vague and leaves a great deal to the agency's discretion. The rules must have a reasonable basis; that is, they may not be arbitrary, capricious, or involve an abuse of discretion, and they must be promulgated in accordance with the APA and with the restrictions laid down in their own enabling or organic act.

Types of Rules

There are three types of rules: substantive (legislative), procedural, and interpretive.

Substantive rules implement or prescribe law or policy, for example, safety requirements for nuclear power plants. They are legally binding and can be enforced in court as though they were primary legislation. The amount of authority that an agency has to promulgate rules varies with the enabling legislation. Some agencies have very broad authority; for example, NEPA states:

> The Administrator is authorized to allow appropriate use of special Environmental Protection Agency research and test facilities by outside groups of individuals and to receive reimbursement or fees for costs incurred thereby when he finds this to be *in the public interest*. 42 U.S.C §4379 [emphasis added]

Other agencies find their authority quite restricted; for example, the Endangered Species Act of 1973 requires that:

> [T]he Secretary shall make a finding as to whether the petition presents substantial scientific or commercial information indicating that the petitioned action may be warranted. If such a petition is found to present such information, the Secretary *shall* promptly commence a review of the status of the species concerned. The Secretary *shall promptly* publish each finding made under this subparagraph in the Federal Register. 16 U.S. C §1533(b)(3)(A) [emphasis added].

The courts have the final word on whether a substantive rule is legitimate.

Procedural rules "describe the organization, procedure or practice requirements of an agency." For example, they may define who is allowed to intervene in an agency adjudication and under what circumstances. The APA does not apply to procedural rulemaking, and indeed, an agency is allowed to go beyond APA and its own organic act in restricting the procedures under which it operates. However, an agency is required to honor these rules once they have been issued. For example, during the Watergate investigation U.S. Attorney General Elliot Richardson appointed Archibald Cox as Special Prosecutor and at the same time issued a procedural rule giving the Special Prosecutor the authority to contest claims of executive privilege. When Cox tried to get President Nixon's tapes and rejected Nixon's claims of executive privilege, Nixon ordered him fired. The first two attorneys general that he ordered to fire Cox refused; the third was Robert Bork, who complied with Nixon's order. The D.C. District Court invalidated the firing on the grounds that the procedural rule was binding.

Interpretive rules are "statements issued by agencies that present the agency's understanding of the meaning of the language in its regulations or the statutes it administers."[6] They are exempt from APA requirements but must be published in the *Federal Register*. They do not add or subtract any information from existing law; they simply give the public a more detailed idea of how the agency intends to act. In this sense they are the administrative equivalent of advisory opinions. It is not clear how binding an interpretative rule is on the agency. On occasion the courts have judged that an interpretive rule was actually substantive and held the agency to it. The safest approach is for the agency to assume that a court will find the rule binding but for the affected party to assume it is not. Why would an agency bother with such an ambiguous process? It allows the administrative agency to make small adjustments to policy without going through the cumbersome rulemaking procedures.

Rulemaking Procedures

There are three basic procedures for making rules: informal rulemaking, formal rulemaking, and hybrid rulemaking.

Informal rulemaking is informal only in contrast to the formal rulemaking. It is also called Notice and Comment Rulemaking and is governed by §553 of APA. This section exempts from the act all military and foreign affairs functions (since these are committed to the executive branch by the Constitution), agency management and personnel, and "public property, loans, grants, benefits, or contracts" (which are covered by a separate statute, the Federal Property and Administrative Services Act).

The informal rulemaking procedure requires the agency to publish a notice of the proposed rule in the *Federal Register*. An exception is allowed if everyone subject to the proposed rule is individually notified, but this exception is rarely used. There are several necessary components of the notice. It must give the time, place, and nature of the rulemaking proceedings and refer to the legal authority under which the rule is made. The notice either provides the term or substance of the proposed rule or gives a description of the subjects and issues involved. Finally, the notice includes an opportunity for written, and sometimes oral, comment by interested parties.

Once the agency has fixed upon the rule, it must publish the text of the rule, and a general statement of its basis and purpose, in the *Federal Register* at least thirty days before the effective date to allow affected parties to come into compliance. Even then, interested persons have the right to ask for an "issuance, amendment, or repeal" of the rule.

This is a relatively simple, informal procedure. There is no formal hearing in which evidence and testimony about the rule is heard. The time period is short; a rule might complete the process in less than sixty days if it is a simple and noncontroversial rule. There is no record required: the agency merely announces its intention, receive comments, and issues the rule. In contrast, formal rulemaking is much more complex.

The distinguishing characteristic of formal rulemaking is the administrative hearing that is required. Several statutes require full hearings as part of the rulemaking process, and a hearing must be held only if the statute explicitly requires one. There is, however, nothing to prohibit an agency from having one voluntarily. Administrative hearings are conducted under the regulations spelled out in sections 556 and 557 of the APA. An administrative law judge presides over these hearings, and his opinion is conveyed to the administrator charged with making the final rule. His opinion must be considered, although it is not binding. Any final rule must be based on the "substantial evidence" criterion: the agency must demonstrate that its position is upheld by "reliable, probative, and substantial evidence" (§556[d]).

There are many arguments to favor the formal process over the informal. The formal record that is generated by the hearing process provides a pedigree for the development of the new regulation. There is full opportunity for public participation and, because there are rules of evidence (although not the same rules of evidence as apply in a criminal trial), all information can be verified. The burden of proof rests with the agency, and the formal hearing provides a record for the interested parties to be sure that the weight of the evidence is sufficient to support the rule.

There are also many counterarguments. Formal rulemaking is costly in terms of both money and time. The flexibility of the administrators is reduced—an evil that the administrative process is designed to avoid. And the process itself, resembling a court trial, is increasingly judicialized. For example, the original APA created independent "hearing examiners" who had specialized knowledge in their own regulatory fields. These hearing examiners have metamorphosed into "administrative law judges" who are attorneys with at least seven years experience presenting cases before federal courts or agencies.

Hybrid rulemaking uses a combination of informal and formal procedures; the impetus for hybrid rulemaking came from the judiciary. Federal courts prefer the administrative agencies to use their rulemaking powers to make policy rather than to use case-by-case adjudicatory powers, because judicial review is simplified when a rule is the basis of the administrative decision. However, the informal process does not require the establishment of a reviewable record. The lack of a formal record complicates the judge's task when reviewing agency action. As the administrative agencies continued to utilize their rulemaking powers, and as the need for regulation increased, in part because of increased environmental regulation, the courts found their job increasingly complex. Deference to administrative expertise was a nice concept, but a court had difficulty judging the "substantial" basis of a rule that was technically complex and lacked a formal record. Partly in self-defense, the agencies began to generate records of the informal rulemaking processes, and the courts, followed by the Congress, applauded.

The keystone of the hybrid process is the record before the administrator. When a record of the rulemaking process has been kept, the court can review the process. The record not only allows judicial review, it also allows peer preview, legislative oversight, and public criticism. Surprisingly, it also increases administrative flexibility because it simplifies changing rules to meet changing circumstances.

Congress has followed the judicial lead, and most rulemaking legislation in the seventies and eighties includes hybrid rulemaking requirements. For example, the Toxic Substance Control Act of 1976 uses hybrid rulemaking:

> Any rule under subparagraph (A), and any substantive amendment or repeal of such a rule, shall be promulgated pursuant to the procedures specified in section 553 of [APA], except that (i) the Administrator shall give interested persons an opportunity for the oral presentation of data, views, or arguments, in addition to an opportunity to make written submissions, (ii) a transcript shall be kept of any oral presentation, and (iii) the Administrator shall make and publish with the rule the finding described in subparagraph (A). 15 U.S.C. § 2604(b)(2)(C).

Generally hybrid rulemaking follows informal rulemaking procedures with several additions on the record: the basis and purpose of the rule, with supporting documentation; evidence that adequate notice was given or made available to all interested parties; sufficient time for comments and alternative interpretations; evidence that the agency did consider and respond to comments; and the reasoning followed by the administrator.

Cost-Benefit Analysis

Substantial presidential efforts have been made to take control of the regulatory process. Since the early seventies, presidents have constrained the powers of the agencies through executive orders. In 1974, President Ford au-

thorized the Office of Management and Budget (OMB) to assess the inflationary impact of proposed rules; in 1978, President Carter issued an order that required, among other things, that agencies ensure an opportunity for public participation in rulemaking, including public hearings, sixty-day comment periods, and wider dissemination of notice of hearings. One of President Reagan's first actions in office was to issue Executive Order 12291 (and later Executive Order 12498), requiring agencies to conduct a cost-benefit analysis of all proposed rules and to choose the least costly alternative. This requirement conflicted with some enabling statutes for environmental legislation and has been challenged in court by environmental groups:

> Not only did these initial changes substantially modify the intent and practice of the APA, they also nullified large portions of substantive law. These changes are also of questionable legality. While the President has authority to oversee execution of the laws by the executive branch, his constitutional authority is "to take care that the laws be faithfully executed," not to devise procedures that make executive agency enforcement of the laws difficult if not impossible.[7]

Executive Order 12291 was applied selectively; cost-benefit analysis was rarely invoked when the proposed regulatory change favored business interests.[8] On 30 September 1993, President Clinton issued Executive Order 12866, revoking Reagan's Executive Order 12291. His new order requires consultation with state, local, and tribal agencies and requires the agencies to impose the "least burden on society" in promulgating regulations. It is too soon to evaluate what impact, if any, the new order will have on the regulatory process; certainly the regulatory changes and budget proposals put forth in Congress during the summer of 1995 have the potential to mask any presidential effect.

Administrative Adjudication

The fifth section of the Administrative Procedure Act deals with adjudication.[9] The specific kind of adjudicatory procedure required in agency processes varies from relatively informal, oral hearings to very structured procedures that resemble formal civil trials. Some statutes require hearings, and it is only these statutes that automatically trigger the full hearing described in the APA. In some circumstances the courts have mandated adjudicatory hearings based on constitutional requirements. Finally, the agencies themselves may have rules independent of their enabling legislation or court decisions that require them to hold hearings. The necessity for hearings originates in the due process clause of the Constitution discussed in chapter 4. When an administrative agency affects a citizen's property rights, the citizen is entitled to a hearing.

The central components of any administrative hearing are notice of the hearing given to all interested parties; the opportunity to be heard by an impartial examiner, to present evidence, and to challenge opposing evidence; to receive a reasoned decision based on a written record; and the right of appeal. These requirements are spelled out in §§ 554–557 of the APA, although the precise nature of a hearing varies with the enabling statute, previous judicial interpretations, and agency regulations.[10]

Judicial Review

The sixth section of the APA deals with judicial review of agency actions.[11] Judicial review is the "power of a court to determine the legality and constitutionality of an action of a government official, agency, or legislative body."[12] Some agency actions are not subject to review. The Supreme Court does not have jurisdiction over all agency actions because the Congress has the power to exempt some activities: "In all the other Cases before mentioned, the Supreme Court shall have appellate Jurisdiction, both as to Law and Fact, with such Exceptions, and under such Regulations as the Congress shall make" (Article III, §2[2]). Section 701 of APA, which defines the application of judicial review of agency actions, exempts actions where the "statutes preclude judicial review" or which have been "committed to agency discretion by law." However, Section 706 (2)(A) of the act forbids arbitrary and capricious action and abuses of discretion. The reviewing courts must determine when an action is committed to agency discretion and when these actions are reviewable under Section 706. The overall effect of these two seemingly contradictory sections is to encourage agencies to maintain records of their actions and interactions.

Courts do not have an unlimited license to oversee agency activities. The scope of judicial review for administrative actions is defined in Section 706:

> To the extent necessary to decision and when presented, the reviewing court shall decide all relevant questions of law, interpret constitutional and statutory provisions, and determine the meaning or applicability of the terms of an agency action.

The court may "compel agency action unlawfully withheld or unreasonably delayed" as well as "hold unlawful and set aside agency action, findings, and conclusions" that are arbitrary, capricious, abuses of discretion, violations of constitutional rights, exceed statutory authority, violate due process, or are unsupported by substantial evidence.

For adjudicatory decisions, the primary judicial question is whether the agency position is supported by substantial evidence. Since most adjudicatory hearings are adversarial and therefore may produce conflicting evidence, a court often has a difficult time determining which evidence is applicable. In formal rulemaking, the scope of review also rests on substantial evidence, while review of informal rulemaking is limited to the "arbitrary and capricious" standard. In hybrid rulemaking, the scope of review is determined by the authorizing statute. For example, the Toxic Substances Control Act cited earlier gives as part of the standard of review:

> Section 706 of [APA] shall apply to review of a rule under this section, except that   (i) in the case of review of a rule under [several sections of the Act] of this title, the standard for review prescribed by paragraph (2)(E) of such section 706 shall not apply and the court shall hold unlawful and set aside such rule *if the court finds that the rule is not supported by substantial evidence in the rulemaking record.* . . . 15 U.S.C. § 2618 (c)(1)(B). [emphasis added]

Controlling Pollution

The preceding sections have shown the importance of the Administrative Procedure Act as a framework for understanding the administrative process in environmental administration. The following sections summarize the current status of air and water pollution regulation. The final portion of the discussion on pollution examines a relatively new regulatory approach to air and water pollution control: pollution rights purchase schemes.

Air Pollution

Aaron Wildavsky defines pollution as *matter out of place,* and this is particularly true of air pollution. An air pollutant develops "when the concentration of a normal component of air or of a new chemical added to or formed in the air builds up to the point of causing harm to humans, other animals, vegetation, or materials such as metals and stone."[13] According to one study, the major sources of air pollution are transportation (49%), industrial processes (13%), fuel combustion in stationary sources (28%), solid-waste disposal (3%), and miscellaneous (7%).[14] Some pollutants are harmful as soon as they enter the atmosphere; these *primary air pollutants* contribute the majority of air pollution in the United States. *Secondary air pollutants* are formed from the chemical reaction of several air components; for example, sulfur dioxide combines with oxygen to form sulfur trioxide, which then combines with water vapor to produce acid rain.

The dangers of air pollution and its dramatic consequences have been known for centuries. In 1273, the king of England tried to reduce air pollution by banning the burning of coal. In 1911, over a thousand Londoners died from coal smoke. London was known as "the Smoke" for good reason, and Sherlock Holmes's romantic "pea-soup" fogs were deadly; in 1952, the infamous Killer Smog killed four thousand Londoners. While this was sufficient to trigger English air pollution control laws, the United States waited through disasters in 1948 (twenty deaths) and 1963 (two hundred dead in New York City) before passing the Clean Air Act in 1970.

In 1970, amendments to the Clean Air Act of 1955 provided the basic structure for the current shape of air pollution control. The 1970 amendments required the national government to set air quality standards that would be achieved through State Implementation Plans (SIPs). The Clean Air Act Amendments of 1977 reinforced federal authority over air quality standards. EPA was required to establish National Ambient Air Quality Standards (NAAQSs) for seven major pollutants: suspended particulate matter (SPM), sulfur oxides, carbon monoxide, nitrogen oxides, ozone, volatile organic compounds, and lead. The cost of meeting the standards was not supposed to be a criterion in setting the standards. EPA had to set two types of NAAQSs: the *primary ambient air quality standards* were designed to protect human health and to provide a margin of safety for the most vulnerable populations such as infants and the elderly, while the *secondary ambient air quality standards* targeted visibility and crops, buildings, and water supplies.

To implement the Clean Air Act, EPA divided the nation into 247 air quality control regions, each of which was supposed to meet the primary standards by 1982. Areas that did not achieve primary standards by 1982 or within whatever deadline extensions were granted were labeled *nonattainment regions,* with restrictions on new plant construction and old plant expansions until emission standards were met.

Of course, some areas of the country were already cleaner than the NAAQSs required, and EPA sought to protect these through a policy of *prevention of significant deterioration* (PSD). Three classes of existing air quality were established. Class I areas, which had the highest existing air quality, were protected from virtually any deterioration. Class II and Class III areas were allowed progressively more pollution, with the NAAQSs being the absolute limit of permissible pollution. Each state was responsible for developing State Implementation Plans (SIPs) to meet federal standards by the late 1980s.

Buying the Right to Pollute

Three approaches to controlling pollution are available to managers: common law remedies such as nuisance suits discussed in chapter 4, the command-and-control regulatory approaches used in clean air and clean water acts, and economic incentives. Unlike most regulatory plans that constrain the private sector, forcing it to utilize and to develop technologies, economic incentives can promote environmental protection by using the market.

Two economic factors that distort the operation of a free market are externalities and free-riders. Simply put, externalities are spillover effects that have an impact on individuals or groups that have not contributed to the project. For example, a factory may dump pollutants into the air, harming the health of local residents. The factory saves the cost of pollution control, but these costs are then borne by others who are external to the factory (both figuratively and literally). Thus the costs of polluting activities are not borne by those who reap the benefits, and polluters have no economic incentives to reduce pollution.

Free-riders are individuals who participate in the benefits of an activity without contributing to the activity's cost and are a special case of externalities; for example, nonresidents who use a tax-supported public park are free-riders. Air pollution provides a good example of the relationship between pollution, externalities, and free-riders:

> There may be many agents who produce the pollution. It can come from automobiles, factories, electrical power plants, and so on. Also, large numbers of individuals "consume" the pollution by breathing air filled with particulates, sulfur dioxide, and oxides of nitrogen. Producers of the externality can also be consumers of air pollution. Anyone who drives a car and lives in an area of low air quality is both a producer and consumer. The reason this public externality arises is simple: Air is an open access resource. Because no property rights to air exist, those who generate air pollution are free to use the air as a waste dump without paying any fees. Once air pollution is generated, large numbers of individuals (animals, vegetation, and property) are affected. Each person affected might be willing to pay something to reduce the pollution, but if he or she did so, others who did not pay would also benefit.[15]

First proposed by Dales in 1968,[16] pollution permits provide transferable property rights for the disposal of waste. The government chooses the level of pollution it is willing to tolerate by issuing Pollution Rights equal to that amount. The rights then become marketable commodities. This strategy is less effective with multiple-source pollution (such as automobiles) and nonpoint pollution (such as agricultural run-off). However, as a substantial proportion of both air and water pollution is generated by single-source industrial polluters, Dales's scheme had great appeal to those with market inclinations. Air pollution was especially amenable to market solutions because the existing regulatory mechanisms were easy to adapt.[17] Title IV of the Clean Air Act Amendments of 1990 applied these strategies to air pollution.

This sort of rights scheme has many advantages. Many business would be more environmentally responsible if their internal affairs and their relations with EPA were modified. While some obstacles to waste reduction are internal to business, others are imposed externally by the government emphasis on emissions control rather than source reduction. In addition to reducing administrative costs, pollution rights schemes encourage business to find alternative ways to reduce emissions and other wastes. They might allow business to focus on waste production, to revamp internal accounting systems to charge pollution to operations and thus encourage improved production technologies, and to improve their internal information management systems.

Under the Reagan administration, industry and the executive branch co-operated to ease federal auto emission standards, to extend EPA deadlines, and in general to relax expansion and enforcement of existing air pollution regulations. The conservatives asserted that the economic cost of clean air was too high,[18] and that the accepted levels of pollution were too low. They charged the regulating agencies with inflexibility. There is some justification for their arguments. Federal policies change even as industry strives to comply, which makes industry tend to avoid compliance as long as possible. Also, prior to the 1990 reauthorization, regulatory strategies focused on emissions rather than on production processes, and there were few economic incentives (or economic slack) for industries to look at internal production and management strategies to stop pollution at its source.

Environmentalists were also critical of EPA, and the chaos in EPA during the first Reagan administration seemed to justify their complaints. Enforcement of existing regulations was problematic, and new regulations were halted or delayed under executive orders requiring cost-benefit analysis and other evaluations not always in agreement with legislative intentions. The environmentalists and the administration were often at odds; "[b]y the end of 1986, environmentalists and key congressional allies had prevented the gutting of the 1970 and 1977 Clean Air Acts but had been unable to persuade Congress to pass any new legislation strengthening air pollution control."[19] All this changed in 1990.

On 15 November 1990, President Bush signed the Clean Air Act Amendments, "departing from a decade of Reagan administration hostility toward new industry regulation . . . [and strengthening] the hand of congressional proponents of clean air legislation, whose proposals had repeatedly been killed or stalled to death at the behest of industry."[20] It was the environmental high point of his administration.

The 1990 Clean Air Act Amendments strengthened existing legislation and added three major new areas to federal regulatory control: acid deposition, reduction of chlorofluorocarbons (CFCs), and increased control of toxic substances in the air.[21] A national permitting program was established and enforcement was strengthened. It also initiated an emissions trading system that applied market-based strategies to the problems of air pollution.

In Title I, the amendments set precise goals for national air quality standards for ozone, carbon monoxide, and particulates. Areas falling under the new standards must satisfy the requirements within firm deadlines. In Title II, the amendments set more and stronger emission standards for cars, trucks, urban buses, and off-road vehicles.

To meet the act's acid deposition requirements in Title IV, industries must achieve a permanent 10 million ton reduction from 1980 levels in sulfur dioxide emissions during a two-phase implementation process to be fully effective on 1 January 2000. This title establishes the innovative emissions trading program: each major coal-fired plant is allocated a set amount of permissible sulfur dioxide emissions that may be traded, bought, or sold. The first government sponsored auction of the rights took place in March 1993. The major purchases was the Carolina Power and Light Company, which bought the rights to emit over 85,000 tons of sulfur dioxide; this represented 57 percent of the permits sold at the auction and cost $11.5 million. The company planned to use the emission rights to delay installation of expensive "scrubbers" at its plants.[22] A delightful contrast occurred in March 1995, when students from seven law schools pooled their resources to buy the rights to 18 tons of sulfur dioxide emissions. The students' plan was ingenious: they intend to let the permits expire, unused, thus reducing pollution and simultaneously driving up the price of other permits.[23] This market-based approach is, for many, a welcome relief from the old command-and-control system of the federal regulatory agencies:

> While a few major environmental organizations, led by the Environmental Defense Fund, consider the new approach a potentially valuable experiment, many more environmental groups regard it as trafficking with the Devil. However, all sides are watching the implementation of Title IV with keen interest. Its fate will become a powerful argument for, or against, the proliferation of future market-based regulatory schemes.[24]

Title VI addresses the problem of stratospheric ozone and global climate protection. The act used the economic incentives and requirements established by EPA under the 1977 amendments to phase out CFCs and halons according to the schedules established in the Montreal Protocol (discussed in chapter 7). This involves complete elimination of CFCs and carbon tetrachloride by the year 2000 and methyl chloroform by 2002. On 1 January 1994, a total ban on aerosols, with exemptions for flammability and safety, went into effect.

The air toxics title was prompted by the information generated from Title III of SARA, the "community right to know" title. The discovery that over 2.7 billions pounds of toxic air pollutants were released annually was a powerful trigger for increasing regulation of air toxics. In a radical departure from previous programs, the new act is technology-based rather than emissions-focused, and 189 substances are now regulated (as opposed to the eight controlled under the old legislation). All pollutant sources must apply Maximum Achievable Control Technologies (MACTs) to their processes. As in the old act, different standards and timetables are established for new and existing sources.

The permitting system and improved enforcement are the last two substantial changes. The operating permits program is "in many ways the most important procedural reform contained in the new law."[25] Polluting sources must obtain an operating permit, states must administer the permitting program, and EPA reviews all programs and may veto any permit. In addition, EPA is required to develop and to implement a federal permit plan if a state fails to comply with the provisions of the act. The fee structure for permits must offset program costs; initial suggestions are for fees of $25 per ton of emission for a five-year permit.

The enforcement provisions are very important and new in clean air legislation.[26] Four provisions are especially noteworthy: the field citation program, the inclusion of endangerment crimes from releases, compliance certification, and the citizen suit provisions. Under the field citation program, inspectors may visit plants to perform inspections of the plants and the plant records. They are empowered to issue citations at once, which may carry fines of up to $5,000. The act establishes civil and criminal liability for releases that endanger the public: "knowingly endangering" the public through a deliberate, illegal release may result in prison terms up to fifteen years and fines to $250,000 for individuals and $500,000 for corporations. Regulated industries are required to certify their compliance with the permit conditions on a regular basis and to provide monitoring and other forms of evidence to support their compliance record. The citizen suit provisions are stronger under the new law; citizen suits may be used to enforce the permits. Citizens may now sue corporations for past violations if the violation is continuing, and penalties may be imposed to require mitigation of harmful effects.

Water Pollution

Water pollution poses an immediate threat to public health, and, because it is usually dispersed over an identified area, water pollution may be more amenable to control than air pollution. Water pollution is "any physical or chemical change in surface water or groundwater that can adversely affect living organisms."[27] The levels of pollution that are acceptable in any water supply depend in part on the use to which the water is put. A waterway used primarily for large ships can tolerate a higher level of pollution than one that provides drinking water. Water for industrial needs does not have to meet swimming water criteria. Environmentalists like to point out that water *could* be used for industrial needs if it met swimming water criteria: the cleaner, the better. Economists talk instead about "beneficent degradation," the desirable level of pollution in a body of water.

Pollution is usually classified as either *point source* pollution, that is, pollution with a readily isolated egress point such as a sewer treatment plant or oil tankers, or *nonpoint source* pollution, which is more difficult to control because it is spread over a large area. The pollution caused by agricultural pesticides in rainwater runoff, for example, is difficult to measure or to identify. Best Management Practices (BMPs) try to reduce the incidence of behavior that causes agricultural nonpoint source pollution, but urban nonpoint source pollution is more difficult to control.

Water supplies are classified as surface water and groundwater. Surface waters such as lakes, river, and oceans are to some extent self-cleansing, although some pollutants are so deadly even in small concentrations that neither dilution nor dispersal is helpful. These surface water systems are easily overloaded, but they are at least accessible. Groundwater is much more vulnerable to pollution and harder to restore. Almost half of the American population and virtually all of the rural population obtain their drinking water from groundwater sources.[28] Over three-fourths of the municipal water systems rely on groundwater.[29]

Although only a small percentage of the nation's groundwater is polluted, the proximity of these contaminated aquifers to population centers means that five to ten million Americans have polluted water sources. This problem may be more severe than reported since many chemicals found in groundwater are not subject to federal standards or testing, and no testing at all is required for private wells. One EPA survey found that almost half of municipal water systems are contaminated with synthetic organic chemicals; a different survey found two-thirds of private wells unsafe for drinking.[30]

There are eight major types of water pollutants: disease-causing agents, such as bacteria; oxygen-demanding wastes, such as manure; water-soluble inorganic chemicals; inorganic plant nutrients; organic chemicals; sediment or suspended matter; radioactive substances; and thermal pollution.[31]

In 1974, the federal Safe Drinking Water Act imposed federal safety standards on the states. Previously, there were no uniform water quality standards for drinking water among the states. The act requires EPA to set standards for drinking water for pollutants with potentially adverse effects on human health. The scope of the act is broad: it applies to water systems with at least fifteen service connections or that regularly serve a minimum of twenty-five people for sixty days each year. Although a "margin of safety" is also mandated, EPA must take technical feasibility and cost into account as well. In 1985, EPA reported that 87 percent of the municipal water systems were in compliance with their standards.[32] However, environmentalists advocated that standards be added for another seven hundred potential pollutants. In 1986, substantial amendments to the Safe Drinking Water Act required EPA to set standards for eighty-three new contaminants by 1989 and for an addition twenty-five by 1991. Despite the federal mandate, many states and localities are unable to meet the law's requirements, and experts do not anticipate improvement in the near future.[33]

The centerpieces of U.S. water pollution control strategies are the Federal Water Pollution Control Act of 1972 and the Clean Water Act of 1977. Amendments to the Clean Water Act were passed in 1981 and 1987, the latter over a presidential veto. Triggered by the *Exxon Valdez* spill, in 1990 the §311 oil spill liability provisions were replaced by the Oil Pollution Act. American waters were supposed to be "fishable and swimmable" by 1983, and discharge of pollutants into navigable waters was to be halted by 1985. This legislation "is the purest example of `technology forcing' in the federal regulatory code . . . [and] serves as an enduring monument to the American politician's belief in the possibilities of social engineering and to the political muscle of the environmental movement in the early 1970s."[34]

Needless to say, these goals were not achieved; however, progress was made in cleaning up the nation's waters. Between 1972 and 1986, almost $45 billion was provided to municipalities by the federal government, supplemented by $15 billion of state and local government funds, to upgrade or to construct municipal wastewater treatment facilities. The federal government no longer provides financial assistance to local governments for upgrading treatment facilities.

The record is a positive one but not unblemished. By 1986, two-thirds of American municipalities had completed construction of their effluent control systems, but of these, 12 percent were still not in compliance. The failure of the remaining one-third to complete construction on schedule is "attributed to fraud, over-building, bureaucratic and construction delays, and a 37% cut in federal funding for water pollution control between 1981 and 1986 by the Reagan administration."[35]

Finally, control of nonpoint sources of water pollution was marginal. Although the water pollution control laws require local and regional planning by the states to reduce nonpoint source pollution, neither goals nor standards have been established, and funding to establish them has not been forthcoming. The national level is no better; there is "no comprehensive legislation, goals, or funding designed to protect . . . groundwater supplies from contamination."[36]

Whether these programs are viewed as partial successes or partial failures, the reasons for the effect are found in the political climate of implementation. First, by assigning the major implementation strategies to the states, the process was opened to the vagaries of state economics and politics. While the intention behind state implementation is to respect the differences between the states, the effect is to blunt the effectiveness of the legislation. Second, EPA had wide discretion in setting the regulatory framework for the water control acts. Third, the action-forcing provisions left EPA vulnerable to claims of technological impossibility, and the immediate stew of litigation that arose from enforcement efforts hampered successful implementation. Finally, water pollution control is protective regulatory policy, and the policy actors include the White House and the senior members of the Congress; their high visibility and the conflicts between them also reduced the effectiveness of implementation efforts.

Toxic and hazardous substances pose qualitatively different problems from the problems of air and water pollutants. Separate regulatory programs to deal with these substances have been established; these are discussed in the next section.

Hazardous and Toxic Substances

The problems associated with the production, use, and disposal of hazardous wastes and chemicals are the result of the high standard of living associated with our industrialized society. Large-scale production of synthetic chemicals did not begin until after the Second World War. Before that, pesticides were the predominant hazardous chemical, and these were under the control of the U.S. Department of Agriculture (USDA) and the Food and Drug Administration (FDA). Today approximately sixty thousand chemicals are commonly used in the United States, resulting in the production of 290 million metric tons of hazardous waste per year.[37] In 1980 alone, one thousand new chemicals were reviewed for manufacture by EPA, but only a few of these chemicals have been tested to determine their potential adverse effects.

Public awareness of the chemical problem was aroused in 1962 by Rachel Carson's book *Silent Spring,* but the more popular issues of air and water pollution dominated environmental action throughout the sixties. Congress was not fully informed about the dangers of accumulating chemicals until 1971, when the Council on Environmental Quality (CEQ) reported on the dangers of toxic chemicals.

Prior to 1976, chemicals and hazardous wastes were controlled and regulated on an individual basis. There was no coordinated attempt to deal with the problem. Chemicals or wastes found in water supplies were regulated under the Federal Water Pollution Control Act of 1972. Chemicals or wastes emitted into the air were controlled by the Air Quality Act of 1967 and the 1970 amendments. Agricultural chemicals and wastes were controlled by the strong 1972 amendments to the Federal Insecticide, Fungicide, and Rodenticide Act of 1947 (FIFRA). If the substance was a residue on food, then it was the responsibility of the FDA.

In 1976, five years after the CEQ report on chemical dangers, Congress enacted two pieces of legislation designed specifically to deal with the problems associated with chemicals and hazardous wastes. The Toxic Substances Control Act of 1976 (TSCA) was designed to identify and to evaluate the environmental and health effects of existing chemicals and any new substance entering the United States market. The Resource Conservation and Recovery Act (RCRA) was designed to control solid waste management practices that could endanger public health or the environment. Both of these laws were implemented slowly due to the underestimation of the chemical and waste problem and the low priority given the issue by the executive branch. Few rules and regulations had been promulgated by the late 1970s and early 1980s. There was also a failure to resolve the problem of leaking and abandoned dumps that presented a threat to human health or the environment. This problem was aggravated because usually no Potentially Responsible Parties (PRPs) could be found to bear the cleanup costs.

The most important acts governing toxic and hazardous substances are the Federal Insecticide, Fungicide and Rodenticide Act of 1947 (FIFRA); the Clean Air Act Amendments of 1970 and the Clean Water Act of 1977; the Resource Conservation and Recovery Act of 1976 (RCRA); the Toxic Substances Control Act of 1976 (TSCA); and the Comprehensive Environmental Response, Compensation, and Liability Act of 1980 (CERCLA or Superfund) and its 1986 amendments (Superfund Amendment and Reauthorization Act or SARA). Each of these statutes follows.

Federal Insecticide, Fungicide and Rodenticide Act of 1947

Although the publicity surrounding pesticide control might lead us to suspect that controlling toxic substances is a relatively new government activity, the federal government has been regulating pesticides since the first labeling act, the Insecticide Act of 1910, was passed. This was repealed in 1947 when the comprehensive Federal Insecticide, Fungicide, and Rodenticide Act (FIFRA) was passed. Like the 1910 act, FIFRA focused on labeling. Originally the Department of Agriculture (USDA) enforced FIFRA, but in 1970, EPA assumed responsibility for administering the act. FIFRA was amended in 1972, 1975, 1978, and 1988. It requires a cost-benefit analysis on regulatory controls; this standard "is unusual among federal environmental statutes: others employ risk-based standards softened only by the availability of control technologies."[38] Persons wishing to sell or to distribute a pesticide must register the pesticide with EPA; the burden of proof of the chemical's efficacy and safety rests with the manufacturer or distributor.

The Clean Air Act and the Clean Water Act

Section 112 of the Clean Air Act provides standards for the emission of hazardous air pollutants. The act contains an extensive list of hazardous pollutants and provisions for revision of the list.[39] Once a standard is promulgated by EPA, all new sources must adhere to the standard. Rather than enforce emission standards, EPA may "issue regulations controlling design, equipment, work practices, or operations."[40]

The Clean Water Act's concerns with toxic substances are more complicated than the Clean Air Act. The original 1972 legislation proved very difficult to implement, and EPA agreed to new methods of control. Codified in the 1977 amendments, the Best Available Technology (BAT) is used to determine effluent limitations. BAT considerations include "the age of equipment and facilities, the process employed, engineering aspects of control techniques, process changes, [cost], and non-water quality environmental impact (including energy requirements). There is no requirement of a balancing between the costs and benefits of effluent reduction."[41] EPA may also impose stronger standards if necessary to provide a margin of safety.

Resource Conservation and Recovery Act

RCRA is focused primarily on solid and hazardous waste, and it is notable for its tracking system of hazardous materials from "cradle to grave," that is, from production to final disposal. This system has standards for generators, transporters, and disposal sites. Generators must keep detailed records and must meet reporting, labeling, and packaging requirements. Transporters, who are also required to meet labeling and records standards, must track materials through a permitted manifest system. The final stage, disposal, includes issues such as location, construction, recordkeeping, and operation of disposal sites.

Enforcement is implemented through the permitting system set forth in §3005. EPA may inspect and can bring both civil and criminal actions for violations. States may assume responsibility for hazardous waste control, and while they may exceed federal standards, they must at least meet federal requirements in their controlling systems.

Toxic Substances Control Act

The intent of TSCA was to fill the gaps between the federal environmental protections statutes that had been enacted between 1970 and 1976; under TSCA, EPA was empowered to regulate new toxic substances, removal of asbestos from schools, radon, and the disposal of polychlorinated biphenyls (PCBs).[42] TSCA gave EPA "broad authority to control chemical risks that could not be dealt with under other environmental statutes."[43]

The main purpose of TSCA is to ensure that manufacturers test the chemicals they market and to allow EPA to regulate the use of chemicals that present unreasonable risks. TSCA emphasizes three policies: data collection, primarily by the industries involved; government authority to prevent risks—especially imminent ones—to public health or the environment; and consideration of economic impacts. Compared to other federal laws, such as those governing air and water, TSCA has not been utilized extensively by EPA.

Superfund and SARA

In 1978, Love Canal, a housing development near Niagara Falls, New York, was declared to be in a state of emergency because long-buried chemicals were seeping into the basements of the public schools and several houses. A high incidence of health problems triggered an investigation that unveiled the presence of 21,900 tons of chemical wastes buried in fifty-five gallon drums.[44] The publicity of Love Canal led to the discovery of thousands of other similar dump sites around the country.

In direct response to the public outcry over Love Canal, the Comprehensive Environmental Response, Compensation, and Liability Act of 1980 (CERCLA or Superfund) was enacted. Superfund is an unusual environmental statute because it does not regulate industry activities. Instead it gives to the president the power to compel cleanup of hazardous substances and to recover the costs of cleanups. The president has delegated his enforcement authority to the EPA by executive order.

Superfund was developed to assure financial responsibility for the long-term maintenance of waste disposal facilities and to provide for the cleanup of old and abandoned hazardous-waste disposal sites that were leaking or that otherwise endangered the public health. This law was designed to close the gap between TSCA and RCRA concerning the closed dumps. Superfund also had provisions to respond to emergency spills of hazardous wastes. A National Priorities List of all uncontrolled hazardous-waste sites was established. Two types of government action were possible under Superfund. First, a removal action, which was primarily an emergency response, had a time limit of six months and a cost limit of $1 million. Second, a remedial action could be undertaken to clean up sites that were not considered an immediate threat to human health but were listed on the National Priorities List. Remedial actions follow the recommendations of the remedial investigations and feasibility studies (RI/FS) and are performed in accordance with the National Contingency Plan (NCP). The NCP under Superfund is an expanded version of the original NCP created in the Federal Water Pollution Control Act of 1972. It includes the hazardous substance response plan, which established procedures and standards for responding to releases of hazardous substances, pollutants, and contaminants. It specifies the procedures, techniques, materials, equipment, and methods to be employed in identifying, removing, or remedying releases of hazardous substances to minimize the damages of the releases.

Superfund allocated $1.6 billion over five years for cleanup, financed primarily by a feedstock tax on certain chemicals and on petroleum. The main accomplishment of Superfund was to develop an understanding of the magnitude of the problem. An Office of Technology Assessment report on Superfund estimated that as much as $100 billion may need to be spent over fifty years to clean up an estimated ten thousand sites.

After four years of Superfund, Congress began to grasp the serious nature of the problem and the lack of desire at EPA under the Reagan administration to get tough with violators.[45] Superfund expired in 1985, and in 1986, Congress passed the Superfund Amendment and Reauthorization Act of 1986 (SARA). SARA expanded the funding of Superfund to $9 billion. This funding included not only an increase in the feedstock tax, but it also added an environmental tax on corporate income over $2 million. This represented a major deviation from the past theory that "polluter pays." SARA set performance deadlines and achievement standards for EPA. It required the completion of 650 RI/FSs and 375 remedial investigations in the five years following enactment. The removal action was expanded to one year in duration and $2 million in cost. Section 206 gave citizens standing to file suit for any violation of CERCLA or SARA, subject to some restrictions. For example, citizen suits are not allowed within sixty days of the notification of the potentially responsible parties of the site violation. Citizen suits are also prohibited if the president is diligently prosecuting the case under CERCLA or RCRA. SARA also allocated $500 million to the leaking underground storage tank (UST) problem. The rights of citizens were expanded in Title III, a freestanding title that required that community planning and right-to-know programs be implemented.

In late 1990, Superfund was added to the congressional budget reconciliation bill during conference negotiations. The special taxes on oil and chemical companies to fund the cleanup operations were extended to 31 December 1995. The purpose for the extension was to avert a repeat of the 1985 slowdown in cleanups; left without taxing authority by the expiration of Superfund, EPA was forced to conserve the $130 million remaining in the fund by reducing its cleanup efforts. During 1994, bills were introduced in Congress to reauthorize and to amend Superfund once again. Although an unusually high degree of consensus had been reached by the various policy actors, Republicans in the House of Representatives blocked the bill.

No one disputes the need for changes in Superfund; it is "a legislative *Titanic* that only the most ardent environmentalists still believe is viable with minor repairs."[46] Superfund was ill-designed from the beginning. The litigation burden is almost insurmountable; the costs of losing a contested Superfund cleanup battle are so high that even inflated legal fees are worth the cost. The application of joint and several liability, which puts all PRPs at equal risk, gives incentives to everyone to fight to the end. Conflict rages over how clean a site must be; the 1994 reform bills would have provided more workable standards as well as allowed consideration of the future uses of the contaminated site.

It is difficult to predict how the Republican-dominated Congress in 1995 will treat the Superfund reauthorizations. The House has been successful in cutting environmental programs, but the Senate has been more moderate. However, "since authorization for the special taxes which support the superfund is due to expire in 1995, we can expect further efforts then to reauthorize and reform CERCLA."[47]

A Recommendation for the Future

In an assessment of environmental progress since the first Earth Day in 1970, William Stevens of the *New York Times* noted that while substantial progress has been made in some areas, such as toxic chemicals and CFC releases, the problems that remain are larger and more complex, and their solutions require dramatic changes in the ways ordinary people live.[48] The developed nations live well but at a high environmental cost; the less developed nations face exploding populations, poor health, and environmental degradation. We have yet to take the full measure of the environmental damage in Soviet-dominated territories.

The antiregulatory posture of the Congress in the mid-1990s has led some environmentalists to predict environmental disaster. This may be an overreaction. First, the shift in the regulatory agencies away from command-and-control toward cooperative, market-driven control strategies seems to be effective; losing regulatory power may be just the incentive needed to push the agencies toward more creative programs. Second, even if every environmental regulatory program were dismantled immediately, pollution levels would not explode. Control technology is still in place, accounting procedures have been institutionalized, new markets for greener products have been established. The laws of physics tell us that bodies in motion tend to remain in motion; similarly, the laws of public policy tell us that established policies tend to remain established. Finally, it is not clear that American business would choose to go on an environmental rampage if its regulatory bonds were loosened.

We might look to Great Britain for an example of government-industry cooperation.[49] In absolute numbers, the improvement in Great Britain's environment in the past has been impressive. Between 1958 and 1978, urban ground concentrations of sulfur dioxide fell by 50 percent. From 1958 to

1981, industrial smoke decreased by 94 percent while in the same period domestic coal smoke was reduced by 80 percent. Water quality has improved; in 1958, 86.1 percent of Great Britain's rivers had both fish and water that was potable after treatment. In 1975, 91.4 percent of the rivers met those standards. Between 1958 and 1980, the kilometers of "grossly polluted" and "poor quality" nontidal waterways decreased by 39 percent, and the length of polluted tidal waterways was reduced by 42 percent.[50] David Vogel attributes this success to three factors: "a highly respected civil service, a business community that was prepared to cooperate with government officials, and a public that was not particularly mistrustful of large corporations,"[51] all factors that are lacking in the United States. The relatively high social status of public officials allows them to deal with industrial managers on an equal footing, and the presumptions of good intentions, on one hand, and economic flexibility, on the other hand, enable the two groups to work cooperatively rather than as antagonists. We probably can do little to elevate the status of our career civil servants, however much they may deserve it, but a positive change of attitude toward business interests and continued development of market-based strategies may prove beneficial in the long run.

Suggested Reading

Battle, Jackson. *Environmental Law* (Volume 2: Water Pollution and Hazardous Wastes; Volume 3: Air Pollution). Cincinnati, OH: Anderson Publishing, 1988.

Bryner, Gary. *Blue Skies, Green Politics: The Clean Air Act of 1990*. Washington, DC: Congressional Quarterly, 1993. A clear and thorough analysis of the evolution of clean air policy in the United States, with a detailed account of the passage of the 1990 Clean Air Act Amendments.

Cohen, Richard. *Washington at Work: Back Rooms and Clean Air*. New York: Macmillan, 1992. A lively account of the passage of the 1990 Clean Air Act Amendments. It also provides a good look at the legislative process.

Dales, J. H. *Pollution, Property & Prices: An Essay in Policy-Making and Economics*. Toronto: University of Toronto Press, 1968. A classic and very readable essay that sets out the concept of pollution rights. He is persuasive even if you are not an economist.

Rosenbaum, Walter A. *Environmental Politics and Policy* (3rd ed.). Washington, DC: Congressional Quarterly Press, 1995. Primarily an undergraduate text, this furnishes as excellent overview of several areas of environmental policy: air pollution, water supply and pollution, toxic and hazardous wastes, energy, and public lands. The discussions on the relationships between science and politics alone make the book worthwhile.

Notes

1. W. F. Dodd, "Administrative Agencies as Legislators and Judges," *American Bar Association Journal* 25 (November 1939): 976.

2. H.R. 986, p. 3.

3. Charles K. Woltz, Preface to *Administrative Procedure in Government Agencies* (Attorney General's Committee Report) (Charlottesville: University Press of Virginia, 1968). This is a facsimile edition of Senate Document No. 8, 77th Congress, 1st Session, 1941.

4. Unless otherwise noted, this material is from Phillip Cooper, *Public Law and Public Administration* 2nd ed. (Englewood Cliffs, NJ: Prentice-Hall, 1988), especially Chapter 5.

5. Florence Heffron and Neil McFeeley, *The Administrative Regulatory Process* (New York: Longman, 1983), pp. 202–204.

6 . Cooper, p. 121.

7. Heffron and McFeeley, p. 251.

8. Walter A. Rosenbaum, *Environmental Politics and Policy* 3rd ed. (Washington, DC: Congressional Quarterly Press, 1995), p. 150.

9. Unless otherwise noted, this section is drawn from Heffron and McFeeley, Chapter 10.

10. Cooper, pp. 173–177.

11. Unless otherwise noted, this discussion is from Heffron and McFeeley, Chapter 11.

12. Heffron and McFeeley, p. 293.

13. G. Tyler Miller, Jr., *Living in the Environment* 5th ed. (Belmont, CA: Wadsworth), p. 423.

14. Miller, p. 424.

15. John Hartwick and Nancy Olewiler, *The Economics of Natural Resource Use* (New York: Harper & Row, 1986), p. 387 (notes omitted).

16. J. H. Dales, *Pollution, Property & Prices: An Essay in Policy-Making and Economics* (Toronto: University of Toronto Press, 1968).

17. The discussion that follows is from Hartwick and Olewiler, pp. 443-445.

18. On August 7 1990, during congressional hearings on the sudden increase in gasoline prices following Iraq's invasion of Kuwait, the head of the American Petroleum Institute charged that the prices went up because environmental controls had ruined the free market!

19. Miller, p. 451.

20. Janet Hook, "Legislative Summary: 101st Congress Leaves Behind Plenty Laws, Criticism," *Congressional Quarterly Weekly Report* 48(44) (3 November 1990), p. 3692.

21. Unless otherwise cited, the material on the 1990 Clean Air Act is from resource materials furnished to accompany *Legal Winds of Change: Business and the New*

Clean Air Act, a video conference on 28 November 1990, presented by EPA, PBS Adult Learning Satellite Service, Public Television Outreach Alliance, and the University of North Carolina at Greensboro.

22. "Carolina Power Is Top Buyer," *New York Times,* 31 March 1993, C2; "CP&L Spends Big to Delay Buying Air 'Scrubbers'," *Greensboro [NC] News and Record,* 31 March 1993, B8.

23. "Law Students Buy and Hold Pollution Rights," *New York Times,* 31 March 1995, B13. Students from the New England School of Law and from law schools at the University of Maryland, City University of New York, Detroit, Duke, and Hamline University spent $3,256. The project was organized by Robert Percival, an environmental law professor at the University of Maryland.

24. Rosenbaum, p. 208.

25. *Legal Winds of Change,* p. 18.

26. This information is drawn from panel remarks by Kathy Bailey, Assistant General Counsel for the Chemical Manufacturers Association during the *Legal Winds of Change* video conference.

27. Miller, p. 455.

28. Rosenbaum, p. 53.

29. Rosenbaum, p. 55.

30. Miller, p. 475.

31. Miller, p. 456.

32. Miller, p. 483.

33. Rosenbaum, p. 227.

34. Rosenbaum, pp. 154–155.

35. Miller, p. 484.

36. Miller, p. 484.

37. USEPA, *Environmental Progress and Challenges: An EPA Perspective* (Washington, DC: Office of Management Systems and Evaluation CPM-222, June 1984), pp. 95 and 82.

38. Roger Findley and Daniel Farber, *Cases and Materials on Environmental Law,* 4th ed. (St. Paul, MN: West, 1995), p. 438.

39. 42 U.S.C.A. 7412 (b).

40. Findley and Farber, p. 137.

41. Findley and Farber, p. 117.

42. Ray Vaughn, *Essentials of Environmental Law* (Rockville, MD: Government Institutes, 1994), pp. 30–31.

43. Bureau of National Affairs, *U.S. Environmental Laws, 1988 Edition* (Washington, DC: Bureau of National Affairs, 1988), p. 145.

44. USEPA, *Environmental Monitoring at Love Canal* (Washington, DC: USEPA, 1982).

45. See Jonathan Lash, Katherine Gillman, and David Sheridan. *A Season of Spoils: The Reagan Administration's Attack on the Environment* (New York: Pantheon, 1984), especially Chapter 2. See also Steven Cohen, "Defusing the Toxic Time Bomb: Federal Hazardous Waste Programs," in *Environmental Policy in the 1980's Reagan's New Agenda*. Edited by Norman Vig and Michael Kraft (Washington, DC: Congressional Quarterly Press, 1984), pp. 273–291.

46. Rosenbaum, p. 253.

47. Roger Findley and Daniel Farber, *Cases and Materials on Environmental Law* 4th ed. (St. Paul, MN: West, 1995), p. 625.

48. William K. Stevens, "The 25th Anniversary of Earth Day: How Has the Environment Fared?" *New York Times,* 18 April 1995, B5.

49. For a more complete discussion of English environmental policy, see Susan Buck, "Environmental Policy in the United Kingdom," in *International Public Policy Sourcebook: Volume 2 [Education and Environment]*. Edited by Frederic Bolotin (New York: Greenwood Press, 1989), pp. 310–333.

50. David Vogel, *National Styles of Regulation: Environmental Policy in Great Britain and the United States* (Ithaca, NY: Cornell University Press, 1986), pp. 22, 153, 157.

51. Vogel, p. 242.

Chapter Six

Managing Wildlife
and Public Lands

Management of wildlife and public lands are related issues that generate complex webs of statutes, regulations, and even international treaties. As in the preceding chapter, it would be impossible to discuss or even to mention every law that affects public lands and wildlife. The purpose of this discussion is not to present the individual provisions of each and every act but rather to acquaint readers with the political context of various policy areas and the general intent behind the major acts and their subsequent implementation and revision.

The chapter is divided into three sections. The section on wildlife discusses federalism, regulating the taking of wildlife, and acquisition and management of wildlife habitat. The section on public lands discusses six periods of federal land history: acquisition, disposal, reservation, custodial management, intensive management, and consultation and confrontation. The chapter concludes with a case study that examines the efforts of the state of Florida to preserve public access to a river claimed as private property by a large, powerful business.

Federal-State Cooperative Wildlife Management

The Rise and Fall of the State Ownership Doctrine

Until the late nineteenth century, wildlife management was essentially *game* management, and conservation was practiced to restore and to protect game animals. The responsibility for game rested with state governments because they were the legal owners of the wildlife. Although partially discredited today, the state ownership doctrine has had a great impact on international, federal, and state wildlife law.[1]

In *Martin* v. *Waddell* (1842), Chief Justice Taney found that the rights to the navigable waters, submerged lands, fish, and wildlife could not have been conveyed by King Charles to the Duke of York as alienable rights because such rights were a public trust. The public character of the rights was passed on the various sovereign states, which therefore also owned the wildlife. Technically this decision applied only to the original thirteen states. However, in 1845, a question arose about the status of wildlife in new states. In *Pollard's Lessee* v. *Hagan* (1845), the Court applied the ruling to newly admitted states as well, citing the legislative convention that new states are admitted on an equal footing with previously existing states.

The state ownership doctrine was challenged again in 1855 in *Smith* v. *Maryland*. The case involved a shipowner who had been taking oysters with a scoop or drag in defiance of Maryland law. Smith's vessel was licensed by the federal government, and he contended that the state law was an unconstitutional interference with the federal power to regulate interstate commerce. The Supreme Court held that because Maryland owned the soil in which the oysters were located, Maryland was allowed to regulate the oyster fisheries. Maryland's claim of state ownership in this case overrode the Commerce Clause. The Court carefully protected its own prerogatives on future related questions:

> Whether this liberty [to take oysters] belongs exclusively to the citizens of the State of Maryland, or may lawfully be enjoyed in common by all citizens of the United States; whether this public use may be restricted by the States to its own citizens, or a part of them, or by force of the Constitution must remain common to all citizens of the United States; whether the national government, by a treaty or act of congress, can grant to foreigners the right to participate therein; or what, in general, are the limits of the trust upon which the State holds this soil, or its power to define and control that trust, are matters wholly without the scope of this case, and upon which we give no opinion.[2]

Of course, the Court was not allowed to leave so many loose ends forever. *McCready* v. *Virginia* (1876) gave Virginia ownership of not only the tidewaters but also the fish and oysters in those waters. At issue was a Virginia statute that forbade non-Virginia residents from planting oysters in the Virginia tidal waters. The Court held that the state was only regulating the common property of the people it represented. This was a substantial expansion of the earlier decisions in *Martin* and *Smith*. However, in 1891, the Court decided that the commonwealth of Massachusetts could regulate fishing in Buzzards Bay, not because it owned the fish but because, absent any conflicting federal regulation, the state probably had the right to regulate within its territorial waters.[3] This represented a change from the strong endorsement of state ownership laid out in *McCready*. The Court was growing cautious, and it seemed to distinguish *McCready* on the basis that *McCready* dealt with shellfish (stationary and imbedded in soil) rather than finfish, which move through waters that are under federal as well as state jurisdiction.

In 1896, *Geer* v. *Connecticut* indicated a return to the notion that the states owned their wildlife and were independent of federal interference in the management of the wildlife. Geer was prohibited under Connecticut law from exporting lawfully killed game birds, and the Court offered three separate arguments to support the state law. First, since the state owned the game, "commerce" within the meaning of the Constitution was—perhaps—not created when the game was killed. Second, even if commerce were created, it was at the most *intra*state commerce, because the Connecticut statute prohibited the export of the game. Finally, even if interstate commerce were occurring, and the statute then an interference with interstate commerce, the right of the state to exercise the police power and to preserve a food supply for its citizens overrode the concerns of the Commerce Clause. Although the Court in *Geer* recognized that some states' rights in wildlife were transferred by the Constitution to the federal government, the case was still used to justify the state ownership doctrine.

The conservation movement was part of the larger Progressive movement at the turn of the century. Disgusted with the excesses of big business, monopolistic control of industry, and machine politics, reformers struggled to protect the rights of the people to the natural resources of the land, not in a spirit of preservation but rather to ensure that the opportunities and benefits held in reserve in these resources were accessible to the general public. The conservation movement was partly a response to the drive for rational and efficient organization of time and resources imposed on many facets of American life during this era. The precepts of Scientific Management in business overflowed into the public sector; government regulation of businesses such as the railroads and the passage of pure food and drug laws was motivated as much by goals of efficiency as by the public interest. The conservation movement also reflected a concern of the American people that the frontier was truly gone; the 1890 Census had formally declared the closing of the American frontier. With the disappearance of the frontier, Americans could no longer accept wasteful exploitation of resources, and the movement to preserve some of the natural world that had partially defined the American experience gained wider acceptance.

In 1900, Teddy Roosevelt's conservation movement was in full cry. The Sierra Club was eight years old, the federal government had passed the Forest Management Act (1897), and the River and Harbor Act (1899) had established a legal basis for controlling some forms of pollution on navigable waterways.[4] The passage in 1900 of the Lacey Act provided federal assistance to state efforts to regulate their wildlife. The Lacey Act prohibits the interstate transportation of any game killed in violation of state law; in addition, it permits a state to prohibit the importation of game lawfully killed in another state. This expanded the holding in *Geer*, which allowed states to prohibit the export of lawfully killed game; the Lacey Act allows them to prohibit the *import* of lawfully killed game.

In 1912, the Court confirmed the expansion of the state power to regulate the taking of wildlife. Justice White, author of the *Geer* opinion, found in *The Abbey Dodge* (1912) that the state ownership doctrine preempted federal wildlife law. This extreme position did not hold for long: in 1926, *Foster-Fountain Packing Company* v. *Haydel* softened *Geer* by holding that once wildlife enters the stream of commerce, the state loses absolute control over that wildlife.

Geer was the high-water mark for state regulation of wildlife. Since then, various Supreme Court decisions have established three constitutional bases for federal regulation of wildlife: the federal treaty-making power, the federal property power, and the federal commerce power.

In 1913, Congress passed the Migratory Bird Act, which declared all migratory game and insectivorous birds to be under federal protection and regulation. Promptly challenged in federal district courts, the act was found unconstitutional.[5] While the United States's appeal was pending, the government concluded a treaty with Great Britain to protect migratory birds, and in 1918, Congress passed the Migratory Bird Treaty Act to implement the treaty. The Supreme Court never ruled on the appeals from the Migratory Bird Act cases.

The states moved promptly to challenge the enabling legislation in court, but use of the federal treaty power complicated their arguments considerably. The landmark case that decided the supremacy of the treaty power over the reserved rights of the states is *Missouri* v. *Holland* (1920). This case arose in federal district court against federal game warden Ray P. Holland, whose enforcement of the Migratory Bird Treaty Act in Missouri was interfering with the amount of state revenues generated by hunting. The district judge found that the treaty-making power of the United States is supreme over state authority, and therefore the Migratory Bird Treaty Act was constitutional. Missouri appealed to the Supreme Court, but the Court upheld the lower court decision. The Migratory Bird Treaty Act was indeed constitutional; the erosion of the state ownership doctrine confirmed in *Geer* had begun.

Although the federal power to regulate wildlife through the treaty provisions of the Constitution had been established, the federal power to hunt or to manage wildlife on federal lands was not so clearly established. The federal government as landowner within state boundaries was held by the states to be simply another property owner and subject to state wildlife regulations. However, in *Kleppe* v. *New Mexico* (1976), the Supreme Court ruled that the federal government had the power to regulate and to protect the wildlife living on federal land.

Until 1977, there was no Supreme Court decision that specified the reach of the commerce clause in federal wildlife regulation. In that year, *Douglas* v. *Seacoast Products, Inc.* determined that a Virginia residency requirement for menhaden fishing was preempted by the federal licenses held by the fishing vessels. In *Douglas* the Court clearly rejected the state ownership doctrine:

> A State does not stand in the same position as the owner of a private game preserve and it is pure fantasy to talk of "owning" wild fish, birds, or animals. Neither the States nor the Federal Government, any more than a hopeful fisherman or hunter, has title to these creatures until they are reduced to possession by skillful capture.[6]

The primacy of the state ownership doctrine was finally laid to rest in the *Tangier Sound* controversy, discussed in chapter 1, which granted fishing rights in Virginian waters to Maryland fishermen:

> In sum, the dilution of the ownership theory has been such that in the Court's analysis of a statutory scheme, "ownership" of a natural resource is but one factor that the Court must consider in determining whether a State has exercised its police power in conformity with federal law and the Constitution.[7]

Federal assumption of control over wildlife was part of a larger effort to centralize national power. Virtually all congressional debates over the Migratory Bird Act and the Migratory Bird Treaty Act focused on the constitutional issues of the proper relationship between the state and federal governments. It is clear from the congressional debates and judicial opinions that everyone was agreed that game in general, and migratory birds in particular, needed protection. They also agreed that the federal acts would provide protection, yet they argued bitterly over the legislation. For the most part, the arguments were not on scientific or administrative grounds but rather on constitutional grounds. Even men who favored the policy ends were driven to object to the policy means.

Using a popular policy agenda to achieve a hidden agenda is an ancient political ploy. Certainly environmental policy is often used to camouflage less respectable goals, partly because environmental issues have such high social appeal. For example, in California, regulation of the state shrimp fishery was as much an attempt to force the Chinese out of business as it was scientific regulation of a natural resource.[8] Similarly, early English game laws were instituted in part to restrict the use of weapons by potential dissidents or criminals.[9]

Having flexed its muscles over migratory birds, the federal government allowed the states to retain some control over wildlife.[10] Throughout much of the twentieth century, the states were given considerable autonomy in choosing how and to what extent they complied with federal guidelines, subject of course to the silken chains of federal money through such programs as the Pittman-Robertson Act (1937), which redistributes a federal tax on ammunition and firearms sales to the states for wildlife restoration, and the Dingell-Johnson Act (1950), which uses a similar strategy to support state sport fisheries.

Federal Aid in Wildlife Restoration (Pittman-Robertson) Act

The Pittman-Robertson Act is a federal-state cooperative endeavor that drew together the same interests that supported efforts to protect migratory birds.[11] Passed in 1937, the bill was unique: a maximum of 8 percent of the funds collected may be used for administration (in fact, administration of Pittman-Robertson averages 6.3 percent[12]), and as a condition of eligibility for federal funds, it prohibits diversion of hunting license fees collected by the states from state fish and game department administration.[13] Thus state fish and game departments that participate in Pittman-Robertson also have a steady source of license revenue; this deceptively simple section of the law has been the basis for one of the most successful environmental laws in the country. Pittman-Robertson was signed by Franklin Roosevelt on 2 September 1937; within the first year, forty-three of the forty-eight states had passed legislation to become eligible for funding.[14]

Although Pittman-Robertson as originally drafted had enormous potential for federal influence on state wildlife management decisions, subsequent amendments have broadened the powers of the state decision makers. In

1946, an amendment allowed up to one-fourth of the state's allocation of federal aid funds to be used to maintain completed projects.[15] Although the states were quick to comply with Pittman-Robertson requirements, Congress was slow to appropriate the full amount of the excise tax due to the Pittman-Robertson program. In the FY 1951 Appropriations Act, Congress finally gave Pittman-Robertson funds a "permanent-indefinite" appropriations status that automatically transferred the excise tax to the Fish and Wildlife Service.[16] In 1955, Congress passed an amendment that permitted grant funds to be used for straightforward wildlife management (rather than discrete projects). Then in 1970, the law was amended in two important areas. First, the federal excise tax on handguns was added to the Pittman-Robertson supply with half of these revenues apportioned for hunter safety programs. Second, the 1970 amendment allowed the states to substitute a "comprehensive fish and wildlife resource management" plan for individual project proposals. Finally, in 1972, sales of archery equipment were included in the tax.

Pittman-Robertson is unusual in its reliance on a tax that is supported enthusiastically by those subject to the tax. In the 1930s, excise taxes in general were being phased out, but the wildlife interests pushed for retention of the excise tax on arms and ammunition.[17] In 1950, manufacturers, sportsmen, conservation groups, and state agencies joined forces once again to defeat the repeal of the federal excise tax on arms and ammunition.[18]

The mechanics of Pittman-Robertson are fairly straightforward.[19] Federal excise taxes are collected on firearms, ammunition, and archery equipment (11%) and on handguns (10%) at the manufacturer or wholesale level. The full amount of the excise tax receipts are automatically appropriated to FWS in the fiscal year following their collection. FWS then makes the funds available to the states through an equitable formula: one-half of the fund is distributed based on the ratio of the land area of the state to the total area of the country, while the second half is distributed based on the ratio of the number of paid hunting license holders per state to license holders nationwide.[20] State grants are limited to a maximum of 5 percent and minimum of 0.5 percent of any one year's total appropriation. The federal-state match for Pittman-Robertson is 75–25 for each project. Any state allocation that is not used within two years automatically reverts to the Migratory Bird Conservation Fund.

By any measure, Pittman-Robertson has been a success. Since 1937, over four million acres of land have been purchased for wildlife restoration and another forty million acres are managed under cooperative agreements. Many species, such as elk, wild turkey, wood duck, white-tailed deer, and pronghorn antelope have been restored; some have been brought back from the brink of extinction.[21] Between 1939 and 1993, revenues to the wildlife restoration account totaled $2,816,543,530; in 1994 the states received $182,081,113.[22]

Federal Aid in Sport Fish Restoration (Dingell-Johnson) Act

Passed in 1950, the Dingell-Johnson Act is modeled on the Pittman-Robertson Act.[23] The act provides federal grants to the states for sport fish restoration and management; amendments in 1970 and 1984 gave states the option of using the funds for recreational boating facilities and public education projects.

Dingell-Johnson has two funding sources. First, paralleling the funding mechanism for Pittman-Robertson, the federal government assesses a 10 percent federal excise tax on sport fishing equipment, yachts, pleasure boats, and imported fishing equipment. Second, a portion of the tax on gasoline purchased for motorboats is allocated to the Dingell-Johnson program. The funds are distributed according to a formula based on geographical area and the proportion of state fishing licenses sold relative to national license sales. Six percent of the federal revenue may be withheld for administration; apportioned funds not spent by the states reverts to the federal government after two years to be used for sport fisheries research. Between 1952 and 1993, the sport fish restoration account receipts totaled $2,285,965,110; in 1994, the states received $174,628,717.[24]

Other Federal-State Programs

A third law analogous to the Pittman-Robertson Act and the Dingell-Johnson Act is the Fish and Wildlife Conservation (Forsythe-Chafee or Nongame) Act of 1980. Forsythe-Chafee is focused on nongame wildlife and fish, and it has never received an appropriation. However, the planning provisions of the act have been integrated with Pittman-Robertson and Dingell-Johnson programs by FWS.

Many natural resource agencies in the federal government have programs with a state component. For example, some national parks allow hunting, fishing, or trapping, and these activities are generally regulated either by the states in which the park is located or according to state regulations. The Forest Service has a State and Private Forestry Program that works with state forestry agencies, private landowners, and forest product industries to improve forest quality; some wildlife habitat is also developed, primarily in the South and Northeast.[25] The Bureau of Land Management makes payments to the states and counties as partial reimbursement for economic activities on BLM lands and to compensate the counties for lost property tax revenues.[26]

Federal Wildlife Programs

Federal wildlife law is distinguished by its dispersal among many federal agencies. The federal agencies with major responsibility for wildlife are the Fish and Wildlife Service (FWS) (Department of the Interior) and the National Marine Fisheries Service in the National Oceanic and Atmospheric Administration (NOAA) (Commerce Department). The National Park Service, the Forest Service, and BLM also have strong roles in this policy area. Because of the interagency activity, the discussions of wildlife management and law are divided into topic areas: regulating the taking of wildlife, regulating commerce in wildlife, acquisition and management of wildlife habitat, protection of marine mammals, and conservation of endangered species.[27]

Regulating the Taking of Wildlife

Although regulation of routine game laws, such as hunting seasons and limits, are state activities, the federal government has the responsibility for species protection. The most important acts dealing with the "taking" of wildlife are the laws protecting migratory birds (for example, the Migratory Bird Treaty Act, the Migratory Bird Conservation Act, and the Migratory Bird Hunting Stamp Act), the Bald Eagle Protection Act, the Wild Free-Roaming Horse and Burro Act, the Marine Mammal Protection Act, and the Endangered Species Act.

Migratory Bird Legislation

The Migratory Bird Treaty Act was passed in 1918 to implement a treaty made with Great Britain on behalf of Canada, providing federal protection through the Secretary of Agriculture for all migratory game birds and insectivorous birds. It also restricted the shipping of birds across state lines if such actions broke the laws of the states in which the birds were taken. The act withstood a court challenge by the states (see previous section), and with that issue settled, the national government proceeded to sign similar treaties with Mexico (1936), Japan (1972), and the Soviet Union (1976).

It was soon clear that simply protecting the birds from hunters was not sufficient to guarantee the supply of birds. Habitat protection was also necessary, and in 1929 the Migratory Bird Conservation Act was passed to create a national system of bird refuges. Few refuges were actually purchased until the Migratory Bird Hunting Stamp Act passed in 1934 and provided funds for habitat protection. Amendments to this act (also known as the Duck Stamp Act) have varied the percentages of revenue allocated for refuge purchase and for management. Some amendments and additional statutes, such as the National Wildlife Refuge System Administration Act (1966), have given the Secretary of Agriculture the authority to permit hunting on the refuges. At the same time as the Duck Stamp Act was passed, Congress enacted the Fish and Wildlife Coordination Act to authorize the Bureau of Biological Survey (precursor to the FWS) to coordinate wildlife refuges on federal water impoundments. These refuges were under the control of the Secretary of Interior.

The opposite side of the bird protection issue is the damage that migrating birds may do to unharvested crops. The 1916 treaty allowed killing birds that endangered agricultural interests, and the Coordination Act was amended in 1946 to permit the Secretary of Interior to work with other agencies to minimize bird damage. The legislative solution was to provide alternative sources of feed for these birds. In 1948, the Lea Act authorized renting or purchasing land for feeding areas, and two other acts (the Waterfowl Depredations Act of 1956 and the Surplus Grain for Wildlife Act of 1961) provided the authority for federal feeding of migrating birds and resident game birds.

The agency with primary responsibility for regulating hunting and commerce in migratory bird species is the Fish and Wildlife Service (FWS). Through the duck stamp revenues and congressional appropriations, FWS is able to purchase land and easements to protect habitat for migrating species. FWS is consulted by the Department of Agriculture and all other federal water resource agencies to ensure that water projects affecting wetlands will not unduly harm the migratory species or their habitat. FWS may authorize killing of birds (as opposed to routine hunting) if agricultural crops or human health are threatened by the birds' activities.[28]

Bald and Golden Eagle Protection Act

This act was passed in 1940 to protect the national symbol of the United States. In addition to protecting the lives and nests of the birds, the Bald Eagle Protection Act prohibits the sale, possession, or transport of bald eagles or of any part of an eagle (such as feathers). After 1959, Alaskan bald eagles were protected by the act, and in 1962, golden eagles were also covered, although state governors may authorize the shooting of golden eagles to protect livestock. Golden eagles were added to the act because immature bald eagles are difficult to distinguish from young golden eagles. The act was also amended in 1972 to prohibit "taking" birds by poison. Penalties for violation of the act are severe: criminal penalties up to $10,000 and two years in jail and civil penalties of up to $5,000 per violation. The civil penalties were also increased in 1972 by the automatic revocation of federal grazing privileges, while at the same time a "citizen bounty" of half of any fine (up to $2,500) was authorized for anyone giving information that leads to a conviction.

After the 1916 Migratory Bird Treaty between Great Britain and the United States was amended in 1972, the Migratory Bird Conservation Act was also changed to protect bald eagles and other raptors. The Endangered Species Act (discussed later in this section) also affords some protection for the bald eagle.

Wild Free-Roaming Horse and Burro Act

Just as the Bald Eagle Protection Act was passed to protect a national symbol, the Wild Free-Roaming Horse and Burro Act of 1971 had a great deal of popular sentiment behind it. The brutal slaughter of wild horses was publicized by the efforts of a few westerners, and the romantic attachment of Americans to horses in general and to symbols of the Old West in particular persuaded Congress to protect the animals on federal lands. Subsequent complications over animals wandering onto private property and the problems for legitimate owners of unbranded animals straying onto federally managed land have been resolved through the courts.

The act protected the horse and burro populations almost too well: populations were expanding rapidly and the animals were beginning to destroy their own habitat. In 1978, the act was amended to permit BLM to remove "excess" animals. At the end of 1985, BLM was holding 9,000 animals in its feedlot corrals,[29] and the removal of excess animals from the range was necessarily slowed.

In 1995, the wild horse and burro program is a resounding success.[30] In the late 1980s, BLM aggressively promoted horse and burro adoption programs in the eastern United States, tripling the adoption rate. By 1989, BLM had completely eliminated its feedlot corrals and had placed all of the adoptable animals. Approximately 3,000 animals were not suitable for adoption, and these were placed in sanctuaries in South Dakota and Oklahoma. Working with concerned interest groups, BLM has placed most of these animals in permanent retirement. In the early 1990s, the South Dakota sanctuary closed, and as the last animals are placed, BLM will close the Oklahoma sanctuary. The wild horse herds have stabilized at 42,000 animals; BLM removes about 9,000 animals per year.[31]

This is an example of a policy area that is especially difficult for Congress. Most Americans are oblivious to the conditions in slaughterhouses, but even a sanitized photo of frightened horses in slaughter conditions will mobilize public opinion. In the early eighties, when the Reagan administration tried to remove wild ponies from the eastern coastal islands to make room for off-road vehicles, the public outcry forced them to reconsider. An issue that is so emotional that school children write letters in protest will also involve their parents. Congress must consider the political context of horse and burro issues more than simply the technical or economic context.

Regulating Commerce in Wildlife

The issue of commerce in wildlife was discussed in some detail at the beginning of this chapter. The key legislation is the Lacey Act, passed in 1900. It had two purposes: "to strengthen and supplement state wildlife conservation laws . . . [and] to promote the interests of agriculture and horticulture by prohibiting the importation of certain types of wildlife determined to be injurious to those interests."[32] Although there is nothing in the language of the Lacey Act to exclude fish, the act was generally considered only in relation to game birds and fur-bearing mammals. In 1926 Congress passed the Black Bass Act to extend Lacey Act–like protections to black bass, an important game fish. Subsequent amendments to these acts have extended the Lacey Act to include "wild animals, birds, and parts or eggs thereof, captured or killed contrary to federal law or the laws of any foreign country."[33]

These acts had important implications for protecting wildlife in foreign countries. In 1930, the Tariff Act supplemented the Lacey Act by requiring that, if the laws of the exporting country protected an animal, the United States consul at the place of export must certify any such animal or any products derived from it before they could be brought in to the United States. Products or animals lacking the certification may be seized. Responsibility for the Lacey Act rests with the Commerce Department and the Tariff Act is administered by the Department of Interior.

Substantial changes were made in these acts in 1981. The Lacey Act Amendments repealed the Black Bass Act and drastically revised the original Lacey Act. The enforcement provisions were enhanced and the general scope of the laws expanded. Now the act extends to all wild animals, including animals bred and raised in captivity, and some plant species. Criminal penalties were also increased: the maximum fine is $20,000 and jail terms range from one to five years. Under the 1981 amendments, these penalties no longer require that the violator "knowingly and willfully" violated the act, so that the government does not bear the burden of proof that the violator intended to break the law.[34]

Conservation of Endangered Species

Since 1969, the federal government has enacted three statutes aimed directly at the protection of endangered species, and the United States has become party to the Convention on International Trade in Endangered Species of Wild Fauna and Flora (CITES), discussed more fully in chapter 7.

The first statute was the Endangered Species Preservation Act of 1966. The strongest provision of this act was habitat protection. Beyond this, it was primarily a statement of good intentions. The most notable limitation was that it did not provide any restrictions on the taking of wildlife, leaving such regulations to the states.

In 1969, Congress enacted the Endangered Species Conservation Act. For the first time, the Secretary of Interior was authorized to list wildlife "threatened with worldwide extinction" and generally to prohibit importing threatened wildlife into the United States.[35] Unfortunately, the 1969 act fell short of providing the kind of legislation that could provide timely protection of endangered species. The Secretary of Interior only listed species in imminent danger of extinction and provided no protection for species approaching the danger point. However, the act did call for an international meeting on endangered species. Held in 1973, the meeting produced the Convention on International Trade in Endangered Species of Wild Fauna and Flora (CITES), which is discussed in chapter 7.

Almost immediately Congress realized that the federal endangered species program was not sufficient. Apart from the Marine Mammal Protection Act, there were no restrictions on taking endangered species, and the constraints on federal activities that might harm species were narrow and embellished with many loopholes. The magnitude of the problem of vanishing species was all too apparent. In 1973, Congress voted almost unanimously to pass the Endangered Species Act.

Implementation for the Endangered Species Act is the responsibility of the Secretary of the Interior for terrestrial species and the Secretary of Commerce for marine species.[36] The actual work is conducted by the Fish and Wildlife Service (Interior) and National Marine Fisheries Service (Commerce). Four key sections of the act provide its basic structure. Section 4 provides the formal listing process used to identify threatened and endangered species; this process allows increased access by interest groups in the protection process. It also provides protection for critical habitats, a departure from previous federal regulatory efforts, and requires the drafting of recovery plans for each listed species.

Section 7 mandates every federal agency to consult with the appropriate secretary before taking any action that might affect a listed species. The "God Squad," one of the more interesting amendments to a federal statute, was added to Section 7 in 1978.[37] This provision established a cabinet-level committee to review the cases in which species protection was in direct conflict with other, compelling federal policy goals. It was first used in the snail darter–Tellico Dam controversy (*TVA* v. *Hill,* the case used in Chapter Four to illustrate law school briefs); the committee ruled in favor of the fish but was later overruled by Congress.[38] The God Squad is rarely convened; by early in 1994, it had only reviewed three proposed exemptions.[39]

Section 9 is the third major section, prohibiting both the taking of listed species and damage to their habitats; Section 11 provides the penalties for violations of the act.

In 1982, responding to Reagan's requirements that FWS consider the economic consequences of listing endangered and threatened species, Congress amended the act to clarify congressional intentions that only scientific factors are to be used to assess the endangered or threatened status of species; the only place in the Endangered Species Act (ESA) for economic factors is in the designation of critical habitat.[40] Even with congressional and public support, progress under the ESA has been marginal. About 50 species are listed each year, and approximately 750 species are listed as endangered or threatened; however, thousands of species are in the queue for review. Despite some highly publicized species recoveries, such as the California condor, sea otter, and bald eagle, the overall recovery rate is poor. On an international scale, the lack of success is even more alarming. Scientists estimate conservatively that 15 percent of all species in the Latin American rain forests will be gone by the year 2000; in the large national parks in the United States between one-quarter and one-third of the large animal species are already gone.[41] According to William Mansfield, the deputy director of the United Nations Environmental Programme, the extinction rate in 1990 was over 150 species per day and "biological diversity faces the worst stage of mass extinction in 65 million years."[42]

Center stage for the past ten years has been the spotted owl, a small, secretive bird, found only in the old-growth forests of the Pacific Northwest. The Northern Spotted Owl has become to the 1990s what the snail darter was to the 1970s. It took a lawsuit to get the bird listed as a threatened species in June of 1990.[43] The policy actors immediately began to jockey for position. The logging interests tried to redefine the issue as jobs for loggers and profits for timber companies and *not* as species protection or biodiversity. The environmentalists, who had long opposed cutting in the old-growth forests because of watershed protection, soil erosion, and a general aversion to extensive cutting of virgin timber, took on the cause of the owl with fervor. The spotted owl became a hot issue in the presidential race between Bush and Clinton. Bush said the ESA was "a sword aimed at the jobs, families, and communities of entire regions like the Northwest,"[44] while Clinton promised to hold a "forest summit" if he was elected. Although he fulfilled his promise, holding the meeting in Portland in April 1993, resolution of the issue was still left to the courts. Both sides agree that the ESA need to be changed, but agreement goes no further.

The issue has continued in the public eye for several reasons. A new international treaty, the Biodiversity Convention, has entered into effect without the participation of the United States, and this engendered a great deal of publicity, especially during the Rio Conference discussed in chapters 2 and 7. The conservative "takings movement" has seized the ESA as a symbol of unconstitutional interference with the property rights of citizens; the decision of the Supreme Court in *Babbitt* v. *Sweet Home Chapter of Communities for a Great Oregon* (1995) that the ESA applied to habitat on privately owned land may prove a Pyrrhic victory for the environmentalists if it spurs previously uncommitted politicians to support weakening the ESA. The issues at stake are clashes of fundamental values that simply cannot be resolved rationally: are animals more important—or perhaps equally important—as people? are species more important than jobs? are the certain, short-term costs of protecting biodiversity worth the possible, long-term benefits of salvaging the gene pool? Certainly the reauthorization battle over the Endangered Species Act will be volatile.

Marine Mammal Protection Act

Clearly the federal government cannot mandate directly an international system of marine mammal protection, but the government can, and did, institute such a program for the territorial waters of the United States. The reasons for such legislation, enacted in 1972, are many. The primary reason was to provide protection and regulation of a commercial resource that was in danger of depletion. Another reason, stressed by ecologists and other scientists, was the ecological importance of marine mammals and the necessity to protect their ecological niche. Finally, an intensive lobbying effort arose from citizens concerned about the harvesting of mammals with apparently extraordinary intelligence and complex social arrangements.[45]

In 1972 Congress enacted the Marine Mammal Protection Act (MMPA), which "articulated policy goals of broad generality and implemented them with specific directions that were neither purely protectionist nor purely exploitive but were almost always complex."[46] With some extremely specific exceptions, the keystone of the act was an absolute moratorium on the taking of marine mammals by United States citizens or by foreigners within the

Fishery Conservation Zone of the United States. State control over marine mammals was preempted.

Implementation of the act was split between the Secretary of Commerce and the Secretary of Interior.[47] The Commerce Secretary, who has delegated this authority to the National Marine Fisheries Service (NMFS), bears responsibility for all cetaceans (whales and porpoises) and for all pinnepedians (seals) except walruses. The Interior Secretary has authority over all other marine mammals (manatees, dugongs, polar bears, sea otters, and walruses) and has delegated responsibility to FWS.

An independent advisory body, the Marine Mammal Commission, was established in the MMPA act. It became the focus of controversy during the first Reagan administration. The members of the commission had previously been highly respected marine scientists appointed by the president on the recommendation of CEQ, the Smithsonian, the National Science Foundation, and the National Academy of Sciences. Reagan chose to appoint members chosen only by CEQ, a debilitated organization controlled by the White House. In 1982, Congress passed a rider to the Commercial Fisheries Research and Development Act that made Marine Mammal Commission appointments subject to Senate confirmation.[48]

MMPA is unique in the rulemaking requirement it attaches to any consideration of a waiver by either secretary. Waivers are extremely specific, applying only to a particular species or population stock and then only to a limited amount. If the secretary is convinced that the proposed waiver will not harm the resource and that the taking is "in accord with sound principles of resource protection and conservation as provided in the purposes and policies" of the act, the secretary may issue regulations to control the waiver and then issue the waiver itself.[49]

The rulemaking process the secretary must follow is the formal rulemaking process described in chapter 5: a full adversarial hearing conducted by an administrative law judge, allowing the presentation of evidence, cross-examination of witnesses, and a full record. The hearing must cover the proposed waiver that will issue *after* the regulations are promulgated as well as the regulations related to it, and the secretary must publish all scientific statements and all relevant studies and recommendations made by the Marine Mammal Commission. These procedural requirements are the most stringent of all the wildlife statutes.[50]

MMPA is not the only legislation that protects marine mammals. The Endangered Species Act of 1973 provides protections for endangered and threatened marine mammals; the Marine Protection, Research, and Sanctuaries Act of 1972 provides habitat protection; and various international treaties, discussed in Chapter Seven, affect marine mammals. Threatened or endangered marine mammals include "the northern sea otter, the southern sea otter, the dugong, all species of manatees and monk seals, the Gulf of California harbor porpoise and blue, bowhead, finback, gray, humpback, right, Sei, and sperm whales."[51]

Private interest groups have been highly visible in the protection of marine mammals. The harp seal hunts in Canada were halted by Greenpeace activists protesting in often bloody confrontations with seal hunters, by protectionists spray painting the young seals to ruin their pelts during the harvest period, by a international boycott of Canadian fish products, and by the distribution of one of the most poignant animal posters ever made: a mother seal nuzzling the skinned carcass of her pup. "Setting on" porpoises by tuna fishermen was halted in 1990 (or at least the tuna companies claimed that the practice had been stopped) due to a consumer boycott of tuna products: 1990 saw "Dolphin Safe" labels in the supermarket. The plight of the whales has been publicized by Greenpeace, whose members cast themselves adrift between whaling ships and their prey. These interest groups are skilled at manipulating the policy process, providing trigger events and using the media to increase public concern over marine mammal issues.

Federal Acquisition and Management of Wildlife Habitat

The federal government owns approximately one-third of the nation's land, but this ownership is heavily concentrated in the western states and Alaska. For wildlife to thrive, habitat must be available and protected. Wildlife habitat comes from three general areas of land management: lands expressly acquired for habitat, the multiple-use lands, and special purpose federal lands such as the National Park System and military bases.

National Wildlife Refuge System

The Migratory Bird Treaty Act originally did not provide for land for bird refuges, but in 1929 new legislation rectified the oversight. Lands acquired under the Migratory Bird Conservation Act of 1929 were originally intended to be "inviolate sanctuaries" for the birds, but amendments have allowed the Secretary of Interior to permit public hunting if compatible with other purposes. The Duck Stamp Act (Migratory Bird Hunting Stamp Act of 1934) provided funds for refuge acquisition; despite acquisition authority in other related acts, the Migratory Bird Conservation Act remains the primary source of authority for wildlife refuge acquisition.

Acquisition and management of the various wildlife areas were scattered about the country and between the numerous land management agencies. The Fish and Wildlife Service administered several different categories, and BLM occasionally shared responsibility with FWS. In 1966 the National

Wildlife Refuge System Administration Act consolidated the various units under FWS but did not provide much guidance for administration. Its major impact was to restrict the transfer, exchange, or disposal of land; to clarify the authority of the Secretary of Interior to accept monetary donations for land acquisition; and to authorize the secretary to permit hunting if hunting was compatible with other uses. Clearly the mandate behind the national wildlife refuges was to manage them as "dominant use" lands rather than as "single use" lands.[52] The system currently encompasses 90 million acres of lands and waters and is administered by the Fish and Wildlife Service.

Wetlands preservation is another important factor of wildlife habitat. Public perceptions about wetlands have changed dramatically since the 1860s when the Swamp Lands Acts gave federal wetlands to the states for development. Today, wetlands are usually purchased under the Migratory Bird Conservation Act with Duck Stamp Act funding. The 1961 Wetlands Act allows advance appropriations to the Migratory Bird Conservation Fund for upland habitat surrounding wetlands and for some wetlands purchase as well. Other funds are available from the Land and Water Conservation Fund, supplied primarily by receipts for offshore oil and gas leases. A third source of wetlands protection is the Water Bank Act, which allows the Secretary of Agriculture to reimburse landowners who protect their wetlands and adjacent uplands.

The federal programs alone do not adequately address the problem of wetland loss to development; state programs funded under Pittman-Robertson and private organizations are a significant factor in wetlands protection. Private organizations such as Ducks Unlimited are vital in the protection of wetlands as wildlife habitat. Ducks Unlimited manages private lands throughout the Canadian-American migratory pathways. The Nature Conservancy acquires wetlands to protect them from development, and the National Audubon Society manages bird refuges. The impact of groups such as these is not limited to their land acquisitions. Their intensive and skillful lobbying and political involvement also provide protection to the wetland habitats.

Multiple-Use Lands

The Forest Service manages 191 million acres, including half the big game and cold-water fish habitat, and habitat for sixty-four threatened or endangered species.[53] Wildlife conservation is a relatively recent addition to the Forest Service's responsibilities; the Multiple-Use Sustained-Yield Act (1960), the Forest and Rangeland Renewable Resources Planning Act (1974), and the National Forest Management Act (1976) include wildlife habitat for both game and nongame species as part of the Forest Service mission. The multiple-use mandate requires federal land management agencies to manage for recreation and wildlife habitat as well as for the specific consumptive use, such as timber harvesting.

Funding, always a problem, received some relief from the 1974 act that amended the Knutson-Vandenberg Act (1930). The original Knutson-Vandenberg Act required private purchasers of Forest Service timber to help pay for reforestation of the logged area. The amendment allowed the funds also to be used for protecting and improving fish and wildlife habitat. Although helpful, the funds have been restricted in use. Secondary impacts of logging activities are not mitigated, an issue that is particularly important in fish habitat management because of the heavy siltation that often accompanies timbering and road building. An additional criticism of the program is that funds are only generated by profitable timber sales; many sales are, on paper, financial losses to the federal government.[54]

The Bureau of Land Management (BLM) is the second agency required to protect wildlife under the multiple-use concept; like the Forest Service, its mandate comes from the Federal Land Policy and Management Act of 1976 (FLMPA). BLM manages about 60 percent of all lands under federal jurisdiction but is largely unknown in the eastern United States. Its lands are leftovers from the land disposals of the nineteenth century (discussed later in the section on federal land history). Most of the productive or economically valuable land was transferred into private hands, so the BLM holdings usually have low productivity and are not found in contiguous blocks of land. This makes BLM land decisions often controversial as they affect adjacent privately held lands as well as blocks of federal land. Technically, BLM manages habitat rather than species (although it does have responsibility for the wild horses and burros), with most management of resident species under state responsibility.

BLM policy implementation is also hampered by the condition of the land it manages. Grazing permits for BLM lands are issued to western ranchers at well below market value. The ranchers then have little incentive to improve or to maintain the public lands. As a result, typically the public grazing lands are not as well kept as the private lands, and political domination by the powerful livestock industry lobby has affected the BLM policy process. Formed in 1946 from the old Grazing Service and the General Land Office, the organizational history of the agency has earned it the nickname of "Bureau of Livestock and Mining." Efforts to reform the grazing laws and permit fees were attempted by Secretary of Interior Bruce Babbitt in the first year of the Clinton administration but foundered against entrenched conservative ranching interests.

Special Purpose Lands

The National Park Service also has a stake in wildlife. The first national park, Yellowstone, was established in 1872. Even then hunting was an issue, and in 1883 the U.S. Army was used to protect the scenery and wildlife in Yellowstone. For the next thirty-three years, the Army tried with varied success to protect the newly established parks from hunting activities. In 1916, Congress enacted the National Park Service Organic Act, which listed wildlife protection as one of the purposes of the national parks.

Until the 1950s, wildlife management in the parks lacked an ecological perspective. "Good" animals were protected, but "bad" ones like wolves and coyotes were killed. In the 1950s, an advisory board was appointed after the conservation community complained about Park Service management practices. In 1963, this group released the Leopold Report, which emphasized an ecological perspective for wildlife management.

The Wilderness Act of 1964 applied to all of the federal land management agencies. Wilderness protection is critical for habitat protection for wildlife, and this act was passed partly to overcome the reluctance of the Forest Service to designate wilderness areas in national forests. Under this act, almost 40 million acres of national parkland alone have been designated as wilderness, and the Park Service has recommended designation of another 25 million acres. The Land and Water Conservation Act, also passed in 1964, provided much needed money to purchase additional parkland.

Military lands were incorporated into wildlife concerns through the Sikes Act Extension in 1974. Primarily aimed at the development of cooperative comprehensive plans with the Departments of Interior and Agriculture and state fish and game departments, the act provides an optional mechanism for cooperative wildlife management on military reservations. The Secretary of Defense may be brought in with the Secretary of Interior and the state agencies to "carry out a program of planning, development, maintenance, and coordination of wildlife, fish and game conservation in military reservations."[55] In 1989, the Department of Defense agreed to work with the Nature Conservancy on land management issues on military installations.

The final category of special lands are the vast holdings of the federal government on the outer continental shelf (OCS). The total area of the OCS is approximately 819.2 million acres or 36 percent of the total dry land area of the United States.[56] The Outer Continental Shelf Lands Act of 1953 asserted national control of the OCS up to 200 miles from the shore, excluding the three-mile territorial limit for the states established in the Submerged Lands Act of 1953.[57] Management is shared between BLM and the United States Geological Survey (USGS), with USGS having primary responsibility for tract-specific geologic, engineering, and economic evaluations.

The enabling legislation was amended in 1978 due to congressional dissatisfaction with Interior's administration of the 1953 Submerged Lands Act. The amendments required more flexible bidding procedures for oil and gas leases; expanded economic planning provisions; increased the role of state and local governments in planning lease sales, exploration, and development; and established a policy to favor small refiners. The 1978 amendments also created an Offshore Oil Pollution Compensation Fund, supported by a barrel tax at the point of production, to mitigate the costs of oil spills.

The OCS Lands Act establishes federal authority only over the mineral resources of the shelf and not over the fishing and navigation rights in the waters above. However, the "living resources" of the shelf may be protected.[58] The 1978 amendments required the Secretary of Interior to conduct a study "to establish information needed for the assessment and management of environmental impacts on the human, marine, and coastal environments" and to "predict impacts on the marine biota which may result from chronic low level pollution of large spills."[59] Although the OCS Lands Act does not convey authority to conserve wildlife, two related acts, the Fishery Conservation and Management Act of 1976 and the Marine Protection, Research, and Sanctuaries Act of 1972, do provide wildlife conservation authority.

Public Lands

The federal lands comprise over 700 million acres, or about one-third of the United States.[60] This statistic is misleading as most of the federal land is in the western states and Alaska. In some western states, the federal government owns over half of the state's land. Thus federal land policies have a great impact on the states, and especially the western states, as well as the national government. Federal jurisdiction over these lands is spread among several agencies (see Table 6-1).

Federal ownership of land arises from two sources. The first is Article I of the Constitution:

> [Congress shall have Power] . . . to exercise [exclusive Legislation] over all Places purchased by the Consent of the Legislature of the State in which the Same shall be, for the Erection of Forts, Magazines, Arsenals, dock-Yards, and other needful Buildings . . . (Article I, § 8, cl. 17).

The power of the federal government over land that it acquired under Article I varies, depending upon reservations placed on the land at the time the land was ceded to the national government or on subsequent changes by Congress.

Table 6-1: Public Lands of the United States

Land	Major Enabling Legislation	Management Agencies
Parks	National Park Service Organic Act	National Park Service (Interior)
Grasslands, grazing, other public lands	[Taylor Grazing Act]; Federal Land Policy and Management Act	Bureau of Land Management (Interior)
Forests	Forest and Rangeland Renewable Resources Planning Act; Multiple-Use Sustained-Yield Act; National Forest Management Act	National Forest Service (Agriculture)
Preservation lands	Wilderness Act; Wild and Scenic Rivers Act; Alaska National Interest Lands Conservation Act	National Forest Service, Bureau of Land Management, National Park Service
Outer continental shelf	Outer Continental Shelf Act	Bureau of Land Management
Wildlife refuges	National Wildlife Refuge System Administration Act	Fish and Wildlife Service (Interior)

The second source of authority over lands is Article IV:

> The Congress shall have Power to dispose of and make all needful Rules and Regulations respecting the Territory or other Property belonging to the United States; and nothing in this Constitution shall be so construed as to Prejudice any Claims of the United States, or of any particular State (Article IV, § 3, cl. 2).

Federal power over these lands is virtually absolute. At one time the states were thought to exercise police power over federal land within their jurisdictions just as they do over any other property owners, but the law is currently interpreted to mean that the federal government has sovereign power over these lands.

In this century, demands on the federal lands have increased dramatically. Increased leisure time, greater mobility, and the popularity of camping and hiking have increased public interest in all forms of outdoor activities, especially in wilderness experiences and wildlife observation. The demand for grazing permits has increased in the West, and shifts in population to the Sunbelt have created an enormous pressure on the water supply and water quality. The competition among uses and user groups is fierce. The outer continental shelf has become increasingly important for mineral production. Demands on the national forests for timber have increased to about ten billion board-feet annually, and the demand continues to rise.[61] Revenues from federal lands are also increasing, primarily as a result of the offshore oil and gas leases, although timber sales are also a significant factor. Since 1950, the income generated by the federal lands has surpassed their total expenditures.[62]

The statutes governing the federal lands are as checkered as the federal land holdings. There is no uniform or controlling statute, which leaves the agencies with a fair amount of discretion but also subject to the vagaries of congressional whims. Although the public perception is that these lands are both managed and used by the federal government, in actuality, most of the benefits from the federal lands go to private concerns through mining, grazing, recreation, and timbering. Mining and oil claims on federal land are developed by private individuals and corporations. Grazing permits are given to ranchers to expand their herds; the federal government does not run livestock on the federal grazing lands. Timber is purchased and cut by private timber companies, not the United States Forest Service. It is from "this interface between public ownership and private use of the same lands that the conflicts with federal policy arise and persist."[63]

The winning hand in these conflicts between public ownership and private use has changed many times since the colonial days. Marion Clawson, director of BLM from 1948 to 1953, divides the history of federal lands into six relatively distinct areas: acquisition, disposal, reservation, custodial management, intensive management, and consultation and confrontation.

Acquisition

The early phase of acquisition was from the beginning of the republic through the 1860s: the Louisiana Purchase; the acquisition of Florida, the Southwest (including the Gadsden Purchase), and the Pacific Northwest; and finally the acquisition of Alaska. While of course these acquisitions had the effect of increasing the lands held by the federal government, their primary purpose was imperialistic; the United States simply chose to purchase rather than to acquire by conquest.

Other forms of land acquisition by the federal government continued through the twentieth century. Under the Weeks Act of 1911, the national forests have been increased by purchases of private lands, and since 1961 the federal government has been purchasing land for national parks. There has been less opposition to these purchases than one might expect because the private sector usually continues to have access to the benefits of the resources.

Disposal

Following the acquisition of large chunks of land, the federal government was eager to begin development on those lands. This necessitated subsidizing railroads to build railways to encourage homesteaders and ranchers to settle on the land. The government also removed Native Americans from the most profitable land, despite legal and moral arguments against such activities. Some land was given to war veterans, and some was auctioned. Some was simply given away to homesteaders who would promise to live on the land and to improve it; eventually, more than a quarter of the public domain was distributed under the Homestead Act of 1862 and later laws such as the Timber Culture Act of 1873, the Desert Land Sales Act of 1877, the Timber and Stone Act of 1878, and the Stock-Raising Homestead Act of 1916. The period of American history from the early nineteenth century until the New Deal, in which land disposal took place, was tumultuous and the "process of land disposal was a lusty affair—a headlong, even precipitous process, full of frauds and deceits, but one which transformed a great deal of land into valuable private property—and one which built a nation."[64]

Reservation

The Progressive Movement, and an increasing demand by the public for conservation measures at the turn of the century, led to an interest in permanent reservation of part of the federal lands. The first large, systematic reservation was the national forest reserves created in 1891 by the Forest Reserve Act.[65] By 1897, nearly forty million acres had been withdrawn for inclusion in the forest reserves. The authority of the president to make these reservations was finally established by the Supreme Court, when it ruled in *United States* v. *Midwest Oil Company* (1915) that "Congress, by failing to challenge a host of 19th century executive withdrawals, had in effect acquiesced to earlier presidents' claims that they held broad implied powers to withdraw public lands from disposal."[66] This presidential power was limited in the Federal Land Policy and Management Act (FLPMA) of 1976, which requires congressional review of proposed withdrawals and imposes other restrictions on the implied executive powers of withdrawal. Other reservations were established by the 1934 Taylor Grazing Act, which placed regulation of grazing on federal lands under the control of the Department of Interior; the department's Division of Grazing joined in 1946 with the General Land Office to become the Bureau of Land Management.

Custodial and Intensive Management

Custodial management has been a characteristic of federal land management from the very beginning of the reservation period. During this period, fed-

eral land management focused on maintaining resources and allowing access
for development, but active management was not a priority. It continues to
reflect the earliest conservationist ideals of Gifford Pinchot, the first head of
the Forestry Service, and his contemporaries. Pinchot wrote in 1910:

> The first great fact about conservation is that it stands for development
> . . . and for the prevention of waste. . . .The natural resources must be de-
> veloped and preserved for the benefit of the many, and not merely for the
> profit of a few.[67]

Dissatisfied with the management competencies in the Department of Interior, Pinchot took his Division of Forestry to the Department of Agriculture, where it has continued to protect timber resources for private industry. The Forest Service emphasized its relationships with lumber concerns,
but it also encouraged recreational opportunities on forest lands.

When the National Park Service was established in 1916, it found itself in
competition with the Forest Service, which was convinced that it was the
logical guardian of the nation's parks. The Park Service responded by stressing its preservationist attitude (in contrast to the Forest Service's conserva-
tionist-utilitarian perspective) and by expanding the parks with Forest Service land as much as possible. During the New Deal, the Park Service
benefitted from the support of Roosevelt's close friend and adviser, Harold
Ickes, who served as Secretary of Interior. Ickes convinced Roosevelt to give
a large portion of the Civilian Conservation Corps to Park Service management. Finally, in 1936, the Park Service won recognition of its recreational
role with the passage of the Park, Parkway and Recreation Act. This act gave
primary responsibility to the Park Service for federal recreation activities on
all federal lands not controlled by the Department of Agriculture. It also
identified the Park Service as the agency responsible for delivering federal
aid for recreation projects to state governments.[68]

From about 1950 to 1960, the Park Service, Forest Service, and other land
management agencies actively encouraged development and use of federal
lands. Intensive management came to the Park Service in 1951 with the appointment of Conrad Wirth as director. He implemented Mission 66, a plan
to upgrade the park facilities and to encourage increased use of the parks.
More than two thousand miles of road were built or upgraded during this
period.[69] New and ambitious visitor centers were established in many parks
and Mission 66 was a success.

The Forest Service was also experiencing good times. Forest sale revenues
increased, and in most years the service showed a profit. During the 1950s,
the Forest Service surplus was over $20 million.[70] Oil and gas leasing, min-
ing, recreation, and grazing all also increased during this period, and in general the national forests experienced an economic boom. The land and its

federal managers experienced increased pressures that in turn led inex-
orably to clashes with interest groups in the 1960s.

Consultation and Confrontation

To some extent, all of the previous phases of public land management continued from 1960 on. However, for reasons outlined in chapter 2, the public
was no longer willing to allow federal agencies to manage resources without
direct public input. Concerns with environmental quality were bound up in
land management issues. Energy mining issues and air quality are interre-
lated, and the preservation of the ocean ecosystems is imperiled by drilling
on the outer continental shelf. Water supplies and watershed management
became connected with safe disposal of hazardous and toxic wastes. All of
these issues increased awareness of the impact of federal land management
policies for both environmentalists and commodity producers.

In 1960 Congress passed the Multiple-Use Sustained Yield Act that provided a legislative foundation for the institutional policies already in place
in the Forest Service. Multiple use is an ambiguous concept that is not clarified in the legislative definitions. This is both a problem and an asset to the
agencies required to manage under its instructions. It is a problem when
uses conflict, as when critical habitat is also prime recreational or mining or
timbering terrain. It is also an asset because, by leaving the term ambiguous, managers have discretion and hence flexibility.

The 1964 Wilderness Act, like the Multiple-Use Sustained Yield Act, was
the result of controversy and compromise. It gave protection to wilderness
areas within the national forests, protecting these areas from Forest Service
redesignation. Lands managed by BLM were also considered for wilderness
designation. Some extractive uses, such as coal mining, were allowed
through the eighties, and charges that the Department of Interior under
James Watt was deliberately building roads to exclude undeveloped land
from wilderness consideration led to dramatic confrontations between environmental groups and Reagan's administration.[71]

Several acts, such as the Forest and Rangeland Renewable Resource Planning Act of 1974 (RPA) and its successor, the National Forest Management
Act of 1976, mandated long-range planning by the management agencies.
The Forest and Rangeland Renewable Resource Planning Act requires that
all renewable resources be assessed every ten years and that a national forest plan be submitted every five years. The Federal Land Policy and Management Act of 1976 (FLPMA) is also a planning act that increased the discretionary powers of BLM. It contains a multiple-use provision, includes
BLM lands in wilderness consideration, and increases the requirements for
public participation that were so characteristic of the legislation of the
seventies.

The trend in federal land legislation was to turn away from agency initiatives and toward congressional initiatives, largely in response to the demands of special interest groups. Even the venerable Park Service was not immune from congressional assertions of power. Congress began to increase its power over the agency during the Nixon years, when the formerly cordial relations between the Park Service and the Congress deteriorated. As other forms of environmental benefits (such as new dams) for constituents decreased, Congressmen increasingly found the national parks to be a vehicle for distributing goodies back home. One critic said:

> The Park Service has become a servant of Congress in the worst sense. It has become Congress' flunky in carrying out its pork barrel chores while it is supposed to be the guardian of the national interest. Unfortunately the Service doesn't have the power to uphold that interest.[72]

During the eighties, public attention shifted to concerns about environmental quality, but the public lands, with their well-established "iron triangles," held their own in the policy process in Washington. Between 1970 and 1980, the number of acres included in the national parks increased by 169 percent. Over one hundred rivers were designated as wild and scenic, and another 10,000 miles were proposed for consideration. The National Wilderness Preservation System added significant amounts of land, primarily in Alaska. Wetlands were not such a success story; over 300,000 acres per year fell to the developers.[73] As of 1995, about one-half of the wetlands in the contiguous states had been eliminated.[74]

The following case study explores the problems faced by the state of Florida and residents of Glades County, Florida, when a local business tried to close access to Fisheating Creek, a river that the residents used for fishing and other forms of recreation. The business claimed it owned the river and the riverbed; the state of Florida disagreed.

Case Study: Fisheating Creek

We have an old joke in the South: Never wrestle with a pig; you get dirty, and the pig enjoys it. The residents of Glades County, Florida, and the state of Florida have been engaged in some serious pig wrestling since 1989.[75]

Fisheating Creek is an undeveloped, nontidal, freshwater waterway that runs fifty-two miles through Glades County in south-central Florida west of Lake Okeechobee. The Lykes family owns 277,000 acres in Glades County, including all the land bordering Fisheating Creek on *both* sides,[76] which perhaps explains why they feel so strongly that the creek is family property. The Lykes family are the sole owners of Lykes Brothers, a conglomerate of businesses extending to real estate, banking, ranching, meat processing, and politics; they own Floridagold orange juice, a shipping fleet, and Peoples Gas (the largest natural gas utility in Florida).[77]

Fisheating Creek has been an important part of the life of Glades County for almost two centuries. The county residents fish and canoe the creek, hunt along its banks, and even are baptized in its brown water. During the Great Depression, many residents survived on food caught from the creek. It is "the center of the county in all things."[78] For many years, Lykes Brothers allowed free access by canoeists, fishermen, and trappers, but in December of 1988, claiming damage from poachers, rustlers, drug dealers, and vandals, Lykes Brothers posted the property. The next month, Lykes Brothers felled about forty cypress trees across Fisheating Creek to block boat access to the creek.

Irate citizens mobilized the community and alerted the media, expanding what had been a local issue to a wider public already concerned about protecting Florida's waterways. The state was already engaged in other legal disputes that sought to clarify ownership of state waterways. In 1980, Florida was involved in a complicated suit to quiet title to land under the Peace River, which Mobile Oil Corporation planned to mine for phosphate.[79] In 1990, the state, joined by the Florida Audubon Society, successfully sued the state Board of Professional Land Surveyors to invalidate proposed rules that changed the way in which the ordinary high water line was measured. This change would have lowered the line that separates privately owned property and state sovereignty lands. At the same time, a bill in the Florida legislature proposed reassessing the navigability of "every disputed waterway in the state—affecting three million acres of shoreline and stream bed" and converting any non-navigable waterway from state sovereignty land to land that could be sold into private hands.[80]

Prior to a public hearing on the closure of Fisheating Creek in May of 1989, Lykes Brothers removed the cut cypress trees, but any goodwill this generated was dispelled when employees videotaped the meeting, then checked the criminal records of citizens who were especially vocal in opposition. Later that summer, the Lykes family invited Tom Gardner, director of the state Department of Natural Resources (DNR), to the ranch for the weekend. South-central Florida was in the midst of a drought, and after he was driven down the creek bed in a four-wheel-drive truck, Gardner decided his department would not provide litigation funding for the Attorney General for Fisheating Creek. After Gardner's announcement, Lykes Brothers placed three gates across the creek.

State Attorney General Bob Butterworth decided to continue without DNR funding. He saw the controversy over Fisheating Creek as both challenge and opportunity:

> Losing the creek case, [said State] Attorney General Bob Butterworth,
> would cripple the state's ability to defend its other waterways from other
> corporate claimants. "Fisheating Creek is no more a local problem," he
> [said], " than Ted Bundy was a local problem."[81]

In 1989, the state sued Lykes Brothers in federal district court under the
Rivers and Harbors Act to force the corporation to remove all the felled trees
and the gates.[82] Because the Rivers and Harbors Act gives exclusive authority to the United States Corps of Engineers to determine navigability, the district court dismissed the case for lack of jurisdiction. After some initial skir-
mishing, the Corps prepared a navigability report, announcing in February
1990 that Fisheating Creek was navigable from Venus, Florida, to Lake Okeechobee, a distance of approximately thirty miles.

Lykes Brothers promptly removed the barriers, applied to the Corps for a
permit under §10 of the Rivers and Harbors Act to maintain fencing and to
install two gates, and filed an appeal in the United States District Court for
the Middle District of Florida against the Corps's ruling. The state was denied permission to intervene in the case. District Judge Kovachevich ruled
that Fisheating Creek was *not* a navigable waterway of the United States.[83]
The Corps of Engineers appealed; the case was argued in the Court of Appeals (11th Cir.) on 21 September 1994. In November 1995, the Court of Appeals affirmed the district court opinion.

While all the federal litigation with the Corps of Engineers was in
progress, the state was continuing the fight in other ways. In the summer of
1993, the state and the corporation began to negotiate state purchase of
43,000 acres bordering both sides of the creek; the price was reportedly as
high as $20 million. The final contract talks broke down over the question
of public access to the entire reach of the creek. Lykes Brothers wanted to
protect their remaining land by allowing access only at designated points,
and the state supposedly insisted on complete access. The state and local
agencies were especially eager to buy and to protect the creeks as part of the
Everglades Restoration Plan.

The state was also engaging in further litigation, this time in state courts.
In September 1993, the state filed a "complaint for trespass damages and
ejectment" against Lykes Brothers in the Glades Country Circuit Court. Their
complaint asserted that "Fisheating Creek throughout all its course is navigable *under Florida common law* [emphasis added] and hence the land underlying Fisheating Creek is sovereignty submerged land . . ., held in trust
for the use and benefit of the people of the State of Florida."[84]

What has been accomplished during the seven years that Florida, the
Corps of Engineers, Lykes Brothers, and the local residents have been

wrestling over Fisheating Creek? Between forty and eighty cypress trees have been cut down, tempers have frayed, and enormous costs in time and resources have been expended on a series of complex litigations that are still unresolved.[85] No final decisions have been made about ownership of Fisheating Creek or access to it. In one sense, everyone is worse off and no one has gained, except perhaps the state has demonstrated it is serious about claiming and protecting sovereignty lands.

At first glance, this is a classic illustration of the policy process at work. Policy entrepreneurs can be found in the citizens of Glades County: "readjusters" who worked to have the injustice of the creek closing remedied. Lykes Brothers might be seen as "exploiters," taking advantage of a few lost head of cattle to trigger change; the state reacted to the events in Glades County to magnify the issue of state sovereignty lands under waterways so they could solve the larger problem of property rights.

It is, however, easy to see Lykes Brothers's point of view. They own the land on both sides of the creek. They have been considered the owners of the creek for decades; in fact, they have been paying taxes on part of the disputed area for many years and could logically argue that since the state has been taxing them, the state has *de facto* acknowledged their ownership. In addition, the original grants of land from the state were not clear: when the deeds were originally given out, landowners—and everyone else—knew which waterways were navigable. The state did a sloppy job of deeding land back and forth, and it did not always cite in the deed what waterways bordering or running through the land were navigable.[86] Lykes Brothers is also justifiably concerned over liability claims from people who might be injured while using the creek; in this day of million-dollar awards for spilling coffee, Lykes Brothers has cause to worry.[87] The behavior of Lykes Brothers does not seem unreasonable; they removed the gates when the Corps issued the navigability ruling, and they were willing to negotiate the land sale.

The federal government is moving away from its command-and-control attitude toward environmental regulation, and we have the evidence of successful cooperation between government and large corporations in Great Britain, where a lawsuit is the last resort and a source of embarrassment to the government agency that must resort to the courts. Did the state have alternatives? Perhaps they were stampeded by the dramatic actions of groups like the Sierra Club, which called for a boycott of Lykes products, and the citizen who used an acetylene torch to remove the steel gates across the creek.[88] Certainly the lack of agreement between DNR and the attorney general's office is an indication of a high level of bureaucratic disfunction in Tallahassee.

We can draw several lessons from this case. First, look for alternatives that may avert litigation. Lykes Brothers acted precipitously when they felled the trees in January of 1989, but state intervention with negotiations might have saved seven years—and counting—of litigation. Second, choose your arena, or—to continue the original Southern story—if you must wrestle with the pig, be sure *you* get to pick the mud hole. It is not clear why the state chose to file first in federal court rather than state court. If, as the state has asserted in the 1993 suit filed in the Florida circuit court, the state has a common law right in the creek under *state* law, then why involve the federal courts, especially when some of the federal district judges have a reputation for favoring big business? Court decisions may reduce later options, and in disputes where both sides have plausible stories, it is unwise to be forced into a rigid position.

The state's explicit goal is to protect and to restore the state's waterways. The contested property is valuable, and the rights and wrongs of the issue are not clear. It might have been better to try the soft approach of bargaining, compromise, and negotiation before beginning a series of high profile court cases.

Suggested Reading

Bean, Michael. *The Evolution of National Wildlife Law* (revised and expanded edition). New York: Praeger, 1983. A *tour de force* that is essential for understanding issues of wildlife and how they relate to other environmental issues.

Clawson, Marion *The Federal Lands Revisited*. Baltimore: Johns Hopkins University Press for Resources for the Future, 1983. Focused on the Forest Service and BLM lands, this book provides an historical as well as contemporary (1983) look at federal lands.

Foresta, Ronald. *America's National Parks and Their Keepers*. Baltimore: Johns Hopkins University Press for Resources for the Future, 1984. A good companion for Clawson's book on the Forest Service and BLM.

Leopold, Aldo. *Game Management*. Madison: University of Wisconsin Press, 1986. This is a reprint of Leopold's classic 1933 work. A great deal of the book is technical information for game managers, but the chapters on the history of ideas in game management, economics, and policy and administration are masterpieces that are well worth reading today.

National Audubon Society. *Audubon Wildlife Report* (annual since 1985). New York: National Audubon Society. If you can only get one of these, get the 1985 edition since it gives the most thorough background for each area. Subsequent editions provide updates on the major wildlife issues. An especially nice feature is the "Featured Agency" of each book, which gives detailed information on the selected agency.

Musgrave, Ruth, and Mary Anne Stein. *State Wildlife Laws Handbook*. Rockville, MD: Government Institutes, Inc., 1993. This is the only comprehensive, relatively current book on state wildlife. It provides an overview of state wildlife laws, an essay on wildlife poaching, and a summary of laws in each state. This is primarily a research tool, but it is an essential one. It is best used in conjunction with a directory such as the annual *Conservation Directory* published by the National Wildlife Federation

Frederick, Kenneth, and Roger Sedjo, eds. *America's Renewable Resources: Historical Trends and Current Challenges*. Washington, DC: Resources for the Future, 1991. An excellent resource for historical background for water, forest, rangeland, cropland, and wildlife resources.

Tobin, Richard. *The Expendable Future: U.S. Politics and the Protection of Biological Diversity*. Durham, NC: Duke University Press, 1990. Thorough, well-documented, and readable discussion of the development of state and federal policies on endangered species and the politics of biodiversity protection.

Notes

1. Unless otherwise noted, this discussion is drawn from Michael J. Bean, *The Evolution of National Wildlife Law* (New York: Praeger, 1983).

2. *Smith* v. *Maryland*, 59 U.S. 71 at 75.

3. *Manchester* v. *Massachusetts*, 139 U.S. 240 (1891).

4. The law specifically prohibited the dumping of nonliquid refuse; this law was never seriously enforced. Stephen Fox, *The American Conservation Movement: John Muir and His Legacy* (Madison: University of Wisconsin Press, 1981), p. 300.

5. *United States* v. *Shauver*, 214 F.154 (E.D. Ark. 1914), *appeal dismissed*, 248 U.S. 594 (1919); *United States* v. *McCullagh*, 221 F. 288 (D. Kansas, 1915).

6. *Douglas* v. *Seacoast Products*, 431 U.S. 265 at 284.

7. *Tangier Sound Watermen's Association* v. *Douglas*, 541 F.Supp. 1287 at 1294.

8. Arthur McEvoy, *The Fisherman's Problem: Ecology and Law in California Fisheries, 1850–1980* (Cambridge: Cambridge University Press, 1986), pp. 117–118.

9. Thomas A. Lund, *American Wildlife Law* (Berkeley: University of California Press, 1980), p. 6.

10. However, the courts have continued to support federal authority over wildlife: for example, federally owned lands within state borders are not subject to state regulation (*Hunt* v. *United States*, 1928), the federal government may kill animals on national land without state permits (*New Mexico State Game Commission* v. *Udall*, 1969), and the interstate commerce clause gives Congress the power to protect wildlife in navigable waters when affected by dredge and fill operations conducted on *privately owned* riparian land (*Zabel* v. *Tabb*, 1970).

11. For the full story of the movement toward Pittman-Robertson, see *Restoring America's Wildlife 1937–1987: The First 50 Years of the Federal Aid in Wildlife Restoration (Pittman-Robertson) Act* (Washington, DC: USGPO [Department of Interior, United States Fish and Wildlife Service], 1987).

12. Statistical Summary for Fish and Wildlife Restoration, Fiscal Year 1994 (booklet), (Washington, DC: USGPO [United States Department of Interior Fish and Wildlife Service, Division of Federal Aid, 1994], Table II.

13. " . . . no money apportioned under this chapter to any State shall be expended therein until its legislature . . . shall have . . . passed laws for the conservation of wildlife which shall include a prohibition against the diversion of license fees paid by hunters for any other purpose than the administration of said State fish and game department." 16 U.S.C. §669e

14. Lonnie Williamson, "Evolution of a Landmark Law," in *Restoring America's Wildlife 1937–1987: The First 50 Years of the Federal Aid in Wildlife Restoration (Pittman-Robertson) Act* (Washington, DC: USGPO [United States Department of Interior Fish and Wildlife Service], 1987), p. 11.

15. Dian Olson Belanger, *Managing American Wildlife: A History of the International Association of Fish and Wildlife Agencies* (Amherst: University of Massachusetts Press, 1988), pp. 50–51.

16. Lonnie Williamson, "Evolution of a Landmark Law," in *Restoring America's Wildlife 1937–1987: The First 50 Years of the Federal Aid in Wildlife Restoration (Pittman-Robertson) Act* (Washington, DC: USGPO [United States Department of Interior Fish and Wildlife Service], 1987), p. 14.

17. Winston Harrington, "Wildlife: Severe Decline and Partial Recovery," in *America's Renewable Resources: Historical Trends and Current Challenges*. Edited by Kenneth Frederick and Roger Sedjo (Washington, DC: Resources for the Future, 1991), pp. 205–246.

18. Lonnie Williamson, "Evolution of a Landmark Law," in *Restoring America's Wildlife 1937–1987: The First 50 Years of the Federal Aid in Wildlife Restoration (Pittman-Robertson) Act* (Washington, DC: USGPO [United States Department of Interior Fish and Wildlife Service], 1987), p. 14.

19. While this material is drawn from a number of sources, it relies primarily on William Chandler, "Federal Grants for State Wildlife Conservation," in *Audubon Wildlife Report 1986*. Edited by Roger Di Silvestro (New York: National Audubon Society, 1986), pp. 177–212, and Belanger (1988).

Pittman-Robertson funds are allocated to the states and to the Commonwealth of Puerto Rico, Guam, American Samoa, Northern Mariana Islands, and the Virgin Islands. Dingell-Johnson funds are also available to the states, Puerto Rico, the Virgin Islands, Guam, American Samoa, Northern Mariana Islands, and the District of Columbia. The focus of this paper is the state-federal relationship, but when discussing administration of Pittman-Robertson, the term "states" is used to refer to all recipients of funds, although there are some administrative differences between the states and territories.

20. Some question arose in the late 1950s over the second allocation formula: how was the term "paid license holder" to be interpreted? Initially the federal government interpreted this as the total number of licenses sold, but some states disaggregated their licenses (separate licenses for bow hunting and muzzle loaders, or for deer and quail) to increase their share. Eventually the position of the Department of

Interior prevailed: an individual license holder was only counted once regardless of how many licenses he held. (*Udall* v. *Wisconsin*, 306 F. 2d 790 [D.C. Circuit 1962] *cert. denied*, 371 U.S. 969 [1963])

21. For example, in 1920, the wood duck was nearing extinction; today it is the most common breeding waterfowl on the American East Coast. Pronghorn antelope increased from 25,000 or fewer in 1920 to over 750,000 today. "Restoring America's Wildlife" (brochure), (Washington, DC: USGPO [United States Department of Interior Fish and Wildlife Service], June 1992), pp. 8–9.

22. Statistical Summary for Fish and Wildlife Restoration, Fiscal Year 1994 (booklet), (Washington, DC: USGPO [United States Department of Interior Fish and Wildlife Service, Division of Federal Aid, 1994], Tables I-a and V.

23. Unless otherwise noted, this material is from William Chandler, "Federal Grants for State Wildlife Conservation" in *Audubon Wildlife Report 1986*. Edited by Roger L. Di Silvestro (New York: National Audubon Society, 1986), pp. 177–212.

24. Statistical Summary for Fish and Wildlife Restoration, Fiscal Year 1994 (booklet), (Washington, DC: USGPO [United States Department of Interior Fish and Wildlife Service, Division of Federal Aid, 1994], Tables I-b and V.

25. Whit Fosburg, "Wildlife and the U.S. Forest Service," in *Audubon Wildlife Report 1985*. Edited by Roger Di Silvestro (New York: National Audubon Society, 1987), pp. 307–341. The budget for this program is not large: in 1980, it was 3.5 percent of the Forest Service budget, but by 1985 it had declined to 2.6 percent. (Calculated from data in *Audubon Wildlife Report 1985*. Edited by Roger Di Silvestro [New York: National Audubon Society, 1985], Appendix M). In contrast, in 1987, 16 percent of the FWS budget was spent on Pittman-Robertson projects with a total of 37 percent ($25 million) for all the FWS federal grants-in-aid to the states. Katherine Barton, "Federal Fish and Wildlife Agency Budgets," in *Audubon Wildlife Report 1987*. Edited by Roger Di Silvestro (New York: National Audubon Society, 1987), pp. 321–354.

26. Katherine Barton, "Federal Fish and Wildlife Agency Budgets," in *Audubon Wildlife Report 1987*. Edited by Roger Di Silvestro (New York: National Audubon Society, 1987), pp. 321–354 .

27. This follows the outline used by Michael Bean, *The Evolution of National Wildlife Law* (New York: Praeger, 1983).

28. The preceding discussion is drawn from National Audubon Society, *Audubon Wildlife Report 1985* (New York: National Audubon Society, 1985) and the 1986 and 1987 reports.

29. National Audubon Society, 1986, p. 15.

30. Telephone interview with Robert Bainbridge, Wild Horse and Burro Advisor to the Director, Bureau of Land Management, 8 August 1995.

31. The animals stay in BLM custody for about three months. Of these about one-third are under three years old, and after medical care and vaccination, they are moved directly to the adoption program. The middle third, three to ten years old, are sent to the horse-breaking programs at western prison facilities (California, Col-

orado, New Mexico, and Wyoming) for training and subsequent adoption. The rest are too old for training and adoption and are placed in permanent retirement. Unlike the adopted animals, horses and burros in "retirement" remain federal property. Current BLM policy is to remove only young, adoptable animals and to return the rest to the range. BLM is developing fertility management programs for the herds, testing a contraceptive shot for mares that prevents pregnancies for two to three years. Robert Bainbridge, telephone interview, 8 August 1995.

32. Bean, p. 105.

33. Bean, p. 108.

34. In 1995, seventeen people in North Carolina pleaded guilty to violating the Act by bringing foxes into the state from Montana, Wyoming, North Dakota, Texas, and Indiana. One trader said, "I didn't know nothing until they raided my home. . . . I was just shocked. They kept talking about the Lacey Act, and I thought, `What is the Lacey Act?'" The foxes were destined for enclosed "fox pens" where they are hunted by hounds. The letters to local newspapers were unanimous in their defense of this sport; an attorney defending one of the pen operators said "It's just good old boys sitting around some fire and carrying on a harmless activity." Jeri Rowe, "Traders Don't Outfox Wildlife Officials," *Greensboro News and Record*, 22 May 1995, B1.

35. Bean, p. 321.

36. Unless otherwise noted, this material is from Ray Vaughn, *Endangered Species Act Handbook* (Rockville, MD: Government Institutes, Inc., 1994).

37. 16 U.S.C. § 1536(e).

38. Led by Tennessee Senator Howard Baker, in September 1979 Congress exempted the Tellico project from the Endangered Species Act (93 Stat. 437, 449–450 [1979]). George Cameron Coggins, Charles Wilkinson, and John Leshy, *Federal Public Land and Resources Law* 3rd ed. (Westbury, NY: Foundation Press, 1993), pp. 805–806.

39. Ray Vaughn, *Endangered Species Act Handbook* (Rockville, MD: Government Institutes, Inc., 1994), p. 15.

40. J. B. Ruhl, "Section 4 of the ESA—The Cornerstone of Species Protection Law," *Natural Resources & Environment* 8(1)Summer 1993: 27.

41. Edward Wolf, "Avoiding a Mass Extinction of Species," in *State of the World 1988*. Lester Brown (Project Director) et al. (New York: Norton, 1988), pp. 103–104.

42. William Mansfield, quoted in "Species Dying Daily, Conservation Group Warns Toxic World," *New York Times* International Edition, 29 November 1990, A9.

43. *Northern Spotted Owl* v. *Hodel*, 716 F. Supp. 479 (W.D. Washington, 1988).

44. Quoted in Norman Vig and Michael Kraft, "Conclusion: The New Environmental Agenda," in *Environmental Policy in the 1990s* 2nd ed. Edited by Norman Vig and Michael Kraft (Washington, DC: Congressional Quarterly Press, 1995), pp. 369–392.

45. Bean, pp. 281–182 (notes omitted).

46. Bean, pp. 282–283 (notes omitted).

47. "This split is a result of Executive Reorganization Plan No. 4 of 1970, which established the National Oceanic and Atmospheric Administration (NOAA) within the Commerce Department and transferred to it most of the functions vested in Interior's Bureau of Commercial Fisheries, including management responsibility for oceanic marine mammals. Marine mammals considered land-oriented remained with Interior's Bureau of Sport Fisheries and Wildlife, which later was renamed the U.S. Fish and Wildlife Service (FWS)." Michael Weber, "Marine Mammal Protection," in *Audubon Wildlife Report 1985*. Edited by Roger Di Silvestro (New York: National Audubon Society, 1985), pp. 189–190.

48. Bean, p. 285.

49. 16 U.S.C. §1371(a)(3)(A)(1976), quoted in Bean, p. 296.

50. Bean, p. 297.

51. National Audubon Society, 1985, p. 187.

52. Bean, p. 125.

53. National Audubon Society, 1985, p. 307.

54. National Audubon Society, 1985, p. 311.

55. 16 U.S.C. §670(a) (1976), quoted by Bean, p. 176.

56. Walter J. Mead, Asbjorn Moseidjord, Dennis Muraoka, and Philip Sorensen, *Offshore Lands: Oil and Gas Leasing and Conservation on the Outer Continental Shelf* (San Francisco: Pacific Institute for Public Policy Research, 1985), p. 7.

57. Texas and the west coast of Florida give state control for three marine leagues or 10.4 miles. These states are entitled to the wider boundary because they held those lands at the time of their admission as states.

58. Bean, p. 177.

59. 43 U.S.C. §1346(a)(1)(Supp. IV 1980) and §1346(a)(3), quoted in Bean, pp. 177–178.

60. Unless otherwise noted, this material is from Marion Clawson, *The Federal Lands Revisited* (Baltimore: Johns Hopkins University Press for Resources for the Future, 1983), especially Chapters 1 and 2.

61. Clawson, p. 11.

62. Clawson, p. 17.

63. Clawson, p. 4.

64. Clawson, p. 25.

65. Although Yellowstone National Park was established in 1872, Clawson (p. 28) notes that this was an isolated instance of reserving land not otherwise in demand. He quotes John Ise (*Our National Park Policy* [Baltimore: Johns Hopkins University Press for Resources for the Future, 1961], pp. 17–18):

> The establishment of Yellowstone was, of course, due partly to the efforts of few of these idealists, several of them men of influence. Reservation was possible because most private interests were not looking so far west at this early

date, for there were no railroads within hundreds of miles of Yellowstone. Lumbermen had moved into the Lake States and were too busy slashing the pine forests there to reach out for timber lands in this inaccessible region; the hunters and trappers were here, but were not an important political force; the cattlemen, who have been in recent years so powerful an influence against some conservation legislation, were not yet invading the Far West in large numbers; the water power interests that have been among the most serious threats to a few later national parks were not interested here. With Indians still a lurking danger, the `poor settlers' had not ventured into this region in great numbers and were not calling for Congressional consideration.

66. Tom Arrandale, *The Battle for Natural Resources* (Washington, DC: Congressional Quarterly Press, 1983), p. 41, citing *United States* v. *Midwest Oil Company,* 236 U.S. 459 (1915).

67. Gifford Pinchot, *The Fight for Conservation* (Garden City, NY: Harcourt, Brace, 1919), quoted in *American Environmentalism: Readings in Conservation History* 3rd ed. Robert Nash (New York: McGraw Hill, 1990), pp. 76–78.

68. Ronald A. Foresta, *America's National Parks and Their Keepers* (Baltimore: Johns Hopkins University Press, 1984), pp. 45–46 (notes omitted).

69. Foresta, p. 54.

70. Clawson, pp. 37–38.

71. See, for example, Perri Knize, "Chainsaw Environmentalism" in *Backpacker* (November 1987), pp. 55–59. The title tells it all.

72. Quoted in Foresta, p. 79.

73. Michael Kraft and Norman Vig, "Environmental Policy from the Seventies to the Nineties: Continuity and Change," in *Environmental Policy in the 1990s.* Edited by Norman Vig and Michael Kraft (Washington, DC: Congressional Quarterly Press, 1990), p. 23.

74. Walter A. Rosenbaum, *Environmental Politics and Policy* 3rd ed. (Washington, DC: Congressional Quarterly Press, 1995), p. 74. For a brief discussion of wetlands policy in the Bush and Clinton administrations, see chapter 2.

75. This case was developed by Nancy Carlson.

76. Brief for Appellant, *Lykes Bros. Inc.* v. *United States Army Corps of Engineers* (No. 93-3179, 11 Cir. 1994).

77. Michael Crook and Ran Henry, "Baloney," *Miami Herald, Tropic* (magazine), 22 April 1990, p. 18.

78. David Guest, Assistant Attorney General, State of Florida, quoted by Crook and Henry, p. 14.

79. *Mobile Oil Corp.* v. *Coastal Petroleum Co.,* 671 F. 2d 419 (1982). This was a very complex appeal from the U.S. District Court for the Northern District of Florida; the court held that the district court lacked jurisdiction and ordered the cases remanded to the state court.

80. Crook and Henry, p. 20.

81. Crook and Henry, p. 14.

82. This discussion comes from Brief for Appellant, *Lykes Bros. Inc.* v. *United States Army Corps of Engineers* (No. 93-3179, 11 Cir. 1994), pp. 6–9.

83. *Lykes Bros. Inc.* v. *United States Army Corps of Engineers,* 821 F. Supp. 1457 (M.D. Fla. 1993).

84. *Board of Trustees of the Internal Improvement Trust Fund of the State of Florida* v. *Lykes Bros. Inc.,* complaint filed 7 September 1993, Fla. Cir.Ct., 20th Cir.

85. The case presented here has been simplified somewhat. Explosive charges of corruption and conflict of interest have permeated this controversy. See Crook and Henry, pp. 8–9, 14–15, 18–20, 22.

86. David Guest, telephone interview with Nancy Carlson, 14 August 1995.

87. When Lykes Brothers operated a commercial fish camp, campground, and canoe concession on the creek, at least one liability suit was successful, although the amount ($3,800) was relatively small compared to the estimated annual profit of $90,000. Crook and Henry, p.18.

88. Crook and Henry, p. 22.

Chapter Seven

International Environmental Policy and Law

Government policymakers are moving toward a more global view of the world environment, triggered by the recognition of problems such as the depletion of atmospheric ozone, global warming, acid precipitation, and destruction of the tropical rain forests. Governments are working cooperatively: large construction projects with impacts that cross national boundaries are now assessed for their international effect. Nations notify each other when transporting toxic materials across national boundaries. Environmental treaties, conventions, and "soft-law" options—customary procedures that are not formalized through treaties or other binding documents—have proliferated.[1]

Governmental approaches to international environmental problems have also been affected by the dominance of economic considerations and economic analysis. Multinational corporations overshadow national governments in many international spheres. National sovereignty often yields to corporate interest in the world economy: never before in world history have corporate interests unconnected with the interests of some nation-state regularly determined international policies.[2] The technological revolution in communications affects government decisionmaking as well, because instant telecommunications, independent of cables and other physical connections, make global assessment of the environment possible. Such electronic information exchange is rapid and difficult to control; this provides equal access to information and a common vocabulary of events and interpretation that may overwhelm regional and national differences.

Although few issues are truly global, many issues have physical impacts that cross national boundaries. Even if a problem were geographically limited, it may have international or global ramifications, such as the changes in weather caused by volcanic eruptions. Some issues are beyond the practical range of any one national government jurisdiction, for example, mining on the deep sea bed and issues of outer space. Other issues are extremely localized but so similar in many jurisdictions that international cooperation is to the advantage of all concerned, for example, containing outbreaks of contagious disease. Finally, some issues are so interactive that international efforts are the only possible solution. For example, destruction of tropical rain forests is believed to affect global climate; this belief has led international financing for developing countries' governments to encourage rain forest protection.

The same issue characteristics described in chapter 3 that bring national issues to the attention of government agendas act upon international issues. Issues that are specific and concrete and that have an immediate impact arouse public concern and attention more readily than general or highly technical issues such as the bio-geo-chemical cycles. The decreasing ozone layer was not a public international issue until its connection to rising rates of skin cancer was suggested. Much of the control of all international policy (not just environmental) is with the developed nations, and their constituencies usually will not become involved with the concerns of developing countries until they perceive some direct impact on themselves.

Just as domestic policies must have initiators and policy entrepreneurs to get an issue on the systemic agenda and then the institutional agenda, the international environmental movement has to expand its concerns to a mass public. First, environmental issues have to become *national* issues. Sovereign nations have many issues of international importance and until there is consensus within the country that environmentalism is important, a nation will not expend its limited international resources to address the problems. Second, the nations need some assurance or expectation that international efforts toward environmental problems could achieve their policy goals. Lynton Caldwell finds this assurance in the "biosphere concept," which sees the earth as one ecosystem or biosphere, with environmental actions having consequences across the globe, and humans as the dominant altering agent.[3] Once the scientific community acknowledged the interdependence of Earth's subordinate ecosystems and the impact of human activity, constructive action was possible.

We may yearn for the simpler days of isolationism, but they are gone, if indeed they ever really existed. The environment has always been connected globally; we were just not fully aware of it. This chapter provides an introduction to international issues as they affect American environmental administration and law. The chapter begins with a discussion of the development of international organizations that have directly affected environmental policy. The second section introduces the global commons, which are resource domains that do not lie within the jurisdiction of one nation. The final section describes the specialized legal regimes that have developed to manage three of the global commons: the oceans, the atmosphere, and Antarctica.[4]

International Organizations

Progress from national agendas to the international agenda was rapid as it became clear that unilateral national actions were not enough to protect endangered species and to halt pollution. For example, Africa cannot protect its endangered species without help from the countries that provide a market for luxury furs. The industrial states cannot prevent acid rain from blowing over their borders, and—as Chernobyl taught the world—no one is safe from radiation once it gets into the atmosphere. Prognosticators foretold worldwide disaster on the horizon.

The United Nations

The United Nations began to respond to these concerns in the mid-sixties. Environmentalism had become a salient issue not just in the United States but also across the globe, especially in other industrialized democracies such as Canada, France, Japan, Sweden, West Germany, and the United Kingdom. These countries had writers like Rachel Carson to expose the dangers of pollution: Jean Dorst in France wrote *Before Nature Dies* (1965), and in Sweden, Rolf Edberg wrote *On the Shred of a Cloud* (1971).[5] The *Torrey Canyon* disaster in 1967 brought home to western Europe the dangers that could result from ignoring the environment.

In 1966, the General Conference of the United Nations Educational, Scientific, and Cultural Organization (UNESCO) adopted a resolution that the *biosphere* was a social concern as well as a geophysical one. At the 1968 Biosphere Conference in Paris, the members declared that environmental concerns, especially issues regarding air, soil, and water pollution in industrialized countries, were becoming critical and that short-term solutions were no longer satisfactory. They also asserted the importance of the social sciences as partners with science and technology to fashion remedies.

In 1969, the secretary-general of the United Nations gave his state of the environment report. He announced that Stockholm would be the site for an international conference on the environment in 1972. For two years the

Preparatory Committee and subcommittees met, and in 1971 they set the final agenda for the conference. The preliminary meetings had produced some consensus on the issues, and when the delegates assembled in Stockholm, they had an agenda designed to promote achievements rather than simply discussion.

Biosphere protection and social and economic development were the two foci of the conference, and the achievements of the Stockholm Conference in these two areas were substantial. First, the United Nations Environmental Programme (UNEP) was established in the Secretariat to provide an integrated mechanism to coordinate worldwide environmental concerns. Second, the delegates achieved general consensus on four major documents: the Declaration on the Human Environment, the Declaration of Principles, 109 Recommendations for Action, and—perhaps most critical of all—a Resolution of Institutional and Financial Arrangements. Of course, all the participants did not accede to all the proposals. France vowed to continue to test nuclear weapons, Japan decided to continue whaling, and the United States refused to commit funds for environmental protection in developing countries. By most accounts, however, Stockholm was a success:

> It avoided foundering on antagonisms born of Third World resentment over First World "injustice." The price of this avoidance was incorporation of environmental protection into the Third World's development priorities. Yet this First World concession introduced a new environmental element into the conventional interpretation of development. The development concept was thus enlarged, and delegates were exposed to evidence that many social and economic problems had environmental connections.[6]

That same year, the United Nations General Assembly adopted the report of the Stockholm Conference. The site of UNEP was moved from Geneva to Nairobi as a concession to the developing nations. By 1974, UNEP was attempting to implement the Stockholm resolutions. UNEP has become the accepted international forum for examining environmental problems, and the existence of a developing country majority in its membership has continued to allay the suspicions of the developing nations. The primary accomplishment has been the promotion of treaties; for example, UNEP helped forge the Convention on International Trade in Endangered Species (CITES) in 1973.

Twenty years passed before another international environmental conference was convened. In the interim, international perspectives on the environment changed significantly. The ecological crisis worsened; scientific knowledge about the environment and its interrelationships increased; the role of poverty as a cause of environmental degradation, especially in developing countries, became clearer; and new formal institutions such as UNEP and the European Community (EC, now the European Union [EU]) became prominent actors in the international arena.[7]

In 1987, the European Community passed the Single European Act.[8] Article 130R is the environmental title of this act; its policy targets are environmental quality, public health, and prudent use of natural resources, with a caveat that actions taken under this section may not interfere with energy resource policies of the member states.[9] The act created the commission that coordinates environmental data from the member states and represents the European Community in negotiations with nonmember states.[10]

Enforcement of environmental policy within the community is a problem. Member states often agree on policy, but there are no formal procedures to ensure that member states carry out the policy correctly, or at all. No sanctions are brought against noncomplying states; legal action can only be brought by other member states.[11]

In June 1992, the United Nations Conference on Environment and Development (UNCED, or the Earth Summit, or the Rio Conference) convened in Rio de Janeiro. It was the largest international conference ever held, with representatives from 179 nations. The nongovernmental organizations (NGOs) held a parallel conference; representatives of more than 2,500 interest groups attended the Global Forum. George Bush was conspicuous by his absence; he refused to attend until he was sure the Climate Change Convention would not impose binding targets on carbon dioxide emissions.[12]

Even without Bush, the American presence was disruptive:

> U.S. opposition to targets and deadlines for limiting emissions of greenhouse gases continued to exasperate leaders from other industrialized countries. . . . But in the end they yielded to the U.S. position in order to secure its signing of the Climate Change Convention. To those who argued that the United States should reduce its consumption of fossil fuels and other natural resources, the Bush administration refused to compromise.[13]

The goals of the conference were ambitious, but "even before the conference opened, the range and complexity of the economic and social problems in achieving these goals proved virtually insurmountable."[14] A major stumbling block was the fight between the developed nations of the North and the less-developed southern countries. The divisions between North and South revolved around financing for environmental initiatives. The developing nations made their position clear: they are unwilling to support environmental controls unless the developed countries provide funding and technology transfers.[15] The Global Environment Facility (GEF), set up by the World Bank, is a first step toward financing the policies set at Rio.

Five major documents resulted from the Rio Conference: Agenda 21, a lengthy document that spelled out comprehensive goals and objectives for the world environment at an estimated annual cost of $125 billion;[16] a nonbinding statement of twenty-seven principles in the Rio Declaration on Environment and Development; the Climate Change Convention; the Biodiversity Convention; and a statement on forest principles. The most significant institutional outcome was the creation of the United Nations Commission on Sustainable Development, whose main purpose is to provide a venue for further discussions on biodiversity.

The Rio Conference has had little impact on American national policy. The nonbinding agreement on climate change has not been honored; the only significant American legislation to address the problems of greenhouse gas emissions is the Clean Air Act Amendments of 1990.[17] Bush refused to sign the Biodiversity Convention, and although Clinton signed the treaty, the Senate has failed to ratify it.

Nongovernmental Organizations

Nongovernmental organizations (NGOs) often have more influence in the design and implementation of international resource regimes than they do in smaller scale resource regimes, particularly when the territorial sovereignty of the affected nations is not threatened.[18] For example, the International Union for the Conservation of Nature and Natural Resources (IUCN) is the "best example of the intermeshing of governmental and nongovernmental organizations concerned with environmental problems."[19] The IUCN is drafting the guidelines for implementation of the Biodiversity Convention. This and other collective organizations (such as the World Wildlife Fund [WWF]) "are now the principal mechanisms for the initiation and formulation of proposals for international environmental efforts."[20]

Often environmental policy networks have large popular bases that cut across national boundaries, and NGOs now have a significant role in the initiation of international environmental programs. For example, the 1992 Global Forum held in conjunction with UNCED generated thirty-three alternate treaties covering a wide array of topics, such as forestry, biodiversity, and climate change.[21]

The scientific community has also had an important role in the formation and legitimation of international regimes. Certainly the Antarctic regime was a child of the scientists; their insistence on the research focus of the regime and the exclusion of military concerns has helped maintain the stability of the regime. Of course, the scientific community has its own agenda in maintaining an avowedly neutral, scientific presence in the global commons regimes. Protection of research funds, government jobs, and access to policy decisions rest on refusing to take sides in political disputes. There is also a culture of political neutrality within the sciences, just as practitioners of public administration frequently claim to hold policy-neutral positions, often in the face of overwhelming evidence to the contrary.

International and Global Commons

Much of human history can be described as an effort by individuals to establish absolute control over items of value, whether land or cattle or jewels or people. The notion of commonly held property has an equally long but less flamboyant pedigree. Communal wells in arid regions, ancient irrigation systems, common pastures in medieval English villages, Shaker settlements in the New World, and neighborhood automobile parking ordinances are all examples of common pool resource regimes. These are, however, small scale; the usual human response to vast areas of valuable resources unfettered by legal rights that the dominant culture recognizes has been appropriation and exploitation as soon and as rapidly as physical force and technology permit. The global commons of the twentieth century are, in large part, an exception.

International and global commons are particular kinds of resource domains that contain common pool resources. International commons are domains shared by several nations; global commons are resource domains to which all states have access. The use of international treaties and other forms of international accommodation is the only way to address the problems raised by the commons. They present especially thorny policy and law problems because there is intense competition for the right to exploit their resources, but there is no established, enforceable law to regulate access and use.

In the past, physical access to international and global commons has been difficult; for example, Antarctica is unbearably cold, the high seas were impossible to monitor, deep outer space was beyond the reach of even our dreams. In addition, the value of the resources within each domain has not always been clear; while the Antarctic seal and whale harvests were profitable, the existence of deep-sea mineral nodules are a comparatively recent discovery, and to date there is little known economic value in deep-space exploration. The political climate has also changed, and developing countries now assert their rights to share in the resources within these global commons.

The first part of this section provides an introduction to property rights in international law. The remaining sections describe the current management regimes for oceans, the atmosphere, and Antarctica.

Property Rights and Regimes

In the American national system of environmental administration and law, property rights are defined by the Constitution and legislation, but in the international arena, rights are less clearly defined in part because there is no clear enforcement mechanism. International law cannot be defined as "the command of the sovereign backed by a sanction" because there is no sovereign, and international sanctions are applied with great reluctance. To understand the acquisition, exploitation, and conservation of resource systems in international environmental law, it is customary—and helpful—to think of property rights in economic terms.[22] The property right to a resource is not a single right but rather a bundle of rights such as the rights of access, extraction, or alienation (sale) of the captured resources; the right to transfer one's other rights to a second person; and the right of inheritance. The specific composition of each bundle of rights varies; for example, as a member of the Antarctic Treaty System, France does not have the right to conduct cold-climate military experiments in Antarctica, but the territorial rights of France in Polynesia do include the right to conduct nuclear tests.

Property rights have two aspects; they are either transferable or nontransferable, and they are either exclusive or nonexclusive.[23] Transferable rights are saleable for goods or money, or are subject to bestowal and removal for services rendered. Some equatorial nations have tried to sell their access rights to geo-stationary orbits, although the international community has not recognized these sales.[24] Nontransferable rights have been removed from individual control by the government or the community of legitimate users; these rights may be assigned to individuals but the individual may not transfer the rights to another. For example, a nation that maintains an Antarctic research presence may not sell its rights to participate in the treaty regime to another state.

Property rights may also be exclusive or nonexclusive. Exclusive rights imply that access to the resource is limited; others can be excluded from the resource. For example, grazing permits for public land are exclusive in that only a limited number of permits are issued, and access to public grazing is restricted to those holding permits. A nonexclusive right gives access to the resource to all the members of a specific pool of users rather than to individuals. For example, all members of the Antarctic Treaty have a nonexclusive right to explore the southern continent. Access to high-seas fisheries has historically been virtually unrestricted; therefore, the right to exploit these fisheries has been nonexclusive. Similarly, access to outer space is open to anyone with the technology to launch a rocket.

In international environmental law, it is important to base political or legal analysis on property rights and the legal regimes that administer them rather than simply on the physical resources. Thus the consideration of ocean fisheries must specify the resource regime: the bundle of rights in the high-seas regime includes the nonexclusive right of virtually unlimited access, while the bundle of rights in coastal fisheries allows only limited access.

Nations choose to share, or to continue to share, a resource domain for several reasons. The costs of defining and enforcing property rights (for example, the time and diplomatic costs of negotiating specific rights for each state) may be more than the individual nations are willing or able to bear. Individual nations may simply be unwilling to accept the consequences of unilateral assumption of property rights; they might be risking economic sanctions or even war. Finally, the resource itself may be difficult to divide (the atmosphere) or it may be in such large supply (the high-seas fisheries in the nineteenth century) that clearly defined property rights seem unnecessary.

Modern international commons were once global commons, but as technology and developing markets made them profitable to exploit, the legal right of access was assumed by states with the technology or the power to enforce it, and then access was denied to other nations. Outer space is the last true global commons; no national property rights have been established in this domain. As technology improves and profitable exploitation becomes feasible, outer space will probably become an international commons subject to a legal regime with exclusionary rights.

Regimes for international and global commons do not develop in a policy vacuum. Nations have many diplomatic concerns and must reconcile domestic interests as well as international ones. For example, the United States refused to sign the Law of the Sea Treaty partly to protect domestic business interests in deep-sea mining. There is also a great deal of uncertainty about the biological data on many common-pool resources. Resource domains such as outer space and the deep seabeds are often inaccessible, and their sheer magnitude prevents collection of accurate information. Relatively straightforward information on populations and breeding habits of many ocean fish, for example, is either lacking or conflicting. It is difficult to set catch limits without knowing how much harvest pressure a fishery can tolerate.

Another problem arises with risk assessment. Risk assessment involves estimating the probability that a given policy will produce harmful results; decision makers have different levels of risk they are willing to accept.[25] The disagreement over the interaction of chlorofluorocarbons and ozone depletion points up this problem; the data were clear but the scientific community could not agree on its interpretation.[26]

It would be impractical to attempt a comprehensive survey of international treaties and understandings that govern environmental concerns. However, management regimes for the global commons affect and are affected by American policies. The following sections describe the management regimes of three global commons: the oceans, the atmosphere, and Antarctica.

Oceans

The oceans regime has evolved gradually and is based on a patchwork of customs and multilateral treaties that address concerns ranging from regulating deep seabed mining to ownership of ocean waters to controlling pollution

The present law of the sea is the result of a series of international conferences. In 1958, the first United Nations Conference on the Law of the Sea (UNCLOS I) passed a series of conventions which, while technically binding only on the nations which ratified them, were in effect codifications of existing customary law. Two years later, in 1960, UNCLOS II was convened to resolve issues that had not been decided at UNCLOS I; a major issue was the size of the territorial seas—the distance from shore that a nation claims as sovereign territory.[27] Little was accomplished at UNCLOS II, although a compromise on the question of fishing zones and the limits of the territorial seas was almost reached.

After several years of preparatory meetings and negotiations, UNCLOS III began in 1973, continuing in a series of twelve sessions over nine years. The task was to design a new legal regime for the oceans. The design of the conference was flawed because it tried to reach agreement on two completely different resource domains: the sea and the deep seabed.[28] The various actors in the international arena, especially the United States and the other major industrialized nations, were watching the arrangements carefully, concerned that whatever was decided for deep seabed mining would set precedent for other global commons such as the Antarctic, outer space, the moon, and the electromagnetic and satellite orbits. Resolution of the seabed issue was almost impossible, and by linking the two, issues of the ocean regime were dragged under as well.

Deep Seabed Mining

Two major questions at this conference revolved around the issue of deep seabed mining: who would actually do the mining and how would the arrangements be financed? The financing issue was a two-part question, dealing first with how to organize the payments (such as fees, royalties, profit shares, etc.) from the miners to the international community and second, how to finance the operations of the international organization. By 1976, a "parallel" system began to emerge with two major components. First, private and state-sponsored organizations were permitted to mine the seabed. Second, the Enterprise (the mining arm of the United Nations created by the new Law of the Sea treaty) could mine for the international community; the Enterprise would have access to minerals, technology, personnel, and money. To ensure an equitable allocation of sites, states or private companies wanting to mine were to apply for two sites, and the Seabed Authority (the claims registry in the United Nations created by the Law of the Sea treaty) would grant one application but keep the second for the Enterprise. This saved the United Nations the cost of exploration, passing the costs on to the technologically developed nations.

This was a suitably balanced solution to the allocation problem, but it did not address the ever-present problems of data uncertainty (investment costs, operating costs, and world market stability). The financial problems for deep seabed mining are enormous, and the lack of information only aggravates the difficulties. Mining firms that would pay royalties to the Enterprise had to worry about extraction costs and the opportunity costs of tying up capital, which increased corporate risks; also the tax rate would be difficult to assess if the technology being taxed was in flux.

In negotiating financial arrangements, the various policy actors had different approaches to their estimations of success and of risk. The developing countries anticipated high returns from the deep seabed mining, so they were more willing to accept risk because the risk (and cost) was practically nonexistent for them. Developed countries were more conservative in their estimates of profits and, because of the high capital investment needed, were assuming a higher risk.

The United States played a major role in UNCLOS III and accepted the parallel system in 1980, but after the election of Ronald Reagan, his administration refused to accede to the arrangements.[29] This change came about for a number of reasons. First, the Americans felt that the seabed mining arrangements set dangerous precedents, especially regarding technology transfer, the Enterprise (a completely new type of international organization), and the mission of the Seabed Authority.[30] In addition, the administration saw alternatives to the treaty; for example, both the United States and Germany passed domestic legislation to govern deep seabed mining, opening the possibility of treaty arrangements outside the United Nations.

The seabed mining regime is designed to be a combination of private property regime and cooperative property regime. The private mining operations could establish leases (a substantial bundle of property rights) but at the price of technology transfer and financing the cooperative regime, contributing costly information on explorations and paying fees to the Enterprise. Now that the treaty has entered into force in November 1994, efforts to implement the seabed regime will begin. The regime will be extremely difficult to implement. While forecasting is an uncertain business, it seems unlikely that the seabed minerals regime will survive without substantial modification.

Living Resources

While preparations for UNCLOS III were under way, several treaties relating to conservation were negotiated.[31] These and the 1980 World Conservation Strategy and the 1982 World Charter for Nature set the stage for the fisheries concerns reflected in the UNCLOS III negotiations.

The issues of conservation and territorial seas are closely linked. They were finally addressed in UNCLOS III. One of the most useful accomplishments of UNCLOS III was the clarification of territorial limits: the twelve-mile limit for the territorial sea; the contiguous zone extended to twenty-four nautical miles;[32] the continental shelf to its natural margin or to two hundred nautical miles, whichever is farther; and an Exclusive Economic Zone (EEZ) not to exceed two hundred nautical miles. The EEZ is subject to the control of the littoral state and the waters are therefore no longer an open-access regime, but this has clearly not been sufficient to promote effective conservation. For example, in May 1992, the northern cod fishery off the coast of Newfoundland was closed because of fisheries depletion. Observers apportion blame generously: inshore fishers blame off-shore trawlers for indiscriminate overfishing, while the off-shore fishermen accuse the inshore fishers of cheating on quotas. Canadians blame the Europeans for taking migratory fish in international waters in violation of the Northwest Atlantic Fisheries Organisation regulations, but Canada has also contributed to the problem by subsidizing its fleet and processing plants since 1977.[33]

In July 1993, a United Nations conference on global fisheries management agreed on the problem but not the solutions. As the fisheries conference emphasized, global fisheries are in a perilous state. The fleets are overcapitalized; in 1991 *The Times* reported that a 40 percent reduction in the European Community (European Union) fleet was necessary to protect the North Sea and Baltic fisheries.[34] This figure optimistically assumes the remaining 60 percent of the fleet would not simply increase their fishing efforts to make up the difference. Efforts to reduce coastal harvests may simply displace the fleets to international waters. The costs associated with monitoring these fleets are substantial; the European Union relies on a computer system that is prohibitively expensive for developing countries to adopt.[35]

Marine Pollution

Marine pollution stems from several sources: discharges from the land and from ships, waste disposal, and oil drilling. Because the ocean currents are found throughout the water column, these pollutants are distributed across the surface of the oceans and from the surface to unmeasured depths. The immediate impact of these pollutants ranges from waste-strewn beaches that are unsafe and unsightly to fishing stocks that are reduced in population or unfit for consumption. It is clear that the ocean cannot be used as an inexhaustible sink for waste disposal or pollution.

Early efforts to contain marine pollution failed; conventions negotiated in 1926 and 1935 never entered into force. In 1954, the International Convention for the Prevention of Pollution of the Sea by Oil (London) was adopted and later amended.[36] In October 1983, the London Convention of 1954 was replaced when the International Convention for the Prevention of Pollution by Ships (MARPOL) entered into force.[37] Although many states that were party to the London Convention have not ratified MARPOL, few of these nations are heavily invested in large-scale tanker operations, so the impact on the marine environment is not substantial.[38] Over 85 percent of the world's shipping fleet have become party to MARPOL.

In the late 1960s, several major coastal spills led to the International Legal Conference on Marine Pollution (1969).[39] From this conference two treaties emerged, both ratified in 1975: the International Convention Relating to Intervention on the High Seas in Cases of Oil Pollution Casualties (Brussels),[40] and the International Convention on Civil Liability for Oil Pollution Damage (Brussels).[41] The International Fund for Compensation of Oil Pollution Damage became effective in 1978.[42] Lynton Caldwell writes that from the slow pace of ratification,

> [the] conclusion follows that although there is international recognition of the harmfulness of ocean pollution, national economic interests have remained powerful enough to handicap or delay action that would impose cost, inconvenience, or responsibility upon shipping interests.[43]

Dumping of hazardous waste at sea is also controlled by treaty. The Convention on the Prevention of Marine Pollution by Dumping of Wastes and Other Matter (London Convention of 1972)[44] and the Convention for the Prevention of Marine Pollution by Dumping from Ships and Aircraft (Oslo Convention of 1972)[45] apply to the high seas and the northeast Atlantic respectively. The London Convention of 1972 distinguishes some highly harmful wastes (the so-called "black list," e.g., organohalogenic compounds, mercury) which are absolutely prohibited from other less harmful products (the "grey list," e.g., lead, arsenic, copper, pesticides),[46] which may be dumped if a permit is obtained. The third category of waste requires only a general permit. The Oslo Convention has a similar structure. The London Convention is widely ratified and applies to all marine areas not considered territorial waters; thus the regime it establishes is clearly a global regime.[47]

Atmosphere

This section has three subdivisions. The first describes the development of national sovereignty over air space and modification of this regime as space technology developed. The second discusses acid deposition ("acid rain"), and the third examines the problems of ozone depletion in the upper atmosphere.

Air Space

Commercial possibilities of air travel were recognized as soon as the Wright brothers flew at Kitty Hawk in 1903. In 1925 the International Technical Committee for Aerial Legal Experts (CITEJA) was created. This association of private law authorities dealt primarily with such issues as liability for aircraft damages and insurance for passengers and luggage, all of which are still important issues over seventy years later. Airmail was soon on the international agenda, and in 1929, the Universal Postal Convention contained a provision to allow the unimpeded passage of mail carried by airplanes.[48] Over the following ten years, numerous renewals and amendments to the existing documents were negotiated.[49] The United States concluded several bilateral agreements and, in 1938, passed the Civil Aeronautics Act to regulate commercial flights over the United States.[50]

In 1913, the British Parliament passed an aerial navigation act that claimed, among other things, British jurisdiction over almost the entire English Channel. France and Germany soon passed similar laws, no doubt in partial anticipation of the aerial combat to come.

The commercial uses of air travel expanded international concerns with the regulation of air space. At first, ocean policy was proposed as a model, with low-altitude air travel (comparable to travel through coastal waters that are adjacent to land) regulated by the states and high-altitude travel an open-access regime. However, it was quickly apparent that military usefulness was not restricted to low-altitude activities, and in October 1919 the

Paris Convention Relating to the Regulation of Aerial Navigation was signed, giving exclusive sovereignty to each nation of the airspace above its territory.[51] This convention not only recognized exclusive sovereignty over national airspace, but it also set certain standards of conduct such as rights of innocent passage (subject to regulation), equal treatment of all nations, and the rights of nations to establish protected zones through which no aircraft might fly.[52] Three years later, an amendment that provided protocols for overflights by aircraft of nonsignatory nations was added.[53] Although the United States did not accede to the convention,[54] it did observe the conditions of the convention on an informal basis. Nor did the United States sign the Spanish-American Convention of Aerial Navigation, finalized in Madrid in 1926 and patterned after the Paris Convention.[55] However, in 1928, the United States signed the Habana Convention, acceded to by nations of the Western Hemisphere plus Spain.[56] The Habana Convention paralleled the Paris Convention of 1919.

Despite efforts in the early days of manned flight to designate airspace free to travel, much as the high seas were,[57] the clear dangers presented by military aircraft during World War I led all nations to assert sovereignty over their adjacent airspace. Since the First World War, the law has been that nations can regulate flight over their own territories or territorial seas. For example, when Francis Gary Powers, an American U2 pilot, was shot down over Soviet territory in 1960, there were no protests that the Russians had acted improperly. Indeed, the American government initially denied that the overflight had occurred, partly in order to maintain its reputation as a law-abiding nation.

In addressing the question of the dividing line between national air space and outer space, changes in technology have played an important role. Access to outer space has clearly been limited only by the technological and financial resources of the user, but access to airspace is governed by rules of national sovereignty. The two areas must be treated differently. At what point does *airspace* stop and *outer space* begin? A clearly defined limit seems difficult to achieve, given changing technology. Human life can be sustained without artificial assistance perhaps as high as ten miles.[58] Conventional aircraft can fly as high as twelve miles.[59] The states themselves have seemed reluctant to establish a firm boundary. One position advocated by the United States was that airspace stopped just below the level of orbiting satellites, for the obvious reasons that if the satellites were included within airspace, they were in violation of national sovereignty throughout most of their orbits. Although the Soviets were much more interested than the United States in establishing a definitive boundary between the two realms, they advocated a use-oriented approach. Their position was that espionage activities were illegal regardless of altitude, but peaceful uses, which did not affect the

rights of the government below, were automatically allowed.[60] This echoes
the notion of innocent passage long accepted on the high seas, but it leaves
to the government the definition of peaceful use. Thus, when the Soviets
shot down a Korean airliner in 1983, they justified the action by charging
that the airliner was engaged in deliberate, illicit reconnaissance.

International controls for atmospheric problems have been extremely difficult to negotiate. Issues of sovereignty have plagued the policy arena from
the start, and scientific data have been both conflicting and confusing. Developed and developing countries have disagreed over acceptable levels of
pollution, with some developing countries viewing air pollution as proof
their country was on the road to industrialization and an improved economy. Pollution control technology has been expensive, and the costs of monitoring and enforcing regulation have been high. Businesses with strong political influence have successfully blocked regulatory efforts. The
transboundary nature of air pollution and other atmospheric problems has
aggravated the difficulties, with transboundary air pollution only one of
many policies subject to international horse-trading. Finally, the lack of established international organizations charged with the coordination of transboundary air policy has delayed progress toward resolution of the problem.[61]

Transboundary air pollution is, strictly speaking, a negative externality
or spillover and not an issue of resource use. However, the impact of such
issues on international law regarding the global commons is significant, in
part because it has clarified the role of scientific research on global environmental policy.

Acid Deposition

Acid deposition ("acid rain")[62] became an international issue when the effects from burning fossil fuels and the airborne effects of radiation became
apparent in countries that had not caused them. Early in the seventies, the
first warning signs appeared when lakes in Sweden began to die: "hundreds
of previously normal lakes had become too acidic to support healthy biological processes; customary plant and animal life, including most native
fishes, were dying or absent."[63] Scientists determined that the acid deposition affecting these lakes had originated in Europe and in other parts of
Scandinavia. In the next twenty years, evidence showed similar and increasing problems with acid deposition throughout the European continent
and North America.

In 1980, the United States and Canada signed a memorandum of intent in-
dicating that each would reduce the sulfur and nitrogen emissions from
coal-fired furnaces that are the major source of acid deposition. However,
the Reagan administration immediately backed away from the agreement

and advocated more study to confirm the connection between coal-fired furnaces and acid deposition. This was a difficult position for the White House
to maintain, given three reports from the American scientific community
that confirmed the connection. First was the report from the Interagency
Task Force on Acid Precipitation, asserting that industrial stacks were the
major source of acid raid in the Northeast. This was followed by a report
from the White House Office for Science: "If we take the conservative point
of view that we must wait until scientific knowledge is definitive, the accumulated deposition and damaged environment may reach the point of irre-
versibility."[64] The third report was from the National Academy of Sciences,
claiming that acid rain could be reduced if the sulfur oxide emissions from
coal-fired plants in the eastern United States were reduced.

Since then the international evidence has mounted. Forests in the eastern
United States are endangered, and in Germany over half of the trees are
damaged from acid deposition. Eastern Europe is also plagued with damaged
areas, the extent of which is becoming apparent as the political regimes
change.

One of the stumbling blocks to international cooperation on stemming
acid rain is that countries have had great difficulty in reaching internal
agreement on their own remedies. Despite growing scientific evidence to
support the peril of acid deposition, public interest in the United States remains low. In the United States, conflicts between industry and environmentalists, among coal-producing regions, and between coal burning and
acid deposition-receiving regions complicate any legislative attempts to deal
with the problem. The Clean Air Act Amendments of 1990 finally put in
place a legislative scheme to reduce acid deposition by half by the year 2000.
Stricter standards were imposed on 110 coal-burning electric utility plants,
and nitrous oxide emissions were also scheduled for reduction.

Some international improvements have been made: the eight nations of
Norway, Finland, Sweden, Denmark, West Germany, Switzerland, Austria,
and Canada agreed to a 30 percent reduction in sulfur discharges by 1993.
In 1988, the European Community agreed to a cutback program for sulfur
emissions. Great Britain, which was the largest producer of sulfur oxides in
Western Europe, agreed to install scrubbers on its sulfur-producing power
plants. In related action, the European Community agreed that by 1992,
small engine vehicles would be required to meet emission control standards
similar to the United States standards. All large cars throughout Europe were
required to be fitted with catalytic converters by 1994.

Ozone Depletion

Another transboundary air pollution issue with global implications is the
diminishing level of ozone in the stratosphere. Ozone shields the planet's

surface from ultraviolet radiation and affects the temperature gradients and weather patterns across the Earth. Stratospheric ozone is reduced by the interaction of chlorine and ozone. Scientists estimate that the ozone layer above the mid-latitudes of the Northern Hemisphere has declined 3 percent since 1970.[65] Lower levels of stratospheric ozone are dangerous because ultraviolet radiation can penetrate to the planet surface more easily. This increases the incidence of skin cancers, reduces some crop yields, and has numerous other negative effects on living organisms. For example, in November 1991, marine scientists announced their finding that the thinning of the ozone layer over Antarctica was harming the single-cell organisms that form the bottom link of the oceanic food chain. The reduction of ozone protection over the southern pole allowed ultraviolet radiation to penetrate more deeply into the ocean, not only reducing the productivity of the phytoplankton but also increasing genetic damage in the organisms.[66]

National action to curtail ozone loss predated the international efforts by several years. In 1974, two scientific studies hypothesized a dangerous connection between release of chlorine from chlorofluorocarbons (CFCs) and the reduction of stratospheric ozone.[67] In 1977, the United States imposed some limits on CFC use under the Clean Air Act Amendments.[68] The Environmental Protection Agency was authorized to regulate "any substance . . . [which] . . . may reasonably be anticipated to affect the stratosphere, especially ozone in the stratosphere, . . . [if] such an effect may *reasonably be anticipated* to endanger public health or welfare. . ." (emphasis added).[69] Federal regulations limited the use of CFCs in aerosols in 1978, and Canada, Norway, and Sweden followed suit.[70] The European Community proposed a slower reduction extended over a longer time; several observers attribute this reluctance to industry pressures and a lack of public interest.[71]

In 1985, compromise was reached through the Vienna Convention for the Protection of the Ozone Layer, which called for an economic workshop, information exchange, and further research.[72] As in the Transboundary Air Pollution Convention, serious questions of economic equity between developing and developed nations were at issue. In 1985, no practical substitute for CFCs was available, and their use in industrial processes and refrigeration were critical in technology transfers to developing countries. This led to a weak convention that was an "empty framework" of vague measures.[73] Nonetheless, the convention is important for its ecosystem approach and its emphasis on prevention rather than simple remedies.[74]

Scientific data continued to accumulate that indicated a dramatic decrease in stratospheric ozone. The world environmental community was shocked at the 1985 reports of an enormous ozone hole over the Antarctic.[75] The hole was so extensive that the scientists had delayed publication while they rechecked the data: American satellite measurements had not observed the dissipation because their computers were programmed to ignore losses of such magnitude as anomalies.[76] The ozone hole is more severe over the Antarctic because the air there is the coldest on earth, and the chemical reaction that removes ozone from the atmosphere is accelerated in cold temperatures.[77] The hole now exposes an area equal to the size of the continental United States.[78] A similar but smaller hole exists over the Arctic.

In 1986, a landmark research report was published by the World Meteorological Organization (WMO) and the United Nations Environment Programme (UNEP).[79] The study confirmed what had been feared: although use of CFCs was not increasing, CFC levels in the atmosphere continued to rise.[80] The models predicted dangerous reductions in atmospheric ozone in the coming years and warned that the contributions of CFCs to global warming were much higher than originally anticipated.[81] Ozone levels have continued to drop even as CFC use is reduced because of the delay in chemical breakdowns and reactions. Scientists estimate that even with projected reductions in CFC releases, the ozone layer will not recover for over a century.[82]

In September 1987, twenty-four nations (including the major CFC-producing countries) plus the European Community Commission signed the Montreal Protocol on Substances that Deplete the Ozone Layer.[83] The protocol is notable because "for the first time the international community reached agreement on control of a valuable economic commodity to prevent future environmental damage."[84] The protocol imposed substantial reductions in the use of CFCs when no replacement chemical was available, bypassing the customary "best available technology" approach in favor of a standard that recognized the urgency of the ozone problem.[85] The protocol was widely accepted by the international community, in part because of the selective incentives built into the protocol; for example, the Soviet Union was "grandfathered" for factories under construction, and developing countries were allowed to delay compliance for ten years.[86] Also, expectations for funding contributions from each country were adjusted according to the United Nations's global assessment scale, which is based on each country's economic, geographic, and demographic characteristics.[87]

Although support for the Montreal Protocol was substantial, the international community soon realized that more stringent deadlines were required. In March 1989, the EC states decided to reduce the production of CFCs by 85 percent with the goal of complete elimination by 2000. This decision exceeded the demands of the Montreal Protocol; a change in the position of the British was the major impetus behind the change.[88] In May 1989, eighty-one nations adopted the nonbinding Helsinki Declaration on the Protection of the Ozone Layer,[89] which urged ratification of the protocol and accelerated phaseouts of CFCs, halons, and other ozone depleting substances.[90]

The Montreal Protocol was revised in 1990. The amendments accelerated the timetable for phasing out CFCs; the United States implemented this change in Title VI of the 1990 Clean Air Act Amendments. They also adopted an incentive program to encourage developing countries to change to CFC substitutes and new technologies as rapidly as possible. A second set of negotiations in 1992 advanced the schedule even further, setting a total ban by 2030 and adding controls for methyl bromide.[91]

The Montreal Protocol represents a major shift in the relationship between scientific certainty and public policy decision making. The political and economic pressures to resist establishing policies to reduce CFCs and related compounds were intense. Richard Benedick, chief United States negotiator for the ozone protection treaties, attributes the success of the negotiations to several factors, among which are the close relationships between atmospheric scientists and the government officials, the education and use of public opinion to sway politicians, leadership from the United Nations Environmental Programme and from financially influential countries such as the United States, and consideration of the needs of developing countries.[92] The protocol "may signal a fundamental shift in attitude among critical segments of society when confronted with uncertain but potentially grave threats that require coordinated international action."[93]

Antarctica

The "highest, driest, windiest, and coldest continent,"[94] Antarctica is so inhospitable that it has no native terrestrial mammals. The region was first explored and exploited in the late eighteenth century, but the development of a regime began late in the nineteenth century. Bound by fairly clear geographical limits and governed by a treaty system that originated with scientific exploration, Antarctica presents the most coherent regime of all the global commons.

Exploration has been limited by technology, and only recently have the polar regions been invaded by quasi-permanent settlements of scientists. The northern polar regions are more accessible than the southern ones, and the comparative proximity of Canada and the Soviet Union has made the Arctic more familiar than the southern continent. The Antarctic is a continent surrounded by an extensive ice pack, unlike the Arctic, which is comprised entirely of frozen ocean. Until recently, the inaccessibility of the Antarctic has made any territorial claims upon its land "largely symbolic," and its chief value has been scientific observation and research.[95]

In 1959 Antarctica was designated an international scientific reserve under the Antarctic Treaty by the twelve nations doing scientific research on the continent (Argentina, Australia, Belgium, Chile, France, Great Britain, Japan, New Zealand, Norway, South Africa, the Soviet Union, and the United States). The seven nations that also asserted territorial claims to the land suspended those claims for thirty years; the treaty is reviewed biannually and the suspensions are still in force.[96] The treaty was intended primarily to prohibit the use of Antarctica for military purposes or for testing and storage of nuclear waste. Recent discoveries that suggest substantial oil and gas supplies on the Antarctic outer continental shelf have strained relations between the signatories. An oil spill in 1989 alerted environmentalists to the dangers that development is bringing to the continent, not the least of which is simple waste disposal by the scientific settlements.

In 1964, the signatories (known as the Consultative Parties) adopted the Agreed Measures for Antarctic Fauna and Flora to ensure protection of the native species. The same year as the Agreed Measures were adopted, Norway resumed seal hunting in the Antarctic. Because there were no binding agreements concerning sealing an additional convention was negotiated: in 1972, the Convention for the Conservation of Antarctic Seals was signed. This convention bans pelagic sealing and sets optimum sustainable yield as an upper limit for harvesting. Although the convention does not meet the standards mandated by the American Marine Mammal Protection Act, the United States Senate ratified the convention to provide at least *some* regulation of commercial sealing in the Antarctic.[97]

In 1980, the Consultative Parties adopted the Convention on the Conservation of Antarctic Marine Living Resources (CCAMLR or the Southern Ocean Convention). In effect in April 1982, the convention was innovative, bringing an ecosystem perspective to resource management. Antarctica is one of the few places where some conservation and sustainability measures have been put in place before the damage was done. This has frequently led to regulatory strategies being planned prior to the regulated activity.

Negotiations for CCAMLR were motivated in part by concern for krill, a small crustacean that lives in the Southern Ocean and is fished extensively by the Japanese and Soviet fishing fleets (and in the eighties by the Poles and West Germans). Probably the most bitter dispute in the Antarctic prior to the oil spill involved this abundant and inexpensive source of protein. The political problems arise because krill is the staple diet of the endangered great blue or baleen whales, which are close to extinction, and for seals, penguins, and some fish. Political pressures became so intense that the Food and Agriculture Organization (FAO) of the United Nations withheld scientific findings to avoid offending the krill-fishing nations. The convention is intended to protect the main ecosystem by requiring that the nations harvesting krill consider the impact on other species when setting catch limits. CCAMLR also expanded the territorial limits of the Treaty System to the Antarctic Convergence.[98] This has raised complicated related issues because part of the area covered by the convention overlaps the recognized territorial limits of several claimant states. Once again, the vague agreements of the Antarctic Treaty to set aside questions of sovereignty were invoked.[99]

As the text of the CCAMLR makes clear, the extension of the convention to the Antarctic Convergence is in recognition of the scope of the Antarctic ecosystem. Where CCAMLR overlaps undisputed territorial claims, the states may impose stricter regulations than required by the commission and may enforce the regulations within the two-hundred-mile limit themselves. To implement CCAMLR, a Commission for the Conservation of Antarctic Marine Living Resources was established. The commission has the authority to adopt conservation measures, including restrictions on the harvest of living marine resources in the Southern Ocean, and it is also empowered to establish marine reserves to protect especially vulnerable species and habitat.

It is significant that the treaty powers chose to regulate krill fishing by convention rather than by additions to the Antarctic Treaty System. This allows nonmember states such as South Korea, which has an interest in krill but virtually no interest in Antarctica, to participate in the extended regime. Thus in a quiet but nonetheless spectacular diplomatic coup, the treaty nations "won recognition of their authority to negotiate resource regimes for the Antarctic."[100]

The legal complexities raised by krill harvests—jurisdiction, access rights, and so on—were important in the exploitation of mineral resources as well. In 1973, trace hydrocarbons were found on the continental shelf of the Ross Sea, and this, coupled with the OPEC oil crisis, raised the stakes on Antarctic resources. The quantity of potential oil and gas remained uncertain, but in 1974, a report written for the U.S. Geological Survey (USGS) estimated 45 billion barrels of oil and 115 trillion cubic feet of natural gas.[101] When these figures were leaked to the press, public interest was intense.[102] Even if the estimates were accurate, the recoverable oil and gas would be significantly less, perhaps one-third of the potential, but the political implications were still substantial. Members of the Antarctic Treaty System were concerned about two issues: jurisdiction over mineral resources, which was not an issue covered by the treaty or any subsequent agreements, and protection of the fragile Antarctic environment.[103] Further complications were raised by the demands of the developing nations to have a share in Antarctic resources.

The first hurdle to be passed by the treaty members was the Law of the Sea (LOS) discussion over seabed mining. In exchange for a guarantee that the treaty powers would discuss Antarctic resources after the Third United Nations Conference on the Law of the Sea, the Group of 77, a coalition of developing nations, agreed to exclude Antarctic resources from the LOS discussions.[104] Pressure for mineral exploitation on the Antarctic continent continues to increase, although a 1988 draft convention dealing with minerals was rejected by two members of the consultative committee. On 5 October 1991, a protocol to the Antarctic Treaty was signed that banned mineral and oil exploration in Antarctica for at least fifty years. The protocol also contained stronger provisions to protect the marine ecosystem from pollution and overharvesting of living resources.[105]

Suggested Reading

Birnie, Patricia, and Alan Boyle. *International Law & the Environment*. Oxford: Clarendon Press, 1993 (paperback). You really can't pick this one up to *read* it, but it is the most thorough, accurate, and clear book available on this subject. An essential addition to your library.

Caldwell, Lynton Keith. *International Environmental Policy*. Durham, NC: Duke University Press, 1984. Extremely thorough discussion of the development and structure of the United Nations's role in environmental matters.

Esty, Daniel. *Greening the GATT: Trade, Environment, and the Future*. Washington, DC: Institute for International Economics, 1994. A comprehensive analysis of the environmental issues in the General Agreement on Tariffs and Trade (GATT). While his recommendations may not appeal to all readers, the book is worthwhile for its discussion of the history of GATT and the annotated list of key cases and multilateral agreements.

Johnson, Stanley, and Guy Corcelle. *Environmental Policy of the European Communities*. London: Graham and Trotman, 1989. This is the only "suggested reading" that I have not read, but Birnie and Boyle describe this as "an exhaustive survey of the policy and lawmaking role of the European Communities" (p. 66, n. 103), and that's good enough for me.

Nugent, Neill. *Government and Politics of the European Community* (3rd ed.). Durham, NC: Duke University Press, 1994. The most up-to-date book about the European Community. Clear discussions on the EC policy process and private interest groups. It is not environmentally focused, but it does discuss some environmental issues.

Ostrom, Elinor. *Governing the Commons; The Evolution of Institutions for Collective Action*. Cambridge: Cambridge University Press, 1990. If I could only have one book on the commons, this would be it. The focus is on small-scale common pool resources. The analytic framework, based on empirical data, has wide application. Very readable.

Peterson, D. J. *Troubled Lands: The Legacy of Soviet Environmental Destruction*. Boulder, CO: Westview Press, 1993. A superb, detailed look at the environmental degradation in the former Soviet Union. It is remarkably readable and essential for understanding the institutions, political processes, and policies that led to such devastation. Highly recommended.

Notes

1. See Peter Sand, *Lessons Learned in Global Environmental Governance* (Washington, DC: World Resources Institute, June 1990). See also Patricia Birnie and Alan Boyle, *International Law and the Environment* (Oxford: Clarendon Press, 1993), p. 10.

2. The modern corporation itself is a recent legal invention. To give a profit-oriented enterprise the legal rights of human beings is a development that does not astonish us only because we have grown accustomed to its face.

3. Lynton Caldwell, *International Environmental Policy* (Durham, NC: Duke University Press, 1984), p. 33.

4. Outer space is also a global commons, but since it is not an environmental policy issue—at least not for this book—it is not discussed in a separate section.

5. Jean Dorst, *Before Nature Dies,* trans. Constance D. Sherman (Boston: Houghton Mifflin, 1970); Rolf Edberg, *On the Shred of a Cloud,* trans. Sven Aham (New York: Harper & Row, 1971).

6. Caldwell, p. 53.

7. Marvin Soroos, "From Stockholm to Rio: The Evolution of Global Environmental Governance" in *Environmental Policy in the 1990s* 2nd ed. Edited by Norman Vig and Michael Kraft (Washington, DC: Congressional Quarterly Press, 1994), pp. 299–321.

8. EC 12 (1986), Cmnd. 9758, UKTS 31 (1988), Cm. 372; 25 ILM (1986), 506. In force 1 July 1987.

9. Birnie and Boyle, p. 66.

10. Birnie and Boyle, p. 67.

11. Tamara Crockett and Cynthia Schultz, "Developing a Unified European Environmental Law and Policy," *Boston College International and Comparative Law Review* 14(2), 1991: 301–317.

12. Norman Vig, "Presidential Leadership and the Environment: From Reagan and Bush to Clinton," in *Environmental Policy in the 1990s* 2nd ed. Edited by Norman Vig and Michael Kraft (Washington, DC: Congressional Quarterly Press, 1994), pp. 71–95.

13. Soroos, pp. 299–321, especially p. 316, notes omitted.

14. Birnie and Boyle, p. 6, notes omitted.

15. As Kim says to Mahbub Ali: "I will change my faith and my bedding, but *thou* must pay for it." Mahbub Ali was so amused that he almost fell off his horse laughing. Rudyard Kipling, *Kim* (New York: Dell, 1959), p. 132. The developed nations did not have a similar reaction.

16. Richard Tobin, "Environment, Population, and Economic Development," in *Environmental Policy in the 1990s* 2nd ed. Edited by Norman Vig and Michael Kraft (Washington, DC: Congressional Quarterly Press, 1994), pp. 275–297.

17. Walter A. Rosenbaum, *Energy, Politics, and Public Policy* 3rd ed. (Washington, DC: Congressional Quarterly Press, 1995), pp. 68–69.

18. Lynton Caldwell, "Beyond Environmental Diplomacy: The Changing Institutional Structure of International Cooperation," in *International Environmental Diplomacy.* Edited by John Carroll (Cambridge: Cambridge University Press, 1988), p. 19.

19. Caldwell, p. 20.

20. Ibid.

21. "Chronological Summary: Events of 1992," *Colorado Journal of International Environmental Law and Policy* 4 (1993): 232.

22. There are hidden dangers in the use of economic analysis: apparently the mere study of economics diminishes cooperative behavior. Reporting on a study by Robert Frank, Thomas Gilovich, and Dennis Regan ("Does Studying Economics Inhibit Co-operation?," *Journal of Economic Perspectives* [Spring 1993]), *The Economist* notes that economists and economics students are less concerned about fairness, give less to charity, and are more likely to cheat than their colleagues in other disciplines. "How do you mean, `fair'?," *The Economist* 29 May 1993, 71.

23. H. A. Regier and A. P. Grima, "Fishery Resource Allocation: An Exploratory Essay," *Canadian Journal of Fisheries and Aquatic Sciences* 42(4): 845–859.

24. Edmund Andrews, "Tiny Tonga Seeks Satellite Empire in Space." *New York Times,* 28 August 1990, 1, C17. It may, however, be possible for these nations to *lease* their space to others.

25. See Mary Douglas and Aaron Wildavsky, *Risk and Culture* (Berkeley: University of California Press, 1982).

26. An interesting case study on this topic is Forest Reinhardt, "Du Pont Freon® Products Division," in *Managing Environmental Issues: A Casebook.* Edited by Rogene Buchholz, Alfred Marcus, and James Post (Englewood Cliffs, N.J.: Prentice-Hall, 1992), pp. 261–286.

27. The "cod war" between Iceland and Great Britain was the trigger event for UNCLOS II. Iceland asserted a twelve-mile limit that excluded the British fishing fleet from its traditional fishing grounds. At one point in the dispute, British fishermen were accompanied in disputed waters by armed escort vessels.

28. Robert A. Goldwin, "Common Sense vs. `The Common Heritage.'" In *Law of the Sea: U.S. Policy Dilemma.* Edited by Bernard Oxman, David Caron, and Charles Buderi (San Francisco: ICS Press, 1983), p. 60.

29. For the British perspective on this behavior, see Marcel Berlins, "US Objections Hold Up Sea Conference," *The Times,* 9 March 1981, 6(b) and Rosemary Righter, "The Law of the Sea: Reagan Tries to Play King Canute," *The Sunday Times,* 26 April 1981, 16(c).

30. Richard Darman, "The Law of the Sea: Rethinking U.S. Interests," *Foreign Affairs 56* (1978): 373–395.

31. Especially important are the following:
1973 Convention on International Trade in Endangered Species of Wild Fauna and Flora (CITES), Washington, 993 UNTS 243; 12 ILM 1085 (1973), in force 1 July 1975;
1979 Convention on the Conservation of Migratory Species of Wild Animals (Bonn),

19 ILM (1980) 15, in force 1 November 1983; 1979 Convention on the Conservation of European Wildlife and Natural Habitats (Berne), UKTS 56 (1982), Cmnd. 8738, ETS 104, in force 1 June 1984; and 1980 Convention on the Conservation of Antarctic Marine Living Resources (Canberra) (CCAMLR), T.I.A.S. 10240; 19 ILM (1980) 837, in force 7 April 1981.

32. Fisheries law within the new contiguous zone is not mentioned in the new LOS treaty; under the Territorial Seas Convention these waters are high seas and therefore open-access fisheries. However, the two hundred nautical mile Exclusive Economic Zone, also established under the treaty, seems to remove that confusion. Birnie and Boyle, p. 518.

33. "Leaving the Feeding Grounds," *The Economist* 7 August 1993: 40.

34. *The Times,* 24 January 1991, 14, cited in Birnie and Boyle, p. 539.

35. Birnie and Boyle, p. 540.

36. 327 U.N.T.S. 3; U.K.T.S. 54 (1958), Cmnd. 595; A.T.S. 7 (1962); C.T.S. 31 (1958); 12 U.S.T. 2989; T.I.A.S. No. 4900. Amended 1962: 600 U.N.T.S. 332; U.K.T.S. 59 (1967), Cmnd. 3354; 17 U.S.T. 1523; T.I.A.S. No. 6109. Amended 1969: U.K.T.S. 21 (1978), Cmnd. 7094; 28 U.S.T. 1205; T.I.A.S. 8508.

37. U.N. Legislative Series ST/LEG/SER.B/18, at 461; U.K.T.S. 27 (1983), Cmnd. 8924; 12 I.L.M. 1319 (1973). Amended by Protocol of 1978 before entry into force, 17 I.L.M. 546 (1978). In force 2 October 1983. Ratification of this treaty was delayed by objections from powerful shipping interests. Lynton Caldwell, *International Environmental Policy* 2nd. ed. (Durham, NC: Duke University Press, 1990), p. 294.

38. Birnie and Boyle, p. 266.

39. The most serious spill was the wreck of the tanker *Torrey Canyon,* which spilled over 100,000 tons of crude oil into the English Channel.

40. U.K.T.S. 77 (1975), Cmnd. 6056; 26 U.S.T. 765, T.I.A.S. 8068; 9 I.L.M. 25 (1970). In force 6 May 1978, 1973 Protocol, 68 *American Journal of International Law* (1974): 577. In force 30 March 1983.

41. 973 U.N.T.S. 3; U.K.T.S. 106 (1975), Cmnd. 6183; 9 I.L.M. 45 (1970). In force 19 June 1976, 1976 Protocol, 16 ILM (1977), 617. In force 8 April 1981.

42. U.K.T.S. 95 (1978); Cmnd. 7383; 11 I.L.M. 284 (1972); Amended 1976, 16 I.L.M. 621 (1977).

43. Lynton Caldwell, *International Environmental Policy* 2nd. ed. (Durham, NC: Duke University Press, 1990), p. 295.

44. 26 U.S.T. 2403; T.I.A.S. 8165. Amended 12 October 1978, T.I.A.S. No. 8165; 18 I.L.M. 510 (1979).

45. 12 I.L.M. 162 (1973).

46. Alexandre Kiss and Dinah Shelton, *International Environmental Law* (Ardsley-on-Hudson, NY: Transnational Publishers, 1991), p. 182.

47. Birnie and Boyle, p. 320.

48. Universal Postal Union, 28 June 1919, 46 Stat. 2523.

49. Paris Convention and amendments renewed, 1929; Second International Diplomatic Conference on Private Air Law (Warsaw Convention), 12 October 1929, 49 Stat. 3000, T.S. No. 876; Sanitary Convention for Aerial Navigation [infectious disease prevention], 12 August 1933, 49 St at. 3279, T.S. No. 901; the Rome Conventions: Convention for the Unification of Certain Rules Relating to Precautionary Attachment of Aircraft [seizure of aircraft as security for debt], 1933, and Convention for Unification of Certain Rules Related to Damages Caused by Aircraft to Third Parties on the Surface, 1933. All cited by Haley, pp. 50–51.

50. 72 Stat. 798 (1958), 49 U.S.C. §1508 (1958). The Civil Aeronautics Authority, later the Civil Aeronautics Board (CAB) was established in the act. It was abolished as part of the Reagan deregulation programs in 1985.

51 The Paris Convention for the Regulation of Air Navigation , 11 L.N.T.S. 173.

52. Andrew Haley, *Space Law and Government* (New York: Appleton-Century-Crofts, 1963), p. 45.

53. 78 L.N.T.S. 439 (1922).

54. The administrative organ for the Convention, the International Commission for Air Navigation, was under the authority of the League of Nations, and the United States was not a member of the league.

55. Haley, p. 48, citing Hudson, *International Legislation* 3 (1931): 2019.

56. 20 February 1928, 47 Stat. 1901, T.S. No. 840.

57. Haley, pp. 42–43.

58. S. Houston Lay and Howard Taubenfeld, *The Law Relating to Activities of Man in Space* (Chicago: University of Chicago Press, 1970), p. 43.

59. Lay and Taubenfeld, p. 43. This becomes symbolically problematic when American pilots receive astronaut wings for flying aircraft such as the X-15 above fifty miles. Lay and Taubenfeld, p. 44.

60. Lay and Taubenfeld, pp. 40–42. One writer in 1944 advocated establishing the line at the distance a state could control. Kelsen, *General Theory of Law and State* 216–217 (1949), cited in Lay and Taubenfeld, p. 45 and note 77. This echoes the ancient notion that national sovereignty over the ocean extended as far as a cannon-shot.

61. Caldwell, *International Environmental Policy* (Durham, NC: Duke University Press, 1990), p. 259; Birnie and Boyle, esp. pp. 387–393.

62. The correct term is acid *deposition* because acid is found in fog and clouds as well as in rain.

63. Walter Rosenbaum, *Energy, Politics, and Public Policy* 2nd ed. (Washington, DC: Congressional Quarterly Press, 1987), p. 117.

64. *New York Times*, 28 June 1983, quoted by Walter Rosenbaum, *Environmental Politics and Policy* (Washington, DC: Congressional Quarterly Press, 1985), p. 135.

65. Kiss and Shelton, p. 339.

66. Keith Schneider, "Ozone Depletion Harming Sea Life," *New York Times*, 16 November 1991, p. 6, col. 6.

67. Chlorine is released from chlorofluorocarbons (CFCs), which are nonpoisonous and relatively inert chemicals used in refrigerants and as aerosol propellants. CFCs are especially stable and can remain in the atmosphere for decades or longer. As solar radiation breaks the CFCs down, chlorine is released that reacts with ozone (O_3) to create oxygen (O_2). The chlorine molecule is then free to react with another ozone molecule, setting off a chain reaction in the stratosphere. Richard Stolarski and Ralph Cicerone, "Stratospheric Chlorine: A Possible Sink for Ozone," *Canadian Journal of Chemistry* 52 (1974): 1610–1615; Mario Molina and F. Sherwood Rowland, "Stratospheric Sink for Chlorofluoromethanes: Chlorine Atom Catalysed Destruction of Ozone," *Nature* 249 (1974): 810–812. Both cited in Richard Elliot Benedick, *Ozone Diplomacy: New Directions for Safeguarding the Planet* (Cambridge, MA: Harvard University Press, 1991) p. 10.

68. Caldwell, *International Environmental Policy* (1990), p. 263.

69. Clean Air Act, 42 U.S.C. §7457(b).

70. Benedick, *Ozone Diplomacy*, p. 24.

71. Markus Jachtenfuchs, "The European Community and the Protection of the Ozone Layer," *Journal of Common Market Studies* 28, no. 3 (March 1980): 263; David Pearce, "The European Community Approach to the Control of Chlorofluorocarbons," Paper submitted to UNEP Workshop on the Control of Chlorofluorocarbons, Leesburg, Virginia, 8–12 September 1986, p. 12. Both cited by Benedick, *Ozone Diplomacy*, p. 24–25. See also Thomas B. Stoel, Jr., Alan S. Miller, and Breck Milroy, *Fluorocarbon Regulation* (Lexington, MA: D. C. Heath, 1980), p. 205; and J. T. B. Tripp, D. J. Dudek, and Michael Oppenheimer, "Equality and Ozone Protection," *Environment* 29, no. 6 (1987): 45. Benedick, *Ozone Diplomacy*, p. 28.

72. Vienna Convention for the Protection of the Ozone Layer, UNEP Doc. 1G.53/5; 26 I.L.M. 1529 (1987). In force 22 September 1988.

73. Birnie and Boyle, p. 406; see generally pp. 404–409.

74. Birnie and Boyle, p. 406.

75. J. C. Farnau, B. G. Gardiner, and J. D. Shanklin, "Large Losses of Total Ozone in Antarctica Reveal Seasonal ClO_x/NO_x Interaction," *Nature* 315 (1985): 207–210.

76. Benedick, *Ozone Diplomacy*, pp. 18–19.

77. Joel S. Levine, "A Planet at Risk," Public Lecture, 20 February 1993, Greensboro, North Carolina. According to Dr. Levine, global warming will do nothing to alleviate this problem as the impact of global warming is felt at the Earth's surface and, in fact, global warming leads to increasingly cold temperatures in the upper atmosphere.

78. Kiss and Shelton, p. 339.

79. World Meteorological Organization et al. (WMO), *Atmospheric Ozone 1985: Assessment of Our Understanding of the Processes Controlling Its Present Distribution* 3 volumes, Global Ozone Research and Monitoring Project, Report No. 16 (Geneva: WMO, 1986).

80. WMO, *Atmospheric Ozone* Ch. 13, cited in Benedick, *Ozone Diplomacy*, p. 14.

81. Ibid.

82. "Ozone-saving Efforts Are Making Headway," *Greensboro News and Record* 26 August 1993, A8.

83. Protocol (to the 1985 Vienna Convention) on Substances that Deplete the Ozone Layer (Montreal), 26 I.L.M. 1540 (1987). In force 1 January 1989.

84. Orval Nangle, "Stratospheric Ozone: United States Regulation of Chlorofluorocarbons," *Environmental Affairs* 16 (1989): 546.

85. Benedick, 1991, p. 1.

86. Peter Sand, "International Cooperation: The Environmental Experience," in *Preserving the Global Environment: The Challenge of Shared Leadership*. Edited by Jessica Tuchman Mathews (New York: Norton, 1991), p. 242.

87. Sand, 1991, p. 245.

88. David Vogel, "Environmental Policy in Europe and Japan," in *Environmental Policy in the 1990s*. Edited by Norman Vig and Michael Kraft (Washington, DC: Congressional Quarterly Press, 1990), p. 273.

89. 28 I.L.M. 1335 (1989).

90. James Koehler and Scott Hajost, "1989: Advent of a New Era for EPA's International Activities," *Colorado Journal of International Environmental Law and Policy* 1(1), Summer 1990: 183.

91. Jacqueline Vaughn Switzer, *Environmental Politics: Domestic and Global Dimensions* (New York: St. Martin's Press, 1994), p. 277.

92. Richard Elliot Benedick, "Protecting the Ozone Layer: New Directions in Diplomacy," in *Preserving the Global Environment: The Challenge of Shared Leadership*. Edited by Jessica Tuchman Mathews (New York: Norton, 1991), pp. 113–153, esp. pp. 143–149.

93. Benedick, "Protecting the Ozone Layer," p. 149.

94. D. W. H. Walton, *Antarctica Science* (Cambridge: Cambridge University Press, 1987), p. 153.

95. Lynton Caldwell, *International Environmental Policy*, p. 254.

96. The seven states asserting territorial claims at the time the Treaty went into force were the United Kingdom, France, Norway, Chile, Argentina, Australia, and New Zealand.

97. Michael J. Bean, *The Evolution of National Wildlife Law* (New York: Praeger, 1983), p. 269.

98. The Antarctic Convergence is the northern boundary of the Antarctic or Southern Ocean. The south Pacific, Atlantic, and Indian oceans converge with the frigid Antarctic water creating a turbulent barrier to marine life and defining the rich Antarctic ecosystem. Deborah Shapley, *The Seventh Continent: Antarctica in a Resource Age* (Washington, DC: Resources for the Future, 1985), p. 2.

99. Shapley, p. 153.

100. Shapley, p. 155.

101. N. A. Wright and P. L. Williams, *Mineral Resources of Antarctica,* Geological Survey Circular 705 (Reston, VA: USGS, 1974).

102. Shapley, p. 125.

103. Shapley, p. 125.

104. Shapley, p. 149.

105. Alan Riding, "Accord Bans Oil Exploration in the Antarctic for 50 Years," *New York Times,* 5 October 1991, 1 and 28.

Afterword

This book was written to explain the history of environmental law, the process by which our laws are made and amended, the role of the agencies in implementing the laws, and the role of the courts in interpreting them. Environmental managers who read this book already have a thorough knowledge of their own policy areas, but it is educational and perhaps comforting to realize that environmental managers in all agencies and in all levels of government face similar issues. Whether those managers are administering a Forest Service timber sale or supervising the cleanup of a Superfund site, their jobs are imbedded in a legal and political context that they must understand if they are to perform their jobs well. The purpose of this book has been to help managers understand that context.

Environmental law, as any other subfield of administrative law, is flexible and depends in large part on the substantive policy being addressed. It includes case law but is not restricted to case law. Environmental law includes a vital discretionary component that operates at every level of the administrative process, including agency and court behavior. Because of its intimate relationship with the legislature, the executive, the courts, and the public, environmental law is intensely political both in its origins and its implementation. Any useful analysis or study of environmental law must include these political relationships.

One important factor that has been emphasized throughout this book is the fluid and historical nature of environmental administration and law. Good managers must know the institutional history of their agencies, their laws, and their programs. For example, the economic pressures to develop the western United States following the Civil War led to the large land dispersal programs, federal subsidies to railroad companies, subsidized grazing permits, and a federal mining law that encouraged mineral exploration and extraction on the federal lands. The legacy of the programs has affected the attitudes of western citizens toward land use for the last century. Regardless of the contemporary intent of Congress in amending old statutes or enacting new legislation, managers must understand the deep-seated cultural attitudes that they will encounter when they try to implement the will of Congress. The managers' role is as much to educate as to regulate if they wish to regulate successfully.

To narrow the example even further, consider the efforts by public land range managers to convince western cattle ranchers to improve range management techniques.[1] Cattle ranchers are by nature individualist and entrepreneurial; they do not take kindly to external controls or to management initiatives that restrict their opportunities for profit. Their cultural biases lead them to prefer to minimize leadership, to exploit their environment, and to follow the economic rationality of squeezing as many cattle as possible onto their allotments. The government land managers, in contrast, are more likely to tend toward hierarchical approaches to resource problems: to defer to their enabling statutes, to implement regulations, and then to enforce the regulations through some combination of economic, civil, or even criminal sanctions. This divergence of cultural biases often led to political impasses or, on occasion, violent resistance.

How might responsible and educated managers respond? First, through public education, they might utilize what Michael Thompson calls *surprise*, which occurs when the accumulated weight of evidence in disagreement with a cultural view breaks through the cultural filter, thereby contradicting existing ideas.[2] In this case, the deterioration of the public range almost past recovery forced some ranchers to realize that nature was not endlessly abundant and resilient. They changed their management strategies from exploitation to control, developing new techniques and technology to structure the grazing environment. A second option was for the hierarchical managers to try to impose some additional form of external controls or regulation on the ranchers. As might have been predicted, there was a concerted effort of resistance from the ranchers by organizing into strong lobbying groups. The ranchers were very successful in their lobbying efforts, but once the immediate threat of external control changes was removed, their dislike of prescriptions led to disintegration of the lobby. The third option is for environmental interest groups, which are usually at odds with public land management agencies, to form a temporary political coalition with the regulating agencies. The administrators, disliking the disorder of depleted ranges and the insult to their control mechanisms, did indeed accept the alliance with the environmentalists. For a short time, the specter of a nonsubsidizing grazing fee to force ranchers to value the land at its true market value was a strong possibility, although the rancher lobby finally prevailed. As one would expect, the *surprise*-based change, small as it is, has endured, but once the environmentalist-manager alliance deteriorated, the unsurprised ranchers reverted to their old ways.

To stay current, managers must be sensitive to political changes in all levels of the policy process: executive, congressional, judicial, public, and personal. Environmental law will respond to changes in presidential leadership and to shifts in power within the legislatures. The impact of the Reagan years on the federal judiciary will be a potent factor for decades, as the lower federal court judges gain experience and prestige. A majority of the Supreme Court now leans to the conservative side in many policy areas. Their impact on property rights has been significant in the last several terms; the long-range impact is still in the realm of speculation.

Managers must also consider their own political agendas when designing environmental law and policy. Ethical managers are constantly aware of their obligation in a democratic society to respond to the demands of elected officials and to the direct inputs of the citizens whose lives they affect. Managers must balance long-term costs and benefits against short-term, and they must be willing to negotiate and to compromise, while at the same time protecting their employees, superiors, and their own positions. It is a challenging task, and managers must bring to bear all the weapons they can muster if they are to do their jobs well and to survive.

Managers are usually trained in their substantive fields of hydrology, silvaculture, fisheries, or civil engineering, but by the time they are managers, their training needs are in public administration. How should a budget be presented for maximum effect? What is a fair hearing? How may the courts respond to a new regulation? Why did something happen, and how can it be changed? These are not questions addressed by technocratic training in environmental specialties; they are the questions solved by applying the techniques of the discipline of public administration. Public administration is a generalist approach to management, and environmental managers are generalists. They have the specific training for their fields, but they need the rigorous, disciplined approach of organization theory and policy analysis as well.

As a new century approaches, environmental management is more complex than ever. In the late nineteenth century, when the conservation movement was first getting under way, the most significant issues were those of aesthetic beauty, land protection, and wildlife management. As industrialization continued, problems of pollution, waste management, and public health became more important, but the old issues of land, wildlife, and beauty did not go away. The movement toward transboundary issues that are resolved in the global community does not mean the previous problems are resolved or set aside.

In the coming century, environmental managers will confront some of the most pressing and vital problems that have ever faced society. Failure will bring tragedy and catastrophe. Success may do nothing more than buy time. Success is most likely to come in increments while failures, like Chernobyl, will loom large in history.

To be successful, environmental managers must take the long view, looking back at the processes and events that have shaped the Earth's environment to its present condition, and predicting how these processes will shape and be shaped by events still unknown. Managers must not be discouraged by the tortoise-like pace of improvement. All around them are signs of encouragement: greater openness in the former Soviet bloc; corporate activism that rewards responsible private management; and international awareness of the global dimensions of environmental problems. Information, and the technology to use it, is available on a scale unimaginable even thirty years ago. If the problems have grown to immense proportions, so has the capacity to forge solutions. This is both a challenge and an opportunity: environmental managers are placed so that, if they are clever and conscientious, they can change the world—or their part of it—for the better. Few of us are so fortunate.

Notes

1.   For a fuller discussion of cultural theory and western cattle ranchers, see Susan J. Buck, "Cultural Theory and Management of Common Property Resources," *Human Ecology* 17 (March 1989): 101–116.

2. Michael Thompson, "The Cultural Construction of Nature and the Natural Destruction of Culture," working paper for International Institute for Applied Systems Analysis, Laxenberg, Austria (1984).

Finding Case Law

After reading this book, you surely have a more comprehensive view of how environmental law is developed and administered.* There are hundreds of court cases that deal with environmental issues. While those mentioned in this book are certainly important, they may not have a direct impact on your own area of environmental policy. So how do you find the cases that will allow you to understand what must be done to meet the guidelines of federal and state government regulations? What is a case citation? What does it mean? Are there different sources for state and federal court cases? This essay provides a beginner's guide to finding case law.

To find a case, you must first know how to read a case citation. For example, a typical *U.S. Reports* citation would look like this: 504 U.S. 555 (1992); this case is *Lujan* v. *Defenders of Wildlife*. Case citations consist of volume numbers (504), a court reporter reference (U.S., which is *U.S. Reports*), page number (555), and year of the opinion (1992). To find the case you would locate *U.S. Reports* in the library, find volume 504 (printed on the spine of the book), and turn to page 555. This will be the first page of the case you are researching. All citations are read like this: a list of the more common reporters and their abbreviations is found in Table 1. Cases may be reported in several reporters; for example, United States Supreme Court cases are found in *U.S. Reports* (official), *Supreme Court Reporter,* and the annotated *United States Supreme Court Reports, Lawyers' Edition.*

---

* This material was prepared by John Ehmig.

Table 1: Citation examples

U.S. Reports	452 U.S. 490 (1981)
U.S. Supreme Court Reports, Lawyers' Edition	87 L. Ed. 626 (1943)
U.S. Supreme Court Reports, Lawyers' Edition 2d	82 L. Ed. 2d 221 (1984)
Supreme Court Reporter	115 S. Ct. 714 (1995)
Federal Cases	19 F. Cas. 1348 (1819)
Federal Reporter	221 Fed. 288 (1915) or 226 F. 137 (1920)
*Federal Reporter, Second Series**	449 F. 2d. 1109 (1960)
Federal Supplement	100 F. Supp. 140 (1965)

*The "second series" or "2d." designation has no legal significance. It just indicates a new series of volume numbers.

There are several ways to find case law. The easiest, at least to those who are fond of computers, is to use the two on-line legal research services, WESTLAW and LEXIS. Both of these services offer full-text coverage of all Supreme Court cases dating back to 1790 and other federal cases found in the earliest volumes of *Federal Cases* (____ F. Cas. ____). Both WESTLAW and LEXIS make the opinions available as soon as they are released by the courts and make any necessary typographical changes, headnotes, or references when the case is ready to be published in print. A case can be searched by any of its citations, by title, or even by subject matter. The major drawbacks to using WESTLAW and LEXIS are, of course, cost and availability. On-line access is restricted to institutions and individuals who have paid a significant annual fee, and cost for each session depends on the number of searches. There are other, more accessible computer alternatives that are currently less complete than WESTLAW or LEXIS but are gaining daily.

Another computer-based source of cases, especially useful for U.S. Supreme Court cases, is the World Wide Web. (The World Wide Web address for the Supreme Court is *http:/www.law.cornell/supct/* and for general law, it is *http:/www/webcom.com/~staber/welcome.html*.) At this time (1995), the Supreme Court cases on the Web are limited to cases decided between 1990 and 1995. The coordinators of Project Hermes, the group responsible for putting the Court on the Internet, are adding more cases to the database and hope eventually to rival WESTLAW and LEXIS for access to Supreme Court decisions. Currently you can search Supreme Court cases by one or both parties (in the example above, the parties are *Lujan,* who was Secretary of Interior under George

Bush, and *Defenders of Wildlife,* an environmental interest group), by topic (wildlife), or by the year in which it was decided (1992). The Cornell information may be accessed by gopher as well as by WWW. There is also a specialized area for law on the Internet that has an environmental law subheading. It is a good place to start when you look for current case law. This page also gives the researcher other environmental law resources from which to choose.

For those who are neither computer oriented nor have access to on-line services, there are still several ways to find case law. The first place to look to find a United States Supreme Court case is in the official reporter of the Supreme Court, the *United States Reports* (___ U.S. ___). *United States Reports* is updated with several new volumes every year; unfortunately advance sheets and volumes appear in print very slowly. Bound versions of Court opinions appear nearly three years after the opinion is issued. Because of the lag between the decision and its publication, several commercial publishers produce unofficial reports that come out much more quickly. *U.S. Law Week,* as its name implies, is the most current. West Publishing Company, which also produces the WEST-LAW computerized service, publishes several unofficial reporters. It publishes the *Supreme Court Reporter* (___ S. Ct. ___), which includes a synopsis of the case and also contains a table of words and phrases to allow you to find a case without knowing a specific case citation or name. A similar reporter that also contains detailed annotations especially useful to lawyers is the *United States Supreme Court Reports, Lawyers' Edition* (___ L. Ed. ___ or ___ L. Ed. 2nd ___), published by the Lawyers Co-operative Publishing Company. These reporters allow lawyers and other interested researchers to have access to decisions in a matter of weeks instead of years.

For federal cases that have not reached the Supreme Court, there are the *Federal Reports* (___ Fed. ___ and, after 1924, ___ F. 2d ___) and the *Federal Supplement* (___ F. Supp. ___). The *Federal Reports* cover selected cases from the U.S. Courts of Appeals, and the *Supplement* covers selected cases from the U.S. District Courts.

State court decisions also have official and unofficial reporters. Like the federal system, most of the official reports are published extremely slowly. Therefore, most researchers rely on the unofficial reports. WESTLAW and LEXIS both contain state court decisions and are excellent sources, if you have access to them. Published reporters include West's National Report System for state court systems, which now has seven reports published according to geographic regions. Some states are large enough that they also have their own supplement to the regions court reports.

These are some of the best sources for case law in the United States, both on the state and the federal level. With the coming of the twenty-first century, more of these cases will be found on computer databases. The printed copies will also be available at most public or university libraries and can also be found in many court house law libraries. Enjoy the search and good luck!

Suggested Reading

Cohen, Morris, Robert Berring, and Kent Olson, *Finding the Law: An Abridged Edition of "How to Find the Law, 9th Ed."* St. Paul, MN: West Publishing Company, 1989. There really is no need to get the unabridged version unless you plan to attend law school. As of August 1995, this is the most recent edition, so it does not contain information on Internet searches.

Acronyms

ABA	American Bar Association
AEC	Atomic Energy Commission
APA	Administrative Procedure Act
ASPA	American Society for Public Administration
BAT	Best Available Technology
BLM	Bureau of Land Management
BMPs	Best Management Practices
BNA	Bureau of National Affairs
CCAMLR	Convention on the Conservation of Antarctic Marine Living Resources (Southern Ocean Convention)
CEQ	Council on Environmental Quality
CERCLA	Comprehensive Environmental Response, Compensation, and Liability Act
CFC	chlorofluorocarbon
CITEJA	International Technical Committee for Aerial Legal Experts
CITES	Convention on International Trade in Endangered Species of Wild Fauna and Flora
DEQ	Department of Environmental Quality
DNR	Department of Natural Resources
EC	European Community (see EEC and EU)

EEC	European Economic Community (see EC and EU)
EEZ	Exclusive Economic Zone
EIS	Environmental Impact Statement
EPA	Environmental Protection Agency
ESA	Endangered Species Act
EU	European Union (see EC and EEC)
FAO	Food and Agricultural Organization (United Nations)
FCC	Federal Communications Commission
FDA	Food and Drug Administration
FIFRA	Federal Insecticide, Fungicide, and Rodenticide Act
FLPMA	Federal Land Policy and Management Act
FONSI	Finding of No Significant Impact (NEPA)
FTC	Federal Trade Commission
FWPCA	Federal Water Pollution Control Act
FWS	Fish and Wildlife Service (United States)
GAO	Government Accounting Office
GATT	General Agreement on Tariffs and Trade
GEF	Global Environment Facility (World Bank)
GOO	Get Oil Out
GPO	Government Printing Office
ICC	Interstate Commerce Commission
IUCN	International Union for the Conservation of Nature and Natural Resources
IWC	International Whaling Commission
LOS	Law of the Sea
LULUs	Locally Undesirable Land Uses
MACTs	Maximum Achievable Control Technologies
MARPOL	International Convention for the Prevention of Pollution by Ships
MMPA	Marine Mammal Protection Act
NAAQS	National Ambient Air Quality Standards
NCP	National Contingency Plan
NEPA	National Environmental Policy Act
NGO	nongovernmental organization
NMFS	National Marine Fisheries Service

NOAA	National Oceanic and Atmospheric Administration
NPL	National Priority List (Superfund)
NPS	National Park Service
OCS	Outer Continental Shelf
OMB	Office of Management and Budget
OPEC	Organization of Petroleum Exporting Countries
OTA	Office of Technology Assessment
PCB	polychlorinated biphenyl
PRP	Potentially Responsible Parties
RCRA	Resource Conservation and Recovery Act
RI/FS	remedial investigations and feasibility studies
RPA	Forest Rangeland Renewable Resource Planning Act
SARA	Superfund Amendment and Reauthorization Act
SCRAP	Students Challenging Regulatory Agency Procedures
SEA	Single European Act
SIP	State Implementation Plan
SPM	Suspended Particulate Matter
TMI	Three Mile Island
TSCA	Toxic Substances Control Act
TVA	Tennessee Valley Authority
UNCED	United Nations Conference on the Environment and Development (1992)
UNCLOS I, II, and III	United Nations Conference on the Law of the Sea (1958, 1960, 1973–1982)
UNEP	United Nations Environmental Programme
UNESCO	United Nations Educational, Scientific, and Cultural Organization
USDA	United States Department of Agriculture
USGS	United States Geological Survey
UST	Underground Storage Tanks
WMO	World Meteorological Organization
WWF	World Wildlife Fund

List of Cases

American Cetacean Society v. Baldridge, 768 D.C. Cir. 426, 604 F. Supp. 1398 (1985).

American Textile Manufacturers Institute et al. v. Donovan, Secretary of Labor, et al., 452 U.S. 490 (1981).

Association of Data Processing Service Organizations v. Camp, 397 U.S. 150 (1970).

Babbitt v. Sweet Home, 115 S.Ct. 714 (1995).

Bi-Metallic Investment Co. v. State Board of Equalization, 239 U.S. 441 (1915).

Bivens v. Six Unknown, Named Agents of the Federal Bureau of Narcotics, 403 U.S. 388 (1971).

Board of Regents v. Roth, 408 U.S. 564 (1972).

Boomer v. Atlantic Cement Co., 257 N.E.2d 870 (1970).

Boyce Motor Lines v. United States, 342 U.S. 337 (1952).

Calvert Cliffs Coordinating Committee, Inc. v. United States Atomic Energy Commission, 449 F.2d 1109, 146 U.S. App.D.C. 33 (1971).

City of Milwaukee v. State, 193 Wis. 423, 214 N.W. 820 (1927).

Dalehite v. United States, 346 U.S. 15 (1953).

Dolan v. City of Tigard, 114 S.Ct 2309 (1994).

Dooley v. Town Plan and Zoning Commission of Fairfield, 151 Conn. 304, 197 A.2d 770 (1964).

Douglas v. Seacoast Products, 431 U.S. 265 (1977).

Dred Scott v. Sandford, 60 U.S.(19 How.) 393 (1857).

Duke Power Company v. Carolina Environmental Study Group, Inc., 438 U.S. 59 (1978).

Euclid v. Ambler Realty Co., 272 U.S. 365 (1926).

First English Evangelical Lutheran Church of Glendale v. City of Los Angeles, 487 U.S. 1211 (1987).

Flast v. Cohen, 392 U.S. 83 (1968).

Fontainebleau Hotel Corp. v. Forty-Five Twenty-Five Inc., 114 So. 2d 357 (1959).

Foster-Fountain Packing Co. v. Haydel, 278 U.S. 1 (1926).

Geer v. Connecticut, 161 U.S. 519 (1896).

Goldberg v. Kelly, 397 U.S. 24 (1970).

Griswold v. Connecticut, 381 U.S. 479 (1965).

Hunt v. United States, 278 U.S. 96 (1928).

Illinois Central Railroad Co. v. Illinois, 146 U.S. 387 (1892).

Just v. Marinette County, 56 Wis. 2d. 7, 201 N.W.2ed. 761 (1972).

Kleppe v. New Mexico, 426 U.S. 529 (1976).

Lochner v. New York, 198 U.S. 45 (1905).

Londoner v. Denver, 210 U.S. 373 (1908).

Lucas v. South Carolina Coastal Council, 112 S.Ct. 2886 (1992).

Lujan v. Defenders of Wildlife, 504 U.S. 555 (1992).

Lujan v. National Wildlife Federation , 497 U.S. 871 (1990).

Lykes Bros. Inc. v. United States Army Corps of Engineers, 821 F. Supp. 1457 (M.D. Fla. 1993).

Manchester v. Massachusetts, 139 U.S. 240 (1891).

Marks v. Whitney, 6 Cal.3d 251, 491 P.2d 374, 98 Cal Rptr. 790 (1971).

Martin v. Waddell, 41 U.S. 367 (1842).

McCready v. Virginia, 94 U.S. 391 (1876).

Miller v. Schoene, 276 U.S. 272 (1928).

Mineral King, see Sierra Club v. Morton.

Missouri v. Holland, 252 U.S. 416 (1920)

Mistretta v. United States, 488 U.S. 373 (1989).

Mobile Oil Corp. v. Coastal Petroleum Co., 671 F. 2d 419 (1982).

Mono Lake, see National Audubon Society et al. v. Department of Water and Power of the City of Los Angeles.

Morris County Land Improvement Co. v. Township of Parsippany-Troy Hills, 193 A.2d 232 (1963).

National Audubon Society v. Department of Water and Power of the City of Los Angeles, 658 P. 2d 709 (1983).

Nebbia v. New York, 291 U.S. 502 (1934).

New Mexico State Game Commission v. Udall, 410 F.2d 1197 (10th Cir.), *cert denied,* 296 U.S. 961 (1969)

New State Ice Co. v. Liebmann, 285 U.S. 262 (1932).

Nollan v. California Coastal Commission, 485 U.S. 943 (1987).

Pennsylvania Central Transportation Company v. New York, 438 U.S. 104 (1978).

Pennsylvania Coal Co. v. Mahon, 260 U.S. 272 (1922).

Pollard's Lessee v. Hagan, 44 U.S. (3 How.) 212 (1845).

Scenic Hudson Preservation Conference et al. v. Federal Power Commission, 354 F.2d 608 (1955).

Shaughnessy v. United States *ex rel.* Mezei, 345 U.S. 246 (1953).

Sierra Club v. Department of the Interior, 376 F. Supp. 90, N.D. Cal. (1974).

Sierra Club v. Department of the Interior, 398 F. Supp. 284, N.C. Cal. (1975).

Sierra Club v. Department of the Interior, 424 F.Supp. 172, N.D. Cal. (1976).

Sierra Club v. Morton, 405 U.S. 727 (1972).

Simon v. Eastern Kentucky Welfare Rights Organization, 426 U.S. 26 (1976).

Smith v. Maryland, 59 U.S. (18 How.) 71 (1855).

Spur Industries v. Del Webb Development, 108 Ariz. 178, 494 P.2d 700 (1972).

Tangier Sound Watermen's Association v. Douglas, 541 F. Supp. 1287, E.D.Virginia (1982).

The Abbey Dodge, 223 U.S. 188 (1912).

United States v. McCullagh, 221 F. 288 (D. Kansas, 1915).

United States v. Midwest Oil Company (1915).

United States v. Shauver, 214 F.154 (E.D. Ark. 1914), *appeal dismissed,* 248 U.S. 594 (1919).

United States v. Students Challenging Regulatory Agency Procedures, 412 U.S. 669 (1973).

Zabel v. Tabb, 430 F. 2d 199 (5th Cir. 1970), *cert. denied,* 401 U.S. 910 (1971).

Legislation

Administrative Procedure Act 1946
5 U. S. C. 551 (1982), 5 U. S. C. 701 (1982)
June 6, 1946, c. 324, 60 Stat. 237

Air Quality Act 1967
42 U. S. C. 7401 (1982)
Nov. 21, 1967, P.L. 90-148, 81 Stat. 485

Alaska National Interest Lands Conservation Act 1980
16 U. S. C. 3101–3233 (1982)
16 U. S. C. 410hh-1 (1982)
43 U. S. C. 1602–1621 (1982)
48 U. S. C. 21 (1982)
Dec. 2, 1980, P.L. 96-487, 94 Stat. 2374

Bald Eagle Protection Act 1940
16 U. S. C. 668 (1982)
June 8, 1940, c. 278, 54 Stat. 250

Black Bass Act 1926 (Interstate Transportation)
16 U. S. C. 851 (1982)
May 20, 1926, c. 346, 44 Stat. 576

Clean Air Act 1970
42 U. S. C. 7401 (1982)
July 14, 1955, c. 360, 69 Stat. 322
Dec. 17, 1963, P.L. 88-206, 77 Stat. 392

Clean Air Act Amendments 1970
42 U. S. C. 7401 (1982)
Dec. 31, 1970, P.L. 91-604, 84 Stat. 1676

Clean Water Act 1977
33 U. S. C. 1251 (1982)
Dec. 27, 1977, P.L. 95-217, 91 Stat. 1566

Coastal Zone Management Act 1972
16 U. S. C. 1451 (1982)
Oct. 27, 1972, P.L. 92-583, 86 Stat. 1280

Comprehensive Environmental Response, Compensation, and Liability Act 1980 [Superfund]
26 U. S. C. 4611 (1982)
42 U. S. C. 9601 (1982)
Dec. 11, 1980, P.L. 96-510, 94 Stat. 2767

Deepwater Port Act 1974
33 U. S. C. 1501 (1982)
Mar. 16, 1974, P.L. 93-627, 88 Stat. 2126

Duck Stamp Act 1934 [see Migratory Bird Hunting Stamp Act]
16 U. S. C. 718 (1982)
Mar. 16, 1934, c. 71, 48 Stat. 451

Endangered Species Act 1973
U.S. Code 1982 Title 16, § 1531 et seq.
Dec. 28, 1973, P.L. 93-205, 87 Stat. 884

Endangered Species Conservation Act 1969
16 U. S. C. 668aa (1982)
Dec. 5, 1969, P.L. 91-135, 83 Stat. 275, §§ 1 to 5

Endangered Species Preservation Act 1966
16 U. S. C. 1531 (1982)
Oct. 15, 1966, P.L. 89-669, 80 Stat. 926, §§ 1 to 3

Energy Policy and Conservation Act 1975
42 U. S. C. 6201 (1982)
Dec. 22, 1975, P.L. 94-163, 89 Stat. 871

Federal Aid in Sport Fish Restoration (Dingell-Johnson) Act 1950
16 U.S.C. §777 et seq.

Federal Aid in Wildlife Restoration (Pittman-Robertson) Act of 1937
16 U.S.C §669 et seq.

Federal Environmental Pesticide Control Act 1972
7 U. S. C. 136 et seq. (1982)
Oct. 21, 1972, P.L. 92-516, 86 Stat. 973

Federal Insecticide, Fungicide, and Rodenticide Act 1947
7 U. S. C. 136 et seq. (1982)
June 25, 1947, c. 125, 61 Stat. 163

Federal Land Policy and Management Act 1976
43 U. S. C. 1702 et seq. (1988)
Oct, 21, 1976, P.L. 94-579, 90 Stat. 2743

Federal Water Pollution Control Act 1972
33 U. S. C. 1251 (1982)
Oct. 18, 1972, P.L. 92-500, 86 Stat. 816

Fish and Wildlife Conservation (Forsythe-Chafee or Nongame) Act of 1980
16 U.S.C §2901 et seq.

Fish and Wildlife Coordination Act 1934
16 U. S. C. 661 et seq. (1982)
Mar. 10, 1934, c. 55, 48 Stat. 401

Fishermen's Protective Act 1967
22 U. S. C. 1971 et seq. (1982)
Aug. 12, 1968, P.L. 90-482, 82 Stat. 729

Fishery Conservation and Management Act 1976
16 U. S. C. 971, 1362, 1801, 1802, 1811–1813, 1821–1825, 1851–1861, 1881 (1982)

Forest and Rangeland Renewable Resources Planning Act 1974
16 U. S. C. 1600 et seq. (1982)
Aug. 17, 1974, P.L. 93-378, 88 Stat. 476

Forest Management Act
16 U. S. C. 1600 et seq. (1982)
Oct. 22, 1976, P.L. 94-588, 90 Stat. 2949

Forest Reserve Act 1891
16 U. S. C. 471 a et seq. (1982)
Mar. 3, 1891, c. 561, § 24, 26 Stat. 1095

Freedom of Information Act 1966 [see Administrative Procedure Act]
5 U. S. C. 552 (1982)
Sept. 6, 1966, P.L. 89-554, 80 Stat. 378, § 1

Government in the Sunshine Act 1976 [see Administrative Procedure Act]
5 U. S. C. 552b (1982)
Sept. 13, 1976, P.L. 94-409, 90 Stat. 1241

Homestead Act 1862
43 U. S. C. 161 et seq.,890–892 (1982)
May 20, 1862, c. 75, 12 Stat. 392

Insecticide Act 1910
7 U. S. C. 136 et seq. (1982)
Apr. 26, 1910, c. 191, 36 Stat. 331

Knutson-Vandenburg Act 1930
16 U. S. C. 576–576b (1988)
June 9, 1930, c. 416, § 1, 46 Stat. 527

Lacey Act 1900 (Game)
16 U. S. C. 701 (1982)
May 25, 1900, c. 553, 31 Stat. 187

Land and Water Conservation Act 1964
16 U. S. C. 460d, 4601-4 et seq. (1982)
Sept. 3, 1964, P.L. 88-578, 78 Stat. 897

Lea Act 1948 (Wildlife Areas)
16 U. S. C. 695 et seq. (1982)
May 18, 1948, c. 303, 62 Stat. 238

Marine Mammal Protection Act 1972
16 U. S. C. 1361 et seq. (1982)
Oct. 21, 1972, P.L. 92-522, 86 Stat. 1027

Marine Protection, Research, and Sanctuaries Act 1972
33 U. S. C. 1401 et seq. (1982)
Oct. 23, 1972, P.L. 92-532, 86 Stat. 1052

Migratory Bird Act 1913
Mar. 4, 1913, c. 145, 37 Stat. 828
repealed 1918

Migratory Bird Conservation Act 1929
16 U. S. C. 715 et seq. (1982)
Feb. 18, 1929, c. 257, 45 Stat. 122

Migratory Bird Hunting Stamp Act 1934 [Duck Stamp Act]
16 U. S. C. 718–718h (1982)
Mar. 16, 1934, c. 71 48 Stat. 451

Migratory Bird Treaty Act 1918
16 U. S. C. 703–711 (1982)
18 U. S. C. 43 (1982)
July 3, 1918, c. 128, 40 Stat. 755
July 31, 1918, 40 Stat. 1812

Multiple-Use Sustained-Yield Act 1960
16 U. S. C. 528 et seq. (1982)
June 12, 1960, P.L. 86-517, 74 Stat. 215

National Environmental Policy Act 1969
42 U. S. C. 4321 et seq. (1982)
Jan. 1, 1970, P.L. 91-190, 83 Stat. 852

National Forest Management Act 1976
16 U. S. C. 1600 et seq. (1982)
Oct. 22, 1976, P.L. 94-588, 90 Stat. 2949

National Park Service Organic Act 1916
16 U. S. C. 1 et seq. (1988)
Aug. 25, 1916, c. 408, 39 Stat. 535

National Wildlife Refuge System Administration Act 1966
16 U. S. C. 668dd, 668ee (1982)
Oct. 15, 1966, P.L. 89-669, 80 Stat. 926, §§ 4,5

Noise Control Act 1972
42 U. S. C. 4901 et seq. (1982)
49 U. S. C. Appendix, § 1431 (1982)
Oct. 27, 1972, P.L. 92-574, 86 Stat. 1234

Outer Continental Oil Shelf Lands Act 1953
43 U. S. C. 1331 et seq. (1982)
Aug. 7, 1953, c. 345, 67 Stat. 462

Park, Parkway and Recreation Area Study Act 1936
June 23, 1936, c. 735, 49 Stat. 1894

Price-Anderson Act 1957
42 U. S. C. 2210 (1982)
Sept. 2, 1957, P.L. 85-256, 71 Stat. 576

Privacy Act 1974 [see Administrative Procedure Act]
5 U. S. C. 552a (1982)
Dec. 31, 1974, P.L. 93-579, 88 Stat. 1896

Resource Conservation and Recovery Act 1976
42 U. S. C. 6901 et seq. (1982)
Oct. 21, 1976, P.L. 94-580, 90 Stat. 2795

Resource Recovery Act 1970
42 U. S. C. 3251 et seq. (1970)
Oct. 23, 1970, P.L. 91-512, 84 Stat. 1227

River and Harbor Act 1899
33 U. S. C. 401, 403, 404, 406–409, 411–415, 418, 502, 549, 686, 687 (1982)

Rivers and Harbors Act 1968
33 U. S. C. 59c-1, 59g–59i, 426i, 562a (1982)
P. L. No. 90-482, 82 Stat 731

Safe Drinking Water Act 1974
42. U. S. C. 300f to 300j-9 (1982)
Dec. 16, 1974, P.L. 93-523, 88 Stat. 1660

Sikes Act 1960 (Conservation on Military Reservations)
16 U. S. C. 670 a et seq. (1982)
Sept. 15, 1960, P.L. 86-797, 74 Stat. 1052
Oct. 18, 1974, P.L. 93-452, 88 Stat. 1369

Stock-Raising Homestead Act 1916
43 U. S. C. 291 et seq. (1982)
Dec. 29, 1916, c. 9, 39 Stat. 862

Submerged Lands Act 1953
43 U. S. C. 1301 et seq. (1982)
May 22, 1953, c. 65, 67 Stat. 29

Superfund 1980 [Comprehensive Environmental Response,Compensation, and Liability Act]
26 U. S. C. 4611 et seq. (1982)
42 U. S. C. 9601 et seq. (1982)
Dec. 11, 1980, P.L. 96-510, 94 Stat. 2767

Superfund Amendment and Reauthorization Act 1986
Oct. 17, 1986, P.L. 99-499, 100 Stat. 1613

Surplus Grain for Wildlife Act 1961
Aug. 17, 1961, P.L. 87-152, 75 Stat. 389

Swamp Land Acts 1849, 1850, 1860
43 U. S. C. 981 et seq. (1982)
Mar. 2, 1849, c. 87, 9 Stat. 352
Sept. 28, 1850, c. 84, 9 Stat. 519
Mar. 12, 1860, c. 5, 12 Stat. 3

Tariff Act 1930
15 U. S. C. 1001 et seq. (1982)
June 17, 1930, c. 497, 46 Stat. 590

Taylor Act 1934 (Grazing)
43 U. S. C. 315 et seq. (1982)
June 28, 1934, c. 865, 48 Stat. 1269

Toxic Substances Control Act 1976
15 U. S. C. 2601 et seq. (1982)
Oct. 11, 1976, P.L. 94-469, 90 Stat. 2003

Water Bank Act 1970
16 U. S. C. 1301 et seq. (1982)
Dec. 19, 1970, P.L. 91-559, 84 Stat. 1468

Waterfowl Depredations Act 1956
July 3, 1956, P.L. 654, c. 512, 70 Stat. 492

Weeks Act 1911 (Protection of Watersheds)
16 U. S. C. 480, 500, 515–519, 521, 552, 563 (1982)
Mar. 11, 1911, c. 186, 36 Stat. 961

Wetlands Act (Waterfowl) 1961
16 U. S. C. 715k-3 et seq. (1982)
Oct. 4, 1961, P.L. 87-383, 75 Stat. 813

Wild Free-Roaming Horses and Burros Act 1971
16 U. S. C. 1331 (1982)
Dec. 15, 1971, P.L. 92-195, 85 Stat. 649

Wilderness Act 1964
16 U. S. C. 1131 et seq. (1982)
Sept. 3, 1964, P.L. 88-577, 78 Stat. 890

Bibliography

Andrews, Edmund. "Tiny Tonga Seeks Satellite Empire in Space." *New York Times,* 28 August 1990, 1, C17.

Andrews, Richard N. L. "Risk-Based Decisionmaking," in *Environmental Policy in the 1990s* 2nd ed. Edited by Norman Vig and Michael Kraft, pp. 209–231. Washington, DC: Congressional Quarterly Press, 1994.

Arrandale, Thomas. *The Battle for Natural Resources.* Washington, DC: Congressional Quarterly Press, 1983.

Attorney General's Committee Report. *Administrative Procedure in Government Agencies.* Preface by Charles K. Woltz. Charlottesville: University Press of Virginia, 1968.

Ault, W. O. *Open-Field Farming in Medieval England.* London: Allen and Unwin, 1972.

Barton, Katherine. "Federal Fish and Wildlife Agency Budgets." In *Audubon Wildlife Report 1987.* Edited by Roger Di Silvestro, pp. 321–354. New York: National Audubon Society, 1987.

Bean, Michael J. *The Evolution of National Wildlife Law.* New York: Praeger, 1983.

Been, Vicki. "Locally Undesirable Land Uses in Minority Neighborhoods: Disproportionate Siting or Market Dynamics?" *Yale Law Journal* 103 (1994): 1383–1422.

Belanger, Dian Olson. *Managing American Wildlife: A History of the International Association of Fish and Wildlife Agencies.* Amherst: University of Massachusetts Press, 1988.

Benedick, Richard Elliot. "Protecting the Ozone Layer: New Directions in Diplomacy." In *Preserving the Global Environment: The Challenge of Shared Leadership.* Edited by Jessica Tuchman Mathews, pp. 112–153. New York: Norton, 1991.

Benedick, Richard Elliot. *Ozone Diplomacy: New Directions in Safeguarding the Planet*. Cambridge, MA: Harvard University Press, 1991.

Berlins, Marcel. "US Objections Hold Up Sea Conference." *The Times,* 9 March 1981: 6(b).

Birnie, Patricia, and Alan Boyle. *International Law & the Environment*. Oxford: Clarendon Press, 1993.

Bolotin, Fredric. *International Public Policy Sourcebook: Volume 2 [Education and Environment]*. New York: Greenwood Press, 1989.

British Information Services. "The London Conference on Substances that Deplete the Ozone Layer." *British Information Services*. New York: British Consulate General, 28 June 1990.

Buck, Susan J. "Cultural Theory and Management of Common Property Resources." *Human Ecology* 17 (1989): 101–116.

Buck, Susan. "Environmental Policy in the United Kingdom." In *International Public Policy Sourcebook: Volume 2 [Education and Environment]*. Edited by Fredric Bolotin, pp. 310–333. New York: Greenwood Press, 1989.

Buck, Susan J., and Edward Hathaway. "Designating State Natural Resource Trustees Under SARA." In *Regulatory Federalism, Natural Resources and Environmental Management*. Edited by Michael Hamilton, pp. 83–94. Washington, DC: ASPA, 1990.

Bureau Of National Affairs. *U.S. Environmental Laws, 1988 Edition*. Washington, DC: Bureau of National Affairs, 1988.

Caldwell, Lynton. "Beyond Environmental Diplomacy: The Changing Institutional Structure of International Cooperation." In *International Environmental Diplomacy*. Edited by John Carroll, pp. 13–27. Cambridge: Cambridge University Press, 1988.

Caldwell, Lynton. *International Environmental Policy*. Durham, NC: Duke University Press, 1984.

Caldwell, Lynton. *International Environmental Policy* 2nd ed. Durham, NC: Duke University Press, 1990.

"Carolina Power Is Top Buyer." *New York Times,* 31 March 1993, C2.

Central Directorate of Environmental Protection. *Pollution Control in England*. London: Department of the Environment, August 1984.

Chandler, William. "Federal Grants for State Wildlife Conservation." In *Audubon Wildlife Report 1986*. Edited by Roger Di Silvestro, pp. 177–212. New York: National Audubon Society, 1986.

"Chronological Summary: Events of 1992." *Colorado Journal of International Environmental Law and Policy* 4 (1993): 232.

Clawson, Marion. *The Federal Lands Revisited*. Baltimore: Johns Hopkins University Press, 1983.

Cobb, Roger, and Charles Elder. *Participation in American Politics*. Boston: Allyn and Bacon, 1972.

Coggins, George Cameron, Charles Wilkinson, and John Leshy. *Federal Public Land and Resources Law* 3rd ed. Westbury, NY: Foundation Press, 1993.

Cohen, Steven. "Defusing the Toxic Time Bomb: Federal Hazardous Waste Programs." In *Environmental Policies in the 1980's Reagan's New Agenda*. Edited by Norman Vig and Michael Kraft, pp. 273–291. Washington, DC: Congressional Quarterly Press, 1984.

Cooper, Phillip. *Public Law and Public Administration* 2nd ed. Englewood Cliffs, NJ: Prentice Hall, 1988.

Cox, Susan Jane Buck. "No Tragedy on the Commons." *Environmental Ethics* 7 (Spring 1985): 49–61.

"CP&L Spends Big to Delay Buying Air `Scrubbers'." *Greensboro [NC] News and Record*, 31 March 1993, B8.

Crockett, Tamara, and Cynthia Schultz. "Developing a Unified European Environmental Law and Policy." *Boston College International and Comparative Law Review* 14(2), 1991: 301–317.

Crook, Michael, and Ran Henry. "Baloney." *Miami Herald, Tropic* (magazine), 22 April 1990, pp. 8–9, 14–15, 18–20, 22.

Dales, J. H. *Pollution, Property, & Prices: An Essay in Policy-Making And Economics*. Toronto: University of Toronto Press, 1968.

Darman, Richard. "The Law of the Sea: Rethinking U.S. Interests." *Foreign Affairs* 56 (1978): 373–395.

Dodd, W. F. "Administrative Agencies as Legislator and Judges." *American Bar Association Journal* 25 (November 1939): 976.

Dorst, Jean. *Before Nature Dies*. Translated by Constance D. Sherman. Preface by Prince Bernard. Boston: Houghton Mifflin, 1970.

Douglas, Mary, and Aaron Wildavsky. *Risk and Culture*. Berkeley, CA: University of California Press, 1982.

Dunning, Harrison, ed. *The Public Trust Doctrine in Natural Resources Law and Management*. Davis: University of California, 1981.

Ecological Society of America. "Environmental Policy Update, July 17, 1995," esanews@umdd.umd.edu.

Edberg, Rolf. *On the Shred of a Cloud*. Translated by Sven Aham. New York: Harper & Row, 1971.

Farnau, J. C., B. G. Gardiner, and J. D. Shanklin. "Large Losses of Total Ozone in Antarctica Reveal Seasonal ClO_x/NO_x Interaction." *Nature* 315 (1985): 207–210.

Findley, Roger, and Daniel Farber, eds. *Cases and Materials on Environmental Law* 4th ed. St. Paul, MN: West, 1995.

Foresta, Ronald A. *America's National Parks and Their Keepers*. Baltimore: Johns Hopkins University Press, 1984.

Fosburg, Whit. "Wildlife and the U.S. Forest Service." In *Audubon Wildlife Report 1985*. Edited by Roger Di Silvestro, pp. 307–341. New York: National Audubon Society, 1985.

Foster, David. "Property Rights Gains Ground." *Greensboro News & Record*. 30 July 1995: A11.

Fox, Stephen. *The American Conservation Movement: John Muir and His Legacy.* Madison: University of Wisconsin Press, 1981.

Gaba, Jeffrey M. *Environmental Law* (Black Letter Series). St. Paul, MN: West, 1994.

Goldwin, Robert A. "Common Sense vs. `The Common Heritage'." In *Law of the Sea: U.S. Policy Dilemma.* Edited by Bernard Oxman, David Caron, and Charles Buderi, pp. 59–75. San Francisco: ICS Press, 1983.

Gonner, E. C. K. *Common Land and Inclosure* 2nd. ed. London: Cass, 1966.

Gore, Albert. *Earth in the Balance: Ecology and the Human Spirit.* Boston: Houghton Mifflin, 1992.

Haley, Andrew. *Space Law and Government.* New York: Appleton-Century-Crofts, 1963.

Hamilton, Michael, ed. *Regulatory Federalism, Natural Resources and Environmental Management.* Washington, DC: ASPA, 1990.

Hardin, Garrett. "The Tragedy of the Commons." *Science* 162: 1243–1248.

Harnish, A. A. et al. *Chief Jospeh Dam Columbia River, Washington Community Impact Reports.* IWR Reports 78-3 and 78-R2. Fort Belvoir, VA: U.S. Army Engineer Institute for Water Resources, 1978.

Harrington, Winston. 1991. "Wildlife: Severe Decline and Partial Recovery." In *American's Renewable Resources: Historical Trends and Current Challenges.* Edited by Kenneth Frederick and Roger Sedjo, pp. 205–246. Washington, DC: Resources for the Future.

Hartwick, John, and Nancy Olewiler. *The Economics of Natural Resource Use.* New York: Harper & Row, 1986.

Heffron, Florence, and Neil McFeeley. *The Administrative Regulatory Process.* New York: Longman, 1983.

Heinzerling, Lisa. "Action Inaction: Section 1983 Liability for Failure to Act." *University of Chicago Law Review* 53 (Summer 1986): 1047–1073.

Henry, Marguerite. *Brighty of the Grand Canyon.* New York: Rand McNally, 1953.

Hook, Janet. "Legislative Summary: 101st Congress Leaves Behind Plenty Laws, Criticism." *Congressional Quarterly Weekly Report* 48(44) 3 November 1990, pp. 3683–3710.

"How do you mean, `fair'?" *The Economist* 29 May 1993: 71.

Hunter, David B. "An Ecological Perspective on Property: A Call for Judicial Protection of the Public's Interest in Environmentally Critical Resources." *Harvard Environmental Law Review* 12 (1988): 311–383.

Ise, John. *Our National Park Policy.* Baltimore: Johns Hopkins University Press, 1961.

Jachtenfuchs, Markus. "The European Community and the Protection of the Ozone Layer." *Journal of Common Market Studies* 28, no. 3 (March 1980): 263. Cited by Benedick, *Ozone Diplomacy* 24.

Keefe, William, Henry Abraham, William Flanigan, Charles O. Jones, Morris Ogul, and John Spanier. *American Democracy: Institutions, Politics, and Policies.* Homewood, IL: Dorsey Press, 1983.

Kingdon, John W. *Agendas, Alternatives, and Public Policies.* New York: Harper-Collins, 1984.

Kipling, Rudyard. *Kim.* New York: Dell, 1959.

Kiss, Alexandre, and Dinah Shelton. *International Environmental Law.* Ardsley-on-Hudson, NY: Transnational Publishers, 1991.

Knize, Perri. "Chainsaw Environmentalism." *Backpacker* (November 1987): 55–59.

Koehler, James, and Scott Hajost. "1989: Advent of a New Era for EPA's International Activities." *Colorado Journal of International Environmental Law and Policy* 1(1) (Summer 1990): 181–187.

Kraft, Michael, and Norman Vig. "Environmental Policy from the 1970s to the 1990s: Continuity and Change." In *Environmental Policy in the 1990s* 2nd ed. Edited by Norman Vig and Michael Kraft, pp. 3–29. Washington, DC: Congressional Quarterly Press, 1994.

Lash, Jonathan, Katherine Gillman, and David Sheridan. *A Season of Spoils: The Reagan Administration's Attack on the Environment.* New York: Pantheon, 1984.

"Law Students Buy and Hold Pollution Rights." *New York Times,* 31 March 1995, B13.

Lay, S. Houston, and Howard Taubenfeld. *The Law Relating to Activities of Man in Space.* Chicago: University of Chicago Press, 1970.

"Leaving the Feeding Grounds." *The Economist* 7 August 1993: 40.

Legal Winds of Change: Business and the New Clean Air Act. Videoconference Resource Materials, presented by Environmental Protection Agency, PBS Adult Learning Satellite Service, Public Television Outreach Alliance, and the University of North Carolina at Greensboro. 28 November 1990.

Levine, Joel S. "A Planet at Risk." Public Lecture, 20 February 1993. Greensboro, North Carolina.

Lockhart, William B., Yale Kamisar, and Jesse Choper. *The American Constitution: Cases-Comments-Questions.* St. Paul, MN: West, 1970.

Lund, Thomas A. *American Wildlife Law.* Berkeley: University of California Press, 1980.

Mazmanian, Daniel, and Paul Sabatier. *Implementation and Public Policy.* Glenview IL: Scott, Foresman, 1983.

McEvoy, Arthur. *The Fisherman's Problem: Ecology and Law in California Fisheries, 1850–1980.* Cambridge: Cambridge University Press, 1986.

Mead, Walter J., Asbjorn Moseidjord, Dennis Muraoka, and Philip Sorenson. *Offshore Lands: Oil and Gas Leasing and Conservation on the Outer Continental Shelf.* San Francisco, CA: Pacific Institute for Public Policy Research, 1985.

Meier, Kenneth J. *Regulation: Politics, Bureaucracy, and Economics.* New York: St. Martin's Press, 1985.

Miller, G. Tyler *Living in the Environment* 5th ed. Belmont, CA: Wadsworth, 1988.

Molina, Mario, and F. Sherwood Rowland. "Stratospheric Sink for Chlorofluoromethanes: Chlorine Atom Catalysed Destruction of Ozone." *Nature* 249 (1974): 810–812. Cited in Benedick, *Ozone Diplomacy* 10.

Naff, John. *Journal of the American Bar Association* 58 (1972): 820, in Christopher Stone. *Earth and Other Ethics.* New York: Harper & Row, 1987.

Nangle, Orval. "Stratospheric Ozone: United States Regulation of Chlorofluorocarbons." *Environmental Affairs* 16 (1989): 531–580.

Nash, Roderick. *American Environmentalism: Readings in Conservation History* 3rd. ed. New York: McGraw-Hill, 1990.

National Audubon Society. *Audubon Wildlife Report.* New York: National Audubon Society, 1985, 1986, 1987.

National Standards Association. *National Directory of State Agencies.* Bethesda, MD: National Standards Association, 1987.

O'Leary, Rosemary. *Environmental Change: Federal Courts and the EPA.* Philadelphia: Temple University Press, 1993.

Ostrom, Elinor. *Governing the Commons.* Cambridge: Cambridge University Press, 1990.

"Ozone-saving Efforts Are Making Headway." *Greensboro News and Record* 26 August 1993, A8.

Pearce, David. "The European Community Approach to the Control of Chlorofluorocarbons." Paper submitted to UNEP Workshop on the Control of Chlorofluorocarbons, Leesburg, Virginia, 8–12 September 1986. Cited by Benedick, *Ozone Diplomacy* 25.

Peters, Guy. *American Public Policy: Promise and Performance* 2nd ed. Chatham, NJ: Chatham House Publishers, 1986.

Peterson, D. J. *Troubled Lands: The Legacy of Soviet Environmental Destruction.* Boulder, CO: Westview, 1993.

Pinchot, Gifford. *The Fight for Conservation.* Garden City, NY: Harcourt, Brace, 1919.

Plater, Zygmunt, Robert Abrams, and William Goldfarb. *Environmental Law and Policy: Nature, Law, and Society.* St. Paul, MN: West, 1992.

Regier, H. A., and A. P. Grima. "Fishery Resource Allocation: An Exploratory Essay." *Canadian Journal of Fisheries and Aquatic Sciences* 42(4): 845–859.

Reinhardt, Forest. "Du Pont Freon® Products Division." In *Managing Environmental Issues: A Casebook.* Edited by Rogene Buchholz, Alfred Marcus, and James Post, pp. 261–286. Englewood Cliffs, NJ: Prentice Hall, 1992.

Restoring America's Wildlife 1937-1987: The First 50 Years of the Federal Aid in Wildlife Restoration (Pittman-Robertson) Act. 1987. Washington, DC: USGPO (United States Department of Interior Fish and Wildlife Service).

"Restoring America's Wildlife" (brochure), Washington, DC: USGPO (United States Department of Interior Fish and Wildlife Service), June, 1992.

ReVelle, Penelope, and Charles ReVelle. *The Environment: Issues and Choices for Society.* Boston: Jones and Bartlett Publishers, 1988.

Riding, Alan. "Accord Bans Oil Exploration in the Antarctic for 50 Years." *New York Times,* 5 October 1991, 1 and 28.

Righter, Rosemary. "The Law of the Sea: Reagan Tries to Play King Canute." *The Sunday Times,* 26 April 1981, 16(c).

Ripley, Randall, and Grace Franklin. *Congress, the Bureaucracy, and Public Policy.* Homewood, IL: Dorsey Press, 1984.

Rodgers, William H., Jr. *Handbook on Environmental Law.* St. Paul, MN: West, 1977.

Rosenbaum, Walter A. *Environmental Politics and Policy.* Washington, DC: Congressional Quarterly Press, 1985.

Rosenbaum, Walter A. *Energy, Politics, and Public Policy* 2nd ed. Washington, DC: Congressional Quarterly Press, 1987.

Rosenbaum, Walter A. *Energy, Politics, and Public Policy* 3rd ed. Washington, DC: Congressional Quarterly Press, 1995.

Rosenbaum, Walter A. "The Clenched Fist and the Open Hand: Into the 1990s at EPA." In *Environmental Policy in the 1990s* 2nd ed. Edited by Norman Vig and Michael Kraft, pp. 121–143. Washington, DC: Congressional Quarterly Press, 1994.

Rowe, Jeri. "Traders Don't Outfox Wildlife Officials." *Greensboro News and Record,* 22 May 1995, B1.

Ruhl, J. B. "Section 4 of the ESA—The Cornerstone of Species Protection Law." *Natural Resources & Environment* 8(1) Summer 1993: 26–29, 67–71.

Sand, Peter. *Lessons Learned in Global Environmental Governance.* Washington, DC: World Resources Institute, June 1990.

Sand, Peter. "International Cooperation: The Environmental Experience." In *Preserving the Global Environment: The Challenge of Shared Leadership.* Edited by Jessica Tuchman Mathews, pp. 236–279. New York: Norton, 1991.

Sax, Joseph. "Public Trust Doctrine In Natural Resource Law: Effective Judicial Intervention." *Michigan Law Review* 68 (January 1970): 473–566.

Sax, Joseph. "Introductory Perspectives." In *The Public Trust Doctrine in Natural Resource Law and Management.* Edited by Harrison Dunning, pp. 6–8. Davis: University of California, 1981.

Schneider, Keith. "Ozone Depletion Harming Sea Life." *New York Times,* 16 November 1991, p. 6, col. 6.

Shapley, Deborah. *The Seventh Continent: Antarctica in a Resource Age.* Washington, DC: Resources for the Future, 1985.

Smythe, Marianne K. "Environmental Law: Expanding the Definition of Public Trust Uses." *North Carolina Law Review* 51 (1972): 316–325.

Soroos, Marvin. "From Stockholm to Rio: The Evolution of Global Environmental Governance." In *Environmental Policy in the 1990s* 2nd ed. Edited by Norman Vig and Michael Kraft, pp. 299–321. Washington, DC: Congressional Quarterly Press, 1994.

"Species Dying Daily, Conservation Group Warns Toxic World." *New York Times* (International edition). 29 November 1990, p. A9.

Statistical Summary for Fish and Wildlife Restoration, Fiscal Year 1994 (booklet). Washington, DC: USGPO (United States Department of Interior Fish and Wildlife Service, Division of Federal Aid), 1994.

Stevens, William K. "The 25th Anniversary of Earth Day: How Has the Environment Fared?" *New York Times,* 18 April 1995, B5.

Stoel, Thomas B., Jr., Alan S. Miller, and Breck Milroy. *Fluorocarbon Regulation.* Lexington, MA: D. C. Heath, 1980. Cited in Benedick, *Ozone Diplomacy,* p. 28.

Stolarski, Richard and Ralph Cicerone. "Stratospheric Chlorine: A Possible Sink for Ozone." *Canadian Journal of Chemistry* 52 (1974): 1610–1615. Cited in Benedick, *Ozone Diplomacy,* p. 10.

Stone, Christopher. *Earth and Other Ethics.* New York: Harper & Row, 1987.

Switzer, Jacqueline Vaughn. *Environmental Politics: Domestic and Global Dimensions.* New York: St. Martin's Press, 1994.

Tinsley, V. Randall, and Larry Nielsen, "Interstate Fisheries Arrangements: Application of a Pragmatic Classification Scheme for Interstate Arrangements." *Virginia Journal of Natural Resources Law* 6 (2), Spring 1987: 265–321.

Thompson, Michael. "The Cultural Construction of Nature and the Natural Destruction of Culture." Working paper for International Institute for Applied Systems Analysis, Laxenberg, Austria, 1984.

Tobin, Richard. "Environment, Population, and Economic Development." In *Environmental Policy in the 1990s* 2nd ed. Edited by Norman Vig and Michael Kraft, pp. 275–297. Washington, DC: Congressional Quarterly Press, 1994.

Tripp, J. T. B., D. J. Dudek, and Michael Oppenheimer. "Equality and Ozone Protection." *Environment* 29, no. 6 (1987): 45. Cited in Benedick, *Ozone Diplomacy,* p. 28.

Trout, James. "A Land Manager's Commentary on the Public Trust Doctrine." In *The Public Trust Doctrine in Natural Resource Law and Management.* Edited by Harrison Dunning, pp. 169–177. Davis: University of California, 1981.

United Church of Christ Commission for Racial Justice. *Toxic Wastes and Race in the United States: A National Report on the Racial and Socio-Economic Characteristics of Communities With Hazardous Waste Sites.* New York: Commission for Racial Justice, United Church of Christ, 1987.

USEPA. *Environmental Monitoring at Love Canal.* Washington, DC: USEPA, 1982.

USEPA. *Environmental Progress and Challenges: An EPA Perspective.* Washington, DC: Office of Management Systems and Evaluation CPM-222, June, 1984.

USEPA. *Unfinished Business: A Comparative Assessment of Environmental Problems.* Washington, DC: EPA, 1987

USEPA, Science Advisory Board. *Reducing Risk: Setting Priorities for Environmental Protection*. Washington, DC: USEPA, September 1990.

USEPA, Office of Policy, Planning and Evaluation. *Environmental Equity: Reducing Risk for All Communities, Vol. 1: Workgroup Report to the Administrator*. Washington, DC: EPA, June 1992.

U.S. General Accounting Office. *Siting of Hazardous Waste Landfills and Their Correlation With Racial and Economic Status of Surrounding Communities*. GAO/RCED-83-168 (June 1, 1983).

Vaughn, Ray. *Essentials of Environmental Law*. Rockville, MD: Government Institutes, 1994.

Vaughn, Ray. *Endangered Species Act Handbook*. Rockville, MD: Government Institutes, Inc., 1994.

Vig, Norman. "Presidential Leadership and the Environment: From Reagan and Bush to Clinton." In *Environmental Policy in the 1990s* 2nd ed. Edited by Norman Vig and Michael Kraft, pp. 71- 95. Washington, DC: Congressional Quarterly Press, 1994.

Vig, Norman, and Michael Kraft. "Conclusion: The New Environmental Agenda." In *Environmental Policy in the 1990s* 2nd ed. Edited by Norman Vig and Michael Kraft, pp. 369–392. Washington, DC: Congressional Quarterly Press, 1995.

Vig, Norman, and Michael Kraft, eds. *Environmental Policy in the 1980s: Reagan's New Agenda*. Washington, DC: Congressional Quarterly Press, 1984.

Vig, Norman, and Michael Kraft, eds. *Environmental Policy in the 1990s*. Washington, DC: Congressional Quarterly Press, 1990.

Vig, Norman, and Michael Kraft, eds. *Environmental Policy in the 1990s* 2nd ed. Washington, DC: Congressional Quarterly Press, 1995.

Vogel, David. *National Styles of Regulation: Environmental Policy in Great Britain and the United States*. Ithaca, NY: Cornell University Press, 1986.

Vogel, David. "Environmental Policy in Europe and Japan." In *Environmental Policies in the 1980's Reagan's New Agenda*. Edited by Norman Vig and Michael Kraft, pp. 257–278. Washington, DC: Congressional Quarterly Press, 1990.

Walker, Jack. "Setting the Agenda in the U.S. Senate." *British Journal of Political Science* 7 (October 1977): 423–445.

Walton, D. W. H. *Antarctica Science*. Cambridge: Cambridge University Press, 1987.

Weber, Michael. "Marine Mammal Protection." In *Audubon Wildlife Report 1985*. Edited by Roger Di Silvestro, pp. 181–211. New York: National Audubon Society, 1985.

Wilkinson, Charles. "Public Trust Doctrine in Public Land Law." In *The Public Trust Doctrine in Natural Resources Law and Management*. Edited by Harrison Dunning, pp. 169–202. Davis: University of California, 1981.

"William Reilly's Green Precision Weapons." *The Economist* 30 March 1991, p. 28.

Williams, Ted. "'Silent Spring' Revisited." *Modern Maturity* (October-November 1987): 46–50, 108.

Williamson, Lonnie. "Evolution of a Landmark Law." In *Restoring America's Wildlife 1937–1987: The First 50 Years of the Federal Aid in Wildlife Restoration (Pittman-Robertson) Act*. Edited by Harmon Kallman, pp. 1–17. Washington, DC: USGPO (United States Department of Interior Fish and Wildlife Service), 1987.

Wolf, Edward. "Avoiding a Mass Extinction of Species." In *State of the World 1988*. Lester Brown (project director), pp. 101–117. New York: Norton, 1988.

World Meteorological Organization (WMO). *Atmospheric Ozone 1985: Assessment of Our Understanding of the Processes Controlling Its Present Distribution*. Geneva: WMO, 1986. Cited in Benedick, *Ozone Diplomacy*, p. 13.

Wright, N. A., and P. L. Williams. *Mineral Resources of Antarctica*. Geological Survey Circular 705. Reston, VA: USGS, 1974.

Wright, Robert R., and Susan Webber Wright. *Land Use in a Nutshell*. St. Paul, MN: West, 1985.

Index